BROWNLOW NORTH

His Life and Work

K. MOODY-STUART, M.A.

"He that cometh to God must believe that He is." HEB. 11.6.

THE BANNER OF TRUTH TRUST
78b Chiltern Street, London, W.1

First Edition, 1878

Popular (Shortened) Edition, 1904

Popular Edition reprinted, with several additions from the text of the first edition, October, 1961

This book is set in 10-point Bookprint and printed and bound in Great Britain by Billing and Sons Limited, Guildford and London

Contents

CHAPTER I

Brownlow North's Earlier Years

BROWNLOW NORTH is a name that has become a household word[1] throughout the length and breadth of Scotland, and also in many of the cities and towns of England and Ireland. It is a name which will be held in grateful remembrance and esteem as that of a man who has influenced by his preaching and teaching the spiritual life of our land more than most have done. It seems therefore unfitting that such a man's life should be allowed to become a thing of the past without some permanent record being preserved of those labours in which he was so unwearied, of that teaching which made such a deep impression upon multitudes, and of that evangelistic ministry which has formed one of the most important factors of the religious, as distinguished from the ecclesiastical, history of Scotland in recent times.

Brownlow North was born on the 6th January, 1810. He was the only son of the Rev. Charles Augustus North, Rector of Alverstoke, Hants, and Prebendary of Winchester, and of Rachel, daughter of Thomas Jarvis, Esq., of Doddington Hall, Lincolnshire. His grandfather was the Hon. and Rev. Brownlow North, D.D., Prelate of the Noble Order of the Garter, who was successively the Bishop of the Sees of Lichfield, Worcester, and Winchester. Mr. North was thus a grand-nephew of Lord North, the celebrated prime minister of George III, not a little of whose characteristic ability and genius,

---

[1] Although these words were written less than a hundred years ago (1878), almost the opposite is true today. Is this just one of the inevitable results of the passing of time or have other factors conspired to make men forget one of the greatest evangelists of the last century? —THE PUBLISHERS.

along with that of other members of the distinguished family to which he belonged, reappeared in him. It is a family which has produced members who have exercised an appreciable influence on the community both in Church and State.

His birth took place at Winchester House, Chelsea, the town house of his grandfather. His father was the Bishop's youngest son; but as his cousin, the Earl of Guilford, had no son, and his elder brother Francis had been long married, and was also childless, the infant boy was welcomed as heir to the earldom; and hearty were the cheers which greeted him, when his father's intimate companion and friend, Christian Schetky, the well-known marine painter,[1] receiving him from the nurse's arms at breakfast, presented him to the company as the future Earl of Guilford. It was these expectations which prevented his being trained for any of the professions, and which thus, as in many similar cases, eventually proved a serious disadvantage to him.

The little boy throve apace, and a story which is told of him when he was five years old, gives evidence of his natural quickness of mind. Walking with his aunt, Lady Lucy North, in the park where the deer were lying lazily basking and browsing, he said to her, after some minutes' silence, "Aunt Lucy, why are you like that big stag there?" "I'm sure I can't tell," replied his aunt. "I don't think I'm a bit like. Tell me why." "Because, Aunt Lucy, you're a great *dear*." To dive to the depths of a long pocket, and extract half-a-crown, was the quick rejoinder of his aunt to his *jeu de mot;* and afterwards with much praise of his cleverness and affection, she related the story as it has since been preserved in the family.

At the early age of nine he went to Eton, when Dr. Keate was headmaster, and remained there for six years, in Dr. Hawtrey's house. He did not distinguish himself there by application to his books, but was known as a first-rate swimmer

---

[1] Schetky when a young man in Rome received the blessing of Cardinal York, the brother of Prince Charles Stuart, and died within two years of Brownlow North's death, at the age of ninety-six. That interview was thus one between two men who were respectively contemporaries of the battle of Culloden and the death of David Livingstone.

and general good fellow by the soubriquet of Gentleman Jack, in contradistinction to a bargee of his name, with whom the Eton boys of that time were familiar. The prayers and pious training of his mother, who was a most godly woman, bore as yet no fruit in the wild and wayward character of her boy, who was strongly averse to all that was good, his influence upon his schoolfellows being exactly the reverse of what she would have desired. His father dying in 1825, young Brownlow was removed from Eton, and went out to Corfu with his cousin, Lord Guilford, who was Chancellor of the Ionian Islands, where he had founded a Theological College, in which it was hoped his young relative might be induced to continue his studies. Nothing, however, seemed able to subdue the wild, high spirits of the lad; and the old gentleman, after finding one day that the window of his classroom had been made the winning-post and last jump of an amateur steeplechase, which Brownlow had got up, regretfully sent him home again, as beyond his control. He was then sent abroad with a tutor, to make, as it was then termed, ' the grand tour; ' but this experiment proved no more fortunate than the preceding, for meeting with his tutor in a gaming saloon the first night after their arrival in Paris, he insisted, under penalty of exposure, that all the books they had brought with them should be left behind in Paris, as unnecessary incumbrances, and afterwards, on the journey to Rome, he won from the miserable tutor at ecarté all the money with which he had been entrusted to defray the expenses of the tour, so that their position became completely reversed; the pupil was now master, and the tutor only tolerated as a useful and humble companion.[1]

On returning from the Continent he joined his mother, who had gone to live at Cheltenham. Here for a time he thoroughly enjoyed himself; for he was at that age (seventeen) very fond of dancing and riding, and both pleasures were here to his hand in perfection. So great an impression did he make upon

[1] It may be mentioned as not unworthy to rank along with other remarkable instances of Divine grace recorded in this volume, that this tutor, who must have had such a bad influence upon his pupil, at a later period gave every evidence of true penitence, and of being renewed in Christ Jesus.

his fair partners, that he proposed to no less than nineteen in one winter, and was accepted by them all! His fond mother had at first considerable difficulty, and felt no little embarrassment in satisfying the expectant mothers-in-law of a future earl that her son was quite a boy, and that nothing serious could be entertained; but after the experience of a few similar situations her replies almost formulated themselves, and it was with difficulty at last that she could refrain from yielding to a strong desire to laugh at the extraordinary absurdity of the whole affair.

His propensity for riding, which developed itself in racing up and down the promenade, a long straight boulevard, which those who know Cheltenham will recollect, had well-nigh brought him to his end, had not a merciful Providence watched over him and intervened to save his life. He was racing with one of his companions, and had just been successful, when his rival challenged him again to another contest, but stipulated they should change sides of the road, owing to some fancied advantage the right side possessed over the left. It was agreed to, and they started at full speed, when, unfortunately, coming down the hill round the corner where now stands the Queen's Hotel, there appeared a travelling carriage and pair of posters. To avoid a collision was impossible, and the horse and rider on the right-hand side went straight into the body of the carriage. The rider was thrown over the top, and taken up senseless, and afterwards died; the horse was so injured that it had to be immediately destroyed. This melancholy event made Cheltenham no longer agreeable to young North; and as he had made the acquaintance during the winter of several Irish families who had come there for the season, and who had pressed him to go and see them in Ireland in the summer, and as he was intimate with some of the officers of the regiment then quartered at Galway, he determined to cross the Channel, and try the attractions of the Emerald Isle. These proved too much for him; for the daughter of a highly-esteemed Protestant clergyman so captivated him, that he induced her to give him her hand, and was married to Grace Anne, second daughter of the Rev. Thomas Coffey, D.D., of Galway, on the 12th of

December, 1828, before he had completed his nineteenth year.
On the 12th of December, 1878, Mr. North would have completed fifty years of wedded life, and those who knew him may
remember how he looked forward to celebrating his " golden "
wedding. The issue of his marriage was three sons, Charles
Augustus, Brownlow who predeceased his father by a short
interval, and Frederic who died in early childhood.

About this period, however, great, and to him most important, changes had taken place in the circle of his relations.
His kind old friend and cousin had died, and had been succeeded in the earldom by his uncle Francis, his father's eldest
brother. Naturally an austere man, he had no sympathy with
the youthful extravagances of his nephew, and when the death
of his wife took place, after nearly thirty years of wedded life,
he told him he would marry again. He was as good as his
word, and marrying a lady some twenty-five years his junior,
he became the father of a family, and though his eldest son
did not live to succeed him, his grandson Dudley Francis became 7th Earl of Guilford.

Mr. North's expectations being thus doomed to disappointment, and his young wife having borne him two sons, the
question as to the maintenance of himself and them asserted
itself persistently and painfully. His sole income was derived
from his fees as registrar of the diocese of Winchester and
Surrey, to which office he had been appointed when quite
young by his grandfather, the Bishop. His work was done by
two local solicitors, who paid him a yearly allowance, and retained the balance of the fees for their services. At that time
he was in receipt of about £300 per annum,[1] a sum quite
insufficient for his habits; so to improve his finances he had
recourse to the gaming-table, with such lack of success that he
lost a larger sum than he could possibly pay; upon which he
left England for Boulogne, taking his wife and children with
him. Here again for some time he amused himself as before;

[1] The very moderate remuneration derived from this post was all
that he ever inherited in the way of means, a fact which it is right to
state, as many had the erroneous idea that he was possessed of a considerable private fortune, and judged him by this mistaken standard.

but finding his funds running low, and wishing for fresh excitement, he sent his wife and children home to his mother, and started off himself as a volunteer for Don Pedro's army in Portugal. Mrs. North then returned for a time to her old home in Ireland. After an interval of several months, Don Pedro's affair being settled, the prodigal returned home, to be forgiven; and in the summer of 1835 we find him going down to Scotland with his brother-in-law, Mr. Hayward, who had taken Abergeldie Castle for the shooting for that year. His wife and two younger children accompanied him; and from that time till his death, with only one interval of any importance, Scotland was the land of his adoption; in it was the home of his choice. Thus, though an Englishman by birth and education, he became almost a naturalised Scotsman, and was greatly attached to the country, and thoroughly conversant with the habits of thought of the people, whom he was destined afterwards to move so deeply and widely to concern about their eternal interests. But as yet his own thoughts and pursuits were running in wholly different channels.

For the greater part of the next four years Brownlow North remained in Aberdeenshire, taking a shooting during the season, and wintering in Aberdeen. It was then that he made his match with Captain Barclay of Ury, to see whom he had ridden over from Aberdeen, in so short a space of time, as he said, that the captain declared it impossible. " Do you call that impossible? " said Mr. North; " I will engage to ride from Aberdeen to Huntly and back at the same rate, that is, eighty miles in eight hours." Captain Barclay replied, " I will say it is impossible; and I will make you a wager of £50 you can't do it." North at once accepted the bet, and the match was settled to come off as soon as could be conveniently arranged. Of course in Aberdeen the coming event was freely talked over, the opinion being pretty general that Mr. North had overrated his own powers and those of the Aberdeen horses. So much so, that at a dinner shortly previous to the match, a young barrister said he was a fool attempting it, and had much better pay forfeit. " A fool you think me! " Mr. North rejoined : " so far do I differ from your opinion, that I will back myself not only to win my match with Captain Barclay, but to do the same feat over again the next day, and win my match with you." The company were astonished; the second match was made. Mr. North rode the eighty miles on three Aberdeen hacks, in hard snow and frost, danced all night at a ball afterwards, and rode and won the second match the following day.

There was another story told about him when shooting over the Huntly moors. Application was made to him one day by a young fellow, half-poacher, half-shepherd, to be allowed to go out with him on the hill, as he had heard that he was a most " tremendous " walker, and that he could find no person who could walk with him, and he should like to try himself what he could do. Mr. North said, " Very well. Meet me tomorrow morning, and I shall be glad of your company for the day." The man came and walked from six in the morning till sundown. Mr. North never used to rest for luncheon then. He came the next day, and the third day, when after a bad day's sport, birds being wild and scarce, on the road home a covey of grouse rose at the foot of a hill, and flew some way up the side of it. Turning to his companion, Mr. North said, " I shall have a try after those fellows." The man looked at him, saw that he was going, sat down on a stone, and cried like a child. He was beaten. He never came out any more. Mr. North certainly was a most untiring sportsman in those days. Every day and all day was his motto, and though never quite in the class of first-rate shots, he was a very good one, and long had a challenge unaccepted, to shoot a match for a month against any man, over two brace of dogs with one gun. One season, in Glenbucket, in six weeks he killed over nine hundred and seventy brace of grouse to his own gun.

It must not be imagined that throughout the course of his gay, pleasure-seeking, ungodly youth he had no upbraidings of conscience, no strivings of the Holy Spirit, and no seasons when he resolved to forsake living for self and sin, and to seek the Lord. On the contrary, like most persons who have been trained to pray at a mother's knee, he was, during his early life, occasionally the subject of deep religious impressions. In his childhood his mind had been stored by her with Divine truth, so that even at an early age he had a correct knowledge of the leading truths of the Gospel of Christ; and this, although long overlaid and apparently dead as well as buried, was yet to spring up in due time, and bring forth much fruit, so that she who sowed, and he who reaped, rejoiced together. These impressions more than once awakened in the bosom of Christian friends the hope that he was yielding himself to the Spirit's teaching, and the Saviour's gracious sway. But, alas! his good resolutions proved but as flaxen cords or green withes to bind the Samson-like force of his old nature; and when temptation came upon him, they were broken as a thread of tow at the touch of the fire, and all his professions and fair promise of amendment turned out, although not insincere at the time, to be as the morning cloud, or the early dew that goeth away. They were fair, but fading and fruitless.

The cause of the deepest religious impression with which he was visited previous to his awakening and conversion, was a conversation which the late eminently godly Duchess of Gordon had with him at her dinner-table at Huntly Lodge in the year 1839.

The following account of this incident was given by her Grace to her friend and pastor, the Rev. H. M. Williamson: " Mr. North was staying in Huntly, engaged in shooting, and utterly careless and ungodly. Some friends of his wrote to me, asking me to take some notice of him, with the view of withdrawing him from his evil ways and companionships. I promised to do so, and gave him an invitation to dinner. When we were at dinner, he sat beside me, and suddenly said to me with much gravity, ' Duchess, what should a man do who has often prayed to God and never been answered? ' I lifted up my heart to God to teach me what to say. I looked him quietly in the face, and said, so as not to be overheard by others, ' Ye ask, and receive not, because ye ask amiss, that ye may consume it upon your lusts ' (James iv. 3). His countenance changed, he became very greatly moved, was very quiet during the evening, and thanked me ere he left."

Not long after this his heart was further softened and impressed by the dangerous illness of his second son, Brownlow,

to whom he was much attached, and by the perusal of a little
book which the Duchess of Gordon had given Mrs. North to
read to her sick child. So deep and apparently hopeful was this
impression, that he determined to change entirely his mode of
life, study at Oxford, and take a degree with a view to entering the English Church. Those who have followed Mr. North's
career hitherto can imagine what force of character, what
energy and perseverance it required to undertake and carry
out such a programme. And as far as depended upon himself
he did so. He came to Cheltenham, consulted with his friend
Frederick Robertson (afterwards of Brighton), who was at that
time an undergraduate at Oxford, and by his advice matricu-
lated to Magdalen Hall as a Gentleman Commoner. He actually
had forgotten his Greek alphabet when he began his self-
imposed task; but such was the power of his memory, so great
his capacity for application, coupled with no ordinary natural
talent, that he passed both his " little go " and " great go "
examinations with credit, and his tutor, Dr. Jacobson, the late
Bishop of Chester, gave it as his opinion that had he entered
into the honour schools, and read for them, with the powers he
had shown he would have taken a fair class. He took his
degree in 1842.

Among his contemporaries at Oxford was the late Archbishop Tait, who in Brownlow North's later years, when he
was preaching as an evangelist in London, received him at
Lambeth Palace, and had pleasure in recalling with him their
old college days. For a considerable time after entering
Oxford he corresponded regularly with the Duchess of Gordon,
who had also written to some of her friends to look after him
there. His life during his residence at Oxford was most
exemplary; but when he was almost ready for ordination, and
had got the promise of a curacy at Olney, the Bishop of Lincoln
was made acquainted by an anonymous letter with some of the
excesses of his early years. Though this might have delayed
his ordination, Brownlow North seems to have felt, when it
was fairly put to him, that the present state of his heart also
rendered him unfit for the holy office of the ministry; for he
afterwards told his friend the Duchess of Gordon that at a

private interview the Bishop said to him, "Mr. North, if I were in your position, and you in mine, would you ordain me?" to which he candidly replied, "My Lord, I would not."

In answer to some interrogations from Mr. Williamson, then minister of the Free Church, Huntly, Mr. North said, that at this time he had been truly and thoroughly awakened, that he had a horrible sense of the demerit of his sins, and of the wrath of God justly due to them, and really purposed to depart from them and turn to God, and did so for a time in outward act. But, he added, " I never apprehended Christ, I never accepted Him as my sin-bearer and my righteousness."

To a Christian lady, a very old friend of his, the late Miss Gordon, sen., of Wardhouse, who knew him intimately both before and after his conversion, he said, when questioned by her concerning this period of awakening, and apparently hopeful impression, which took place after she knew him : " The house was swept and garnished, but *empty*; and the last state of that man was worse than the first. Think of the love of Jesus in coming to me after that! "

While he did not enter the Church as he intended to do on going to Oxford, the course of studies which he pursued with that view proved eventually of the greatest advantage to him as a mental discipline, and as furnishing him with that acquaintance with the evidences of revealed religion which he afterwards displayed, as well as with the other branches of an Arts curriculum.   It also enabled the Free Church of Scotland, without departing widely from her ordinary procedure, to recognize him publicly as a preacher of the gospel.

We have recounted thus fully the sad history of this period of spiritual impression, of good resolutions, and temporary reformation, to which Mr. North freely referred in private to his friends, not to lead any to think lightly of the great sin of grieving the Spirit of God, but while warning them of the danger of so doing, duly to magnify the greatness of that Divine grace which afterwards laid hold on one who had so grievously resisted His strivings, and had so backslidden when he was almost within the kingdom.   There is also a close connection between his own experience at this period and his subsequent religious history and public teaching. It also to some extent explains, taken along with his mother's training, how it was that he possessed such a full and clear knowledge of the way of salvation, and the main truths of Scripture, as to be able within about a year of his saving change to address meetings, without falling into any doctrinal errors which he might afterwards have had to retract.

After this he threw himself openly into his old life of pleasure and of sin. He forgot God, days without number, and wished that God would forget him. In 1845 he again took moors in Scotland, this time in Inverness-shire, when he resided at Glen Spean for three years—afterwards at Dalmally in Argyllshire, when his second son Brownlow married Miss McDonald Macalister, of Inistrynich. Mr. North lived to see them both die before him, and it is in her grave that his body now rests. In 1850 he took Dallas moors, and made that house his residence. His influence and example upon his friends and associates, and upon the whole neighbourhood of his residence, was very pernicious. To a large extent he cast off even that form of godliness which many worldly and ungodly persons retain out of deference to the feelings of the religious portion of the community. The Rev. W. Bathgate, late Congregational minister at Forres, when he saw the streets thronged with eager crowds going to hear Brownlow North preach, said to a friend, that he could not but recall the Sabbath mornings when at the same hour as the worshippers were flocking to the House of God, he had seen him drive in his dog-cart through these streets, with rod and basket behind him, going to spend the day in fishing on the river Findhorn. In his public addresses he acknowledged to the full the evil of his course of pleasure-seeking, irreligion and sin.

At the same time he was not without some good points in his character. He is spoken of by one who knew him at that time as generous towards cases of distress, and this natural kindliness of character and generosity of disposition remained with him to the end.

Another beautiful trait in his character was his devoted love to his mother, who, as we have seen, was a very earnest Christian. He was also very candid and honest, and far removed from making any profession which was not thoroughly genuine. A Christian relative[1] of his having heard an impressive sermon on the words, " Let me die the death of the righteous," at once thought of Mr. North, whose conversion she had much at heart, and on reaching home wrote down portions of the sermon, which she thought might prove of use to him, and with earnest prayer sent them to him while he was visiting worldly acquaintances in the Highlands. Mr. North's answer soon came back, and so far as she can recall it was, " To die the death of the righteous we must live the life of the righteous, dear Auntie, and I am not prepared for that yet."

While quite careless as to religion he so far had a reverence for its claims, that he has stated in public that " there never was an hour in his life, so far as he knew, when he would have remained in the same room with a man who was talking open infidelity and blasphemy."

At this time, then, he had deliberately rejected the great salvation, and as he afterwards confessed before multitudes of awe-struck listeners, he had virtually said to God, " I must have my sins : I know the consequences, but I accept them; I accept damnation as my portion." And the Lord had been just in judging, if He had taken him at his word.

This course of life continued till the autumn of 1854, when he was nearly forty-five years of age.

[1] Miss Gordon of Wardhouse.

CHAPTER II

Brownlow North's Conversion

THE 12th of August, 1854, found Mr. North busy once more upon the Dallas moors; and to show that his hand had not yet lost its cunning, on the 14th, after the other sportsmen had all started for distant beats, he went out, and with only his muzzle-loading gun brought in fifty brace and a bird as his contribution to the day's total. His son Brownlow claimed fifty-one brace for himself, and it was always an undecided point as to who capped the bag on that day.

But now the Spirit of God was about to revive impressions in his mind and heart with much more than their old power, to imprint them on that living tablet in such a manner as that they should never be effaced. His long-suffering was not exhausted, though that of most Christians would have been so.

In the beginning of November, 1854, while he had still health and vigour to relish sport as much as ever, his thoughts were wandering away to his relation to his offended God. Prayer was still ascending for him, and there was one watching to drop the word in season; for though Mr. North had the night of his startling arrest so vividly impressed upon his mind as to regard it as the whole process of his awakening, Miss Gordon recalled the following important reminiscence : —

" Before his conversion he was spending the day in Elgin, and dined and stayed all night at my house. Our conversation, as it often did, took a serious turn. Sometimes he broke it off hastily, saying, ' You always draw me on to make admissions which make you think me better than I really am.' But this evening he seemed depressed, and after some minutes' silence he exclaimed, ' I have a great mind to give it all up and go to

17

Blackwell,' meaning, I supposed, intimacies in the Highlands where he went every Christmas, most hurtful to him, but which no entreaties could prevail on him to give up. I said, ' Who is Blackwell? ' He said, ' An evangelical clergyman of the Church of England, a nephew of my mother's, a good and pious man.' I earnestly urged him to do so, and there for the time it ended." We may explain that soon afterwards, in the period of his spiritual distress, he did go up to visit the Rev. Edward Blackwell, at Amberley Rectory, whose experienced Christian counsel, then and always after, was much valued by him, and whose views of the doctrines of Divine grace appear, to a large extent, to have influenced and moulded Mr. North's own.

Mr. North then said to Miss Gordon, "You never come to see us now at Dallas; you promised my mother you would never give us up." Miss Gordon promised to come, perhaps that week, and on leaving he said to her, " Remember your promise."

In a day or two she received a note from Mrs. North, imploring her to come to them, and saying that the night before her husband had been very ill, and that she thought it was something on his mind, and if it were, he would open his mind to her, and that he had requested that she should be written for.

That had been the night of Brownlow North's remarkable awakening, the circumstances of which were often related by him in public. We shall here narrate it as it was given from his own lips to the students of the Edinburgh University in March, 1862 :—

"It pleased God," he said, " in the month of November, 1854, one night when I was sitting playing at cards, to make me concerned about my soul. The instrument used was a sensation of sudden illness, which led me to think that I was going to die. I said to my son, " I am a dead man; take me upstairs." As soon as this was done, I threw myself down on the bed. My first thought then was, Now, what will my forty-four years of following the devices of my own heart profit me? In a few minutes I shall be in hell, and what good will all these things do me, for which I have sold my soul? At that moment I felt constrained to pray, but it was merely the prayer of a coward, a cry for mercy. I was not sorry for what I had done, but I was afraid of the punishment of my sin. And yet still there was something trying to prevent me putting myself on my knees to call for mercy, and that was the presence of the maidservant in the room, lighting my fire. Though I did not believe at that time that I had ten minutes to live, and knew that there was no possible hope for me but in the mercy of God, and that if I did not seek that mercy I could not expect to have it, yet such was the nature of my heart, and of my spirit within me, that it was a balance with me, a thing to turn this way or that, I could not tell how, whether I should wait till that woman left the room, or whether I should fall on my knees and cry for mercy in her presence. By the grace of God I did put myself on my knees before that girl, and I believe it was the turning-point with me. I believe that if I had at that time resisted the Holy Ghost—of course, I cannot say, for who shall limit the Holy Ghost?—but my belief is that it would have been once too often. By God's grace I was not prevented. I did pray, and though I am not what I should be, yet I am this day what I am, which at least is not what I was. I mention this because I believe that every man has in his life his turning-point. I believe that the sin against the Holy Ghost is grieving the Spirit once too often."

On the following day he announced publicly to his friends staying in the house, and to others by letter, that from that instant he had become a changed man, a resolution to which in the strength of the Saviour he was enabled to adhere.

When his friend, who had been so suddenly summoned to Dallas, reached the house, she found Mr. North in his dressing-room, at his writing-table. He seemed as if just risen from a long illness, and was very gentle and subdued in manner. He said to her little but " I am, dear auntie, I trust, by the grace of God, a changed man, and I have been writing to some of my former companions, to tell them of the change." In the evening, between nine and ten o'clock, he came and joined the family; a bell rang, and she was astonished to see the household assemble for prayers. He read a portion of God's Word, and made some remarks on it, as if it had been the habit of his life. His manner had no excitement in it, but a gentle gravity. By prayer and reading of the Scriptures he strove to find God and pardon and peace; but during many, many months he rose night after night from his bed, that he might retire in agony of soul to the dressing-room, and there engage in earnest supplication. Some years afterwards, when visiting Dallas with a friend, he went into the billiard-room, and pointing to the chimney-piece said that when in that room he had been so suddenly awakened he took his cigar from his mouth, and laid it down there, never to be touched again. For though he had been in the habit of constant smoking from the time he was twelve years of age, and became so addicted to it that he often even took a cigar in his mouth when he went to bed, and fell asleep with it between his lips, he never afterwards touched the weed or took a billiard cue in his hand.

The announcement made by Brownlow North to his old friends of his sudden change, whether orally or in writing, created no small sensation among them. Some thought he had gone out of his mind, others thought it was a temporary impression or excitement, and that it would soon pass off; and this was specially the case with those of them who were acquainted with his previous convictions and temporary reformation: while in some of the newspapers it was even said, after he began his public work, that the whole thing was done for a wager, and that he had taken a bet to gather a certain number of thousands or ten thousands of hearers in a given time. So little do carnal men understand the workings of the Spirit of God, even when they see the most striking and manifest proofs of it. Not only did worldly people stand in doubt of him, but Christian people stood aloof from him for a time, and he underwent the trying ordeal of St. Paul, when he essayed to join himself to the disciples, recorded in Acts ix. 26, to whose case his own experience of God's sovereign awakening power had borne a very marked resemblance. Mr. North recorded this similarity of his case to that of Saul of Tarsus in a marginal note on John iv. 27, "Upon this came Jesus' disciples, and marvelled that He talked with the woman." " It is often a marvel to disciples in every age the people Christ speaks to. When Paul was converted, they were all afraid of him, and believed not that he was a disciple. So it was with Brownlow North, and no wonder; yet for all that he does believe that the Lord has spoken to him. To Him be the gratitude and the glory ! " So on the remark of Festus to Paul at his trial (Acts xxvi. 24), that the apostle was " beside himself " and " mad," Mr. North notes from his own experience, " Christians in all ages have been called mad; but who was the most mad, Paul or Festus? " and at ver. 22, when Paul said that it was by the help of God that he had continued from the day of his conversion until that day, he doubly underlines Paul's words and adds, " It was God who enabled him to continue. Give Him the glory, and trust in Him. And He will enable me."

But some at least of his old Christian friends, who had known the history of his careless godless days, and the history of his religious impressions, stood by him and encouraged him at this crisis of his life. Especially was this the case with Miss Gordon, who writes in September, 1877, after describing her arrival at Dallas and the evening family worship : " He was soon obliged to go on a mission of kindness promised to godless friends (for he was by nature kind and generous). His family were fearful for his health and he did not seem fit to go, for such a mental revolution had acted on his frame; but no one else I found could do it. I asked him to let me hear soon from him. He wrote from Inverness, having gone there on Saturday to catch the Fort William boat early on Monday, (formerly he always went on the Sabbath), and his note contained a few words. ' I have been twice to the Free Church. I am kept. Yours, etc.' And ' *I am kept* ' were long the last words in his notes to me."

It was probably on this very journey to or from his destination in the steamer on the Caledonian Canal that by his altered appearance he attracted the attention of the men on board the ship. For in the year 1866, when in conversation with the steward of one of these steamers, the writer happened to mention the name of Brownlow North, the steward said to him, "Do you know him, sir?" and on our replying in the affirmative, and asking if he knew him, or had heard him preach, he said he had seen him on board the steamer shortly before and shortly after his change, and that he never in his life saw such an alteration in any man. In going northward he attracted his observation by the great amount of spirits he consumed, and the general recklessness of his bearing, while in returning he was so pulled down and weakened, that he had to lean heavily on a staff in coming on board, and seemed very solemn and very much shaken, like a man who had just recovered from a fever. Then he learned that what had so pulled him down and so shaken his stalwart frame was no bodily illness, but distress of soul; and he seemed thoroughly satisfied that it must have been a very deep and very severe anguish of spirit that had produced such an effect on his outward frame, that, as he said, he would hardly have known him for the same man.

Thus suddenly arrested, awakened, and reformed, it must not be supposed that Brownlow North as rapidly found peace in believing in the Saviour. As we have already indicated, he underwent a very severe and prolonged period of deep spiritual conflict, which made the strong man become feeble through the intensity of his emotion and the protractedness of his distress. With him it was of a truth the strong man striving, and striving with all the powers of his being, and the faculties of his mind and spirit, to enter in at the strait gate; while he wrestled not only against the flesh and blood of his old nature, but, as he himself felt, 'against principalities, against powers, and against the rulers of the darkness of this world,' (Eph. vi. 12). His being brought through such a severe ordeal, and kept for so long travelling through the Valley of the Shadow of Death, was probably due in part to his having so long resisted the strivings of the Divine Spirit, but in part also to the design of the Almighty to fit him by his own experience to enter into the sympathies and spiritual difficulties of multitudes of anxious souls, by giving him a deep knowledge of the deceitfulness and sinfulness of the human heart, and of the countless snares and devices of the wicked one. Certain it is that not a few of those men of God who have been the honoured instruments of turning many to the saving knowledge of Jesus, and delivering them from the bondage of sin and corruption, were led in like manner through fire and through water, before they were brought out into the wealthy place. The cases of Martin Luther and John Bunyan, along with others, will at once suggest themselves to many of our readers.

During this long period he read nothing but the Bible, not even looking at the newspaper. The Rev. Charles G. Scott, afterwards of Harrow Road Church, London, who was working in the parish of Dyke at the time of Mr. North's conversion, mentions that Mr. North told him that at that time he was so engrossed with the concerns of his soul, and although the Crimean War was raging, its thrilling events were all unknown to him: so that one day when the country had been ringing with the details of the battle of Inkerman, happening to be travelling on the outside of a stage-coach, he overheard a conversation about the great battle which had been fought on the 5th of November, and of which he knew nothing, so entirely absorbed was he in the greater and more terrible conflict that was raging within his own breast.

He has stated in public that at this season he often put himself upon his knees, or stretched himself upon his rug, with his mouth in the dust, seeking to get hold of the truth that the Person he called God heard him. At last he was enabled to realize this fact by reasoning with himself that if God had been present with him since he was a child and knew every act he had done, then surely He must know what was passing now, and must be present though he did not see Him.

Mr. North also states that during this period he was very much afraid of God and of Christ. As an instance of this he has recorded that, five or six weeks after his awakening, a Christian friend was sitting with him, and asked him if he ever prayed for the coming of Christ; to which he replied, " No, I should be afraid. Suppose He were to come, I should be in dreadful fear." " Well," said the friend, " we are told to do it." They talked together, and his friend showed him that there was a positive command to pray for His coming. Soon after they united in prayer. Mr. North joined in the supplication, and when he concluded, his friend reminded him to pray for Christ's coming. To this Mr. North replied that he did not desire it, and therefore it would be hypocrisy to ask for it. His friend said, " Pray God to make you wish for it. Tell him the truth." Mr. North then reasoned with himself, that he had accepted His atonement, had laid the burden of his sins upon Him, that if the Redeemer came, He would come as his Saviour, therefore he felt he could honestly desire it, and he prayed, " Come, Lord Jesus! " This incident also evinces that thorough genuineness and transparent honesty which characterized the whole of his religious life from its very commencement.

In the month of December, 1854, he went up and visited his mother, spending Christmas with her, and remained with her for a short time, when she rejoiced over the answer to her long interceding for his salvation, and was filled with thankfulness over her son who had been dead and was alive again, who had been lost and was found. He was much encouraged by his saintly mother saying to him, " Brownlow, God is not only able to save you, but to make you more conspicuous for good than ever you were for evil! "

It was in this prolonged period of anxiety of soul that many of the truths which he afterwards preached with such amazing fervour and force were written by the Spirit of the living God upon the tablet of his heart, and burned into the very texture of his being. It was now that the thought of eternity was ever present to his distracted mind; now that he was taught that God is, when tempted long and sorely to doubt it; now that he was brought to realize not only God's existence, but His immediate presence beside him, so that he foresaw the Lord God always before him, and believed that he could not escape from His presence. It was now that he learned to hang for his life upon the naked word of God, feeling that only that which had divine authority, and was fully inspired by the Spirit of God, could afford ground for hope or confidence to a sinner such as he was; now that he was led to sound the depths of corruption within himself, and learned that he was absolutely helpless towards God, and that he must be renewed by the Holy Ghost. It was now also that he was taught at last to believe in the atoning sacrifice of the Son of God as sufficient to cleanse from all sin, even from sins so scarlet-coloured and doubly-dyed as his had been. Now the lesson came home that the sinner is justified instrumentally by faith, and not by his own feelings, that what is subjective and changeable can never be the ground of an unchanging state of reconciliation, or of a peace which will bear the brunt of many a hellish battery, and stand unshaken amid the changing circumstances, the drifting tides, and the driving storm or sunshine of an unstable world. During these weary months he had many difficulties about the truth of God's Word, and he tells us that he had to humble himself, and though a middle-aged man, to enter into the kingdom of God like a little child.

One of his difficulties was about the divine and human natures of Jesus Christ. One day, about three weeks after his awakening, he was reading John v. 16-30, after having sought the Holy Spirit's teaching. After reading the words "My Father worketh hitherto, and I work," his thoughts wandered from the passage before him, and he began to meditate about the deep things of the Divine Word, and after thinking for a long time on these abstruse subjects he was aroused by a violent headache. "I had been thinking," he says, "probably for hours about the plainly revealed but unexplained mysteries of God, and was no wiser; they still remained unrevealed and still unexplained, and all the fruit of my thinking seemed a headache." After a time he began to think again, and said aloud to himself, "Brownlow North, do you think by your own reason or deep thinking you can find out God or know Christ better than the Bible can teach you to know Him? If you do not, why are you perplexing your brains with worse than useless speculations? Why are you not learning and holding on by what you learn from the Scriptures? You are shut up to one of two things, you must either make a god and a religion for yourself, and stand or fall eternally by it, or you must take the religion of Jesus Christ as revealed to you in His Word. You cannot receive a little of God's teaching and a little of your own, you cannot believe on the Lord Jesus Christ and the wisdom of your own heart at the same time. Choose then, now and for ever, by which you will stand or fall." He then struck his hand forcibly upon his open Bible, and said, " God helping me, I will stand or fall by the Lord Jesus Christ. I will put my trust in His truth, and in His teaching as I find it in the written Word of God; and doing that, so sure as the Lord Jesus Christ is the truth, I must be forgiven and saved." After that, he tells us he ceased to try to reconcile apparently opposing doctrines of Scripture, or those that were above his reason, submitting his intellect like a child to the teaching of God's Word and Spirit. (See " Christ the Saviour and Christ the Judge.")

He tells us that on the day here referred to, the 21st verse of John v. struck him very powerfully as he read, " The Son quickeneth whom He will." He saw it was a certainty that if he received the kingdom of God as a little child, since Christ could quicken whom He would, He could quicken him. At least he felt that he *might* be saved, for he had found one who was able to save anybody, and therefore could save him. Still fierce temptations beset him, and much darkness beclouded his soul for many months after this.

In the month of March, 1855, he let his house and moors at Dallas, and went to reside in the town of Elgin, where he attached himself to the ministry of the late Rev. Donald Gordon, minister of the Free Church and son of the well-known Dr. Robert Gordon of Edinburgh. Of Mr. Gordon's ministrations he always spoke most thankfully, and gratefully acknowledged the spiritual help which he derived from them. One who was at the time a member of the congregation writes : " Mr. North on his arrival in Elgin, seemed in great distress of mind, so overwhelming was the sight of himself which he had got. At the time Mr. Gordon was lecturing through St. Mark, and Sabbath by Sabbath the subjects of the lectures that came in course seemed to suit Mr. North's case so startlingly, that I think I see him now with his eyes riveted on the speaker, and sometimes for very gladness of heart I have seen the tears run down his face in church."

Miss Gordon, of Wardhouse, in recalling this time, says, " In the spring of the year, Mr. and Mrs. North came to stay with me. His health was very much shaken. Mr. Gordon, the Free Church minister, was much with him, but he lived in his little study which I had prepared for him, and except for meals and family worship we seldom saw him. He took long walks, and gave a tract to every one he met, at first with diffidence, but he said he never had but one refusal. His time in the house was occupied in studying the Word and in prayer. He sometimes got up in the night, went to his study, and prayed aloud, I would say, agonized in prayer." The Rev. Adam Lind, United Presbyterian minister in Elgin, wrote : " For some time after coming to Elgin, he lived in great retirement, deeply engrossed with his Bible, and abounding in private prayer. I saw him occasionally, and had ample opportunities of observing the workings of his mind; and the mark of true grace which struck me first in his case was the spirit of profound humility, penitence, and adoring gratitude. He seemed like one unable to get out of the region of wonder and amazement at the sovereign kindness of that benignant Being who had borne with him so long in his sin, and such sin, and so much sin; and not only borne with him, but shielded him, and held him back from self-ruin, at length arresting him in his career of folly and wickedness, and bringing him to Himself, a pardoned penitent, a returned prodigal." The Rev. H. M. Williamson wrote. " The first time I saw him was in the Free Church, Elgin, then under the ministry of Mr. Gordon. I was preaching on the Fast-day, and he was present. I had scarcely reached the pulpit when I was arrested by his appearance. Indeed, I was so fascinated, that I felt considerably disturbed during the service. There was the exhibition of such character, such a strength of will, the lines of a life for self and evil, an air of unrest and a hungry look of soul, that cannot be described, as with lowering brows he looked into the speaker and listened to every utterance. When I came down from the pulpit I asked Mr. Gordon, ' Who is that remarkable person, and what is his strange history?   He looks as if he had been a servant of evil, and yet he looks as if yielding wholly to God.'   Mr. G. replied, ' Oh, that is Brownlow North; he has been remarkably awakened, and we trust really brought to God.' "

During these long dark months he was often sorely tempted to deny the very being of God, and to find relief in atheism from the accusations of conscience and the weary struggles of his soul towards the light for which he was vainly, as it seemed to him, groping. We have heard him tell how at this momentous period of his history the suggestion that there was no God, and that His existence was a mere fable, often so persistently pressed itself upon him even when on his knees in prayer, that he felt as if Satan were at his elbow, constantly whispering, " *There is no God, there is no God!* " that he would then have to rise from his knees, and walk up and down the little gravel path in his back garden at Elgin for hours, almost like one demented, iterating and reiterating the words, " *God is, there is a God,*" in reply to these temptations of the devil or of his own heart; until, enabled once more to realize His existence, he returned to his devotion. It might be when he went out into the street upon some business, perhaps before he was aware, his faith in the existence of God again would fail, and, plunged into a sea of doubt and distress, he would return to repeat his whole wrestling and struggling until God satisfied him once more of the truth of His existence. It was a trying ordeal to go through; but when once the way of escape from this temptation was opened to him in God's good time, it left his foot planted upon a rock which never trembled beneath him, and gave him a manly, almost a titanic grasp of the truth of the being of God, which added vivid colour and character to all his lifelong preaching. We shall refer to this again in its own place.

At one critical time during this period of soul-conflict he stated in one of his addresses that the question, " Believest thou that I am able to do this? " was made a word of life to him. He writes: " I was very near death; I was almost despairing. The only thing that kept my head above the water was the promise,' Him that cometh to me I will in no wise cast out.' I repeated it again and again, and prayed very earnestly, when the word came to me with such power, and with such a rebuke, ' Believest thou that I am able to do this,' He *was* able, and I believed Him, and He did it."

That text, John vi. 37, was one which he never wearied of quoting, to which he never failed in public and in private to direct the anxious and returning sinner, and no words are oftener written on the pages of his private Bible than those which, like the old woman, he could mark as both 'tried and proved,' " *Him that cometh to me I will in no wise cast out.*"

At length he was delivered out of all his distresses and perplexities through the Word and by the Spirit of God. We shall best give the description of his deliverance in his own words. " I had risen from my bed in my soul agony, for I was many months in trouble about my soul, though I need not have been as many hours, if I had only had faith to believe in Jesus Christ, and to make my own heart a liar; but my own heart told me that I was the chief of sinners, that Paul, who called himself the chief, was not to be compared—no, neither was he —to me, and that there could be no hope for me; and for months I believed my own heart. One night, being unable to sleep, I had risen and gone into my closet to read the Bible. The portion I was reading was the third chapter of Romans; and as I read the twentieth and following verses, a new light seemed to break in on my soul. ' By the deeds of the law there shall no flesh be justified in God's sight.' That I knew. But then I went on to read, ' But now, *now,* the righteousness of God *without the law* is manifested, being witnessed by the law and the prophets; even the righteousness of God which is by faith of Jesus Christ *unto all and upon all them that believe: for there is no difference.*' With that passage came light into my soul. Striking my book with my hand, and springing from my chair, I cried, ' If that scripture is true, I am a saved man ! That is what I want; that is what God offers me; that is what I will have.' God helping me, it was that I took : THE RIGHTEOUSNESS OF GOD WITHOUT THE LAW. It is my ONLY hope."[1]

[1] From *The Lord our Righteousness.*

Now could Brownlow North utter with a depth and fulness of significance which few could surpass, the inspired song which a few years afterwards became the favourite and characteristic hymn of praise of young converts in the Great Irish Revival of 1859-60.

> " He took me from a fearful pit,
>   And from the miry clay;
> And on a rock He set my feet,
>   Establishing my way.
>
> He put a new song in my mouth,
>   Our God to magnify :
> Many shall see it, and shall fear,
>   And on the Lord rely."
>
> Psalm xl. 2, 3 (Scottish Version).

So terrible had been the protracted spiritual conflict from which he now emerged, that looking back on it after ten years he stated on one occasion in public that he wished his worst enemy might be spared going through the same ordeal. He also said that his friends had sometimes feared that his reason might give way under the severity of the strain upon his mind and spirit.

We have heard it remarked by some that a great part of the influence afterwards wielded by Brownlow North, and by others who like him had gone great lengths in the service of sin and Satan, was owing to the very fact that they had so long and openly served " the world, the flesh, and the devil," whose service they afterwards as openly renounced; and that on this account they made more effective preachers of the gospel than those who had been more under the control of restraining grace. While not denying that the conversion of a John Newton, a Colonel Gardiner, or a Brownlow North, and their subsequent zeal for their Lord and Saviour, have been the means of arresting others who like them were living without the fear of God in the world, we are sure that the service of sin is in all cases very bitter, and must always have bitter fruits and baneful consequences, even in those cases in which

God may in His all-wise and almighty grace bring good out of evil. Where the conscience has been cleansed from flagrant sin by the sweet sprinkling of the all-atoning blood of the great propitiation, the memory must through life retain sin's dark stains and saddening recollections; evil has been done to others, which it may be impossible ever wholly to undo; and habits have been formed through a long course of sinful indulgence which are most injurious to the man himself. The want in Mr. North of such entire and constant self-denial, as distinguished from Christian self-surrender, as has characterized such men as the Rev. Robert M. McCheyne and Mr. North's dear and attached friend and fellow-labourer, Hay Macdowall Grant, of Arndilly, may perhaps be traced to the long course of years during which he lived for and worshipped self before the idol was broken and he was led to worship God. This beautiful trait in the Christian character is indeed rarely found in its perfection, but is very attractive and influential wherever it is present in a marked degree. It always must be " an evil thing and a bitter " to have openly forsaken the Lord our God; and when the iniquity is freely pardoned, and the yoke of the transgressions broken, the scars from the yoke and the marks of the chains often remain.

It was ever with deep sorrow and humiliation that this man of God on occasion alluded to himself as being like the man who was above forty years of age on whom the miracle of healing was showed (Acts iv. 22). On the first page of the New Testament which he began to use on New Year's Day, 1855, is the affecting inscription, written apparently at first in pencil, and afterwards traced in ink: "*B. North, a man whose sins crucified the Son of God.*" And his words and manner alike in alluding to his having been as one born out of due time proved that his deepest feeling was—

> " Alas, that I so lately knew Thee,
>   Thee so worthy of the best;
>   Nor had sooner turned to view Thee,
>   Truest good, and only rest!
>   The more I love, I mourn the more
>   That I did not love before."

CHAPTER III

First Private Efforts to Save Souls

THE grace of God in the heart of man very soon betrays its presence. It is the imparting to the soul of the mind of Christ, which desires the welfare of our brother as well as the glory of our God. In its own nature it is expansive and communicative. It is like light, whose property it is to shine; like salt, whose nature it is to communicate to foreign substances its saltness; like seed, which ever seeks to reproduce itself; like water, which descending from above into an earthly heart, becomes therein a well of water springing up to everlasting life. These are not accidents, but are essential properties of grace wherever found. The soul that was dead, when made alive is made a new centre and spring of life amid a world of death. Christ's people are the immortal seed which is destined to fill the world's face with fairest fruit. Life loves to work; and where there is no work there is no life, or only weak and dying life.

We need not wonder then to find that Brownlow North, as soon as he had seen the Saviour, desired to point Him out to others; as soon as he had tasted of the living water, sought to lead others to the fountain's brink and to persuade them to stoop down and drink. The wonder would have been had it been otherwise. His energy of character, natural gifts, and power of mind, combined with special grace vouchsafed to him, made him the powerful preacher he afterwards became; but grace, native and simple, made him, what it makes every true recipient, anxious within his present sphere to use each opportunity to commend his Saviour by lip and life to all with whom he came in contact.

He has told us that it was about eleven months after his

awakening at Dallas, when he strongly felt it to be his duty
to do some service for the Lord. For two months before this
he had shut himself up in his own room, reading the Bible and
praying. He then said to himself that he must do something
for God but felt that he could not. The thought suggested
itself to his mind that he might at least distribute tracts, but
he felt that to do so would make himself ridiculous, and that
the people would laugh at him and call him mad. At last he
resolved to try, and putting a number of tracts into his pocket,
he went into the most secluded part of Elgin, in which he was
living. The first person he met with was an old woman, who
amazed him by accepting his tract without laughing at him.
To another old woman whom he saw coming down the road
he presented another tract, and she received it with thanks.
The third he gave to a policeman, who said, "Thank you,
Mr. North." He recorded it as his experience after fourteen
years' trial, that only on one occasion was a tract refused, and
that was by a professed infidel, and yet he had systematically
given away tracts to persons of all ranks, in all sorts of places.
Very few Christians can be preachers like Brownlow North,
but there are none who cannot be tract distributers.

Like most other persons, he found it no easy thing to serve
the Lord and try to do good to the souls of others, especially
at the commencement of his course. There is often opposition
in our own hearts before we can humble ourselves even to
hand a tract to an acquaintance or to an unknown fellow-
passenger, and sometimes, though rarely, we may find our
proffer of a tract resented as a liberty. Mr. North met with
some opposition at first, even in giving away tracts. The Rev.
Dr. Fergus Ferguson mentions that once in Glasgow, when he
had preached a public sermon in which he referred to Mr.
North as a remarkable trophy of Divine grace, a gentleman
asked to be introduced to him at the close of the service, and
told him that he came from a district in the West Highlands,
in which Mr. North had resided a considerable time before
his conversion, and that he recollected his returning there after
his great change, and trying, by giving away tracts, to undo
some of the evil he had done. The people, probably doubting

B

the sincerity of his repentance, avoided him and his tracts. Mr. North bore this with beautiful humility, as a cross which perhaps he deserved to bear. But he was not on this account discouraged or weary in well-doing, but left the tracts lying in prominent places on the roads, and on windy days put them under stones, that the wind might not blow them away and that that other wind, that bloweth where it listeth, might gain access to some poor sinner's heart.

He always continued the practice of tract-distribution, although to the last he often found it a trial to do so. We have heard him say that, after he had served the Lord for years, it sometimes cost him half an hour's internal struggle before he could muster courage to offer a tract to a gentleman travelling in a railway carriage with him. Once on arriving at Ramornie to visit his friend, Sheriff Maitland Heriot, he mentioned that in crossing the ferry to Tayport in the steamer he saw a group of gentlemen talking; his conscience told him that he ought to embrace the opportunity, and speak, or give a tract to them; but then it would be much more pleasant and easy to do nothing. This went on for some time, but at last the feeling that it might be a matter of eternal life or death gained the victory, and approaching them he offered each of them a tract, which was accepted quite politely, and he found that some of the company had recognized him, and would rather have been surprised if he had remained quiet. Following out his views of the usefulness of these short messengers of truth he wrote afterwards a number of pointed and powerful tracts on the leading truths of salvation, which, as will be seen from this volume, have been greatly blessed to souls.

About this time he began to visit among the sick poor of Elgin, particularly those connected with Mr. Gordon's church. A friend who knew him well at that time writes : " I remember his supplying the very poor and bedridden with many little comforts, such as introducing gas into their cheerless rooms, and paying for it himself. I have myself gone with him to see some of these poor creatures and I shall never forget some of these visits, one in particular, to a poor wretched old body, who had been unable to leave her bed for years. Mr. North

would take a little stool, sit down at her unlit fire, and peel
oranges for her, and this in a room where the surroundings
were too disgusting even to mention. After that time, I, for
one, felt that I could not be in his company for a quarter of an
hour without being benefited by it. We all loved him much."

Once, in Aberdeen, in January, 1863, when speaking of this
time, in drawing a contrast between the promptings of the
flesh and the promptings of the Spirit, he said, " When I first
came to know the Lord, the Spirit said to me ' Brownlow North,
there's that woman in the porter's lodge; you ought to go and
speak to her about religion.' But the flesh said, ' Do nothing
of the sort; keep what you've got to yourself.' But the Spirit
gave me no rest till I went to the woman at the porter's lodge,
and read the Bible to her, and told her what the Lord had
done for my soul. Then again the Spirit said to me, ' There's
the washerwoman in the town, you know; you should go to
her, and read and pray with her also.' But the flesh said,
' Do nothing of the sort; she will likely think that she has
more religion than you have.' Still the Spirit would give me
no rest till I read and prayed with the washerwoman also."
In these early visits he seems to have confined himself to
giving away tracts, reading the Bible, and occasionally en-
gaging in prayer.

The first time, according to his recollection, when he went
to speak to anyone directly about the soul, was on being sent
for in November, 1855, by a woman who carried his letter
bag, to speak to her dying niece. Feeling this to be a call from
God, he went to the house. He found that she was a Christian,
and drawing rapidly near her end. The poor dying girl said
to him, " Oh, sir, never mind me; but say something through
me to my father, for father is a bad man." He addressed
himself to her father, who seemed impressed, as was also his
wife, by his words, and by the solemn circumstances they were
in. Two careless persons who happened to be present were
interested in what Mr. North said, and returned to hear him
speak whenever he visited the house. The father became a
reformed man. The news of this spread among the neighbours,
and they flocked into the dying girl's room whenever Mr.

North was present. After this had gone on for several days, a woman came to him, and said, " O, sir, I wish you would come and speak to my husband, as you are speaking here; for he is a bad man too, and I think you might do him good." He agreed to go and converse with the man; and on leaving, he asked him to return, saying that he would gather ten or twelve of his fellow-workmen, who were journeymen shoemakers, to listen to him. He addressed the little gathering of shoemakers as requested, who were so interested that they asked him to come and speak to them again, and on coming on the evening named, he found the room crowded with some fifty or sixty people. The shoemaker who had asked him to give the address afterwards died rejoicing in Jesus, as did also his wife. Thus drawn by providential leading into this work, he soon found himself holding a cottage meeting every evening of the week, and once spoke in a granary to about two hundred people.

Mrs. Macdonald, the widow of the Rev. John Macdonald of Calcutta, went to one of these little gatherings one evening. She could get no further in than half-way up the stairs, and told a friend that she had heard nothing like it since she listened to her father-in-law, the " Apostle of the North ".

From various quarters we have received testimony to the interest that was awakened and the good that was effected by these visits to the sick, and little cottage-meetings held in Elgin and its immediate neighbourhood. Mr. John Kintrea, referring to these meetings, wrote:—" In addition to his Elgin cottage-meetings, which were at this time almost nightly, he held weekly meetings in Bishopmills, a loft having been got for the purpose; and although the place was capable of holding a good number, such was the desire to hear him, that the loft was crowded before the hour of meeting, numbers having to go away unable to get a hearing.

" Sometimes, after conducting these little services, one of the office-bearers of the Free Church would convoy him home, to whom he often expressed his fears lest he should, in holding such meetings, be travelling beyond the line of duty, and trespassing upon the sphere belonging to the ministry. Yet he could find no satisfactory reason to his own mind for refusing calls to go and speak at such gatherings when invited to do so. At this time this subject seemed to occupy his mind a good deal, and he appeared to be looking up for light and guidance."

It was now that Mr. John Gow, late town missionary in Elgin, became acquainted with Mr. North. Mr. Gow had long been in the habit of visiting the patients in Gray's Hospital on Sabbath afternoons. One night, as he was returning home, a gentleman, whom he did not know, put two tracts into his hand, and on mentioning the circumstance next day to some of his acquaintances, he learned that it was a gentleman recently converted, who had begun to hold cottage-meetings through the town, and that he was to hold one on the following Tuesday in a room in Masson Lodge Close. Accordingly Mr. Gow went to the meeting, which he much enjoyed, and at the close was introduced to Mr. North as a brother worker. Mr. North invited him to another of his addresses which he had arranged to give in Fraser's Close, and at the same time expressed a wish to accompany him to Gray's Hospital, which he did the following Sunday, and on several succeeding ones.

A short time after Mr. North told him that he thought a Scripture-reader would be very useful in Elgin, and asked him if he were willing to undertake the duties, which after careful consideration he decided to do. Mr. Gow began his work as missionary in March 1856, and prosecuted it till his sudden death in the spring of 1878, not without tokens of the Master's blessing. After some years Mr. Robert Brander, banker, Elgin, most liberally made over the sum of £1,000, the interest of which was to be applied to the annual salary of the missionary.

Thus from the very first Mr. North not only threw himself heart and soul into hard and earnest work for his Saviour, but exerted himself to secure the co-operation both of voluntary assistants and of stated and regular labourers; realizing the immense strength of Satan's kingdom in the earth, and that to attack it with any hopes of solid and lasting victory demands all the combined strength, wisdom, and zeal of the soldiers of the cross.

Having at first scruples about the propriety of one who was

merely a layman doing so much in the way of addressing his fellow-men, even in these small meetings, he spread the whole matter before the Lord in prayer, asking him to close the door if it were not in accordance with His will that he should thus address his fellow-sinners. Waiting and watching the indications of Providence for an answer to his prayer, he received an increasing number of requests to speak, and heard of an increasing number of cases of spiritual impression.

About this time another providential circumstance led him to believe that the Lord was calling him to speak, and not to hold his peace. He had gone up, as he told the Rev. C. H. Scott, to England to see his beloved mother, now rejoicing over the conversion of her prodigal, her long prayed for, and now penitent son, and, when in London, he went on a Sunday afternoon to see a Morayshire young man, who had been appointed secretary to a Young Men's Christian Institute. This young man had himself been converted in a sudden and remarkable manner; and, filled with zeal for God and love to souls, used to spend his Sunday afternoons in street preaching. When Mr. North called on him, he was just preparing to visit one of his stations situated at King's Cross, and asked Mr. North to accompany him. They went together. The young man took up his station at his accustomed corner, and after devotional exercises began to address a promiscuous but not very numerous assembly. His words did not *tell,* and were received at first with indifference, and soon with angry opposition and a torrent of foulest blasphemy. Mr. North was beginning to doubt the wisdom of thus casting pearls before swine, and giving occasion to the worst blasphemy he had ever listened to, when several voices were heard calling upon him to speak. "We'll hear that stout man with the dark eyes." Thus called on, he felt constrained to speak. Instantly every eye was fixed on him. He riveted and retained the attention of all; and when he met the blaspheming sophistry of the infidel, he manifestly carried the bulk of his audience along with him. When addressing to them a closing personal appeal, he was forced to stop through sheer exhaustion and want of breath. Many cried out, "Go on, sir; we want to hear more."

But he was physically unable to say more. On which an old man exclaimed, " Sir, your words should be written in letters of gold ! "

Mr. North was encouraged by this essay at addressing publicly a most unwilling audience on the state of their souls, and by his success in apparently interesting and impressing them.

Shortly after this, in May 1856, he left Elgin for a little, by the doctor's advice, to take rest and recruit his strength, which was worn out by the multitude of his daily cottage-meetings and visitations, and went to Dallas, his old residence, where he was looking forward to worship in the Free Church on the following Lord's Day. The Rev. W. Davidson, the minister, was called away from home, and no supply could be got for the pulpit. Mr. North was told that there would be no sermon unless he consented to address the people, and was urgently pressed to agree to do so. After objecting to speak in a regular place of worship, on the ground of not being ordained, he agreed that if one of the elders read a chapter and conducted the devotional exercises, and called on him to give an address, he would do what he could. The people were impressed both by what they heard and by what they saw; for they saw one who had for years lived in their midst a reckless and godless life, now standing up and warning them to flee from coming wrath, to which his own eyes had eighteen months before been suddenly opened. On the Monday morning following there was a great flood in the river, and two little children, trying to cross it on a plank, were washed off and drowned. This sad event plunged the village into mourning, and as the minister was from home the father came and entreated Mr. North to comfort the bereaved mother. He did so. The bodies of the little children were recovered from the cruel flood on two successive days of suspense and sorrow, and as each little corpse was carried to the door of the dwelling which they had left together in health and happiness, a sympathizing crowd accompanied each sorrowful procession, and Mr. North addressed them, impressing more deeply the truths which he had preached the previous Sabbath. Towards the end of the week the minister returned home. Finding his people impressed by the services, and being asked soon after to go and preach elsewhere, he agreed to do so, and constrained Mr. North again to address his people. The church was crowded, people flocking from a distance to hear the new preacher and his rousing message. Among the audience were two men from Forres, about eight miles off, who carried home with them the tidings of this work of awakening. In consequence a deputation was sent to ask him to give an address in the Free Church there. He presented the same objections as he had done to Mr. Davidson; but the people would take no denial, and he went and held several evening services. The first night he had a large and earnest audience, the next night the church was full, after which passages, staircases, and doorways were thronged with eager and anxious listeners. We are told by one who knows the locality well that permanent good was effected at that time, and that the fruits of that, as of other revival movements, may still be traced.

Mr. North on several occasions was at pains to explain the position he then occupied. "Don't think," he said, "that I am intruding into the office of the holy ministry. I am not an authorized preacher, but I'll tell you what I am; I am a man who has been at the brink of the bottomless pit and has looked in, and as I see many of you going down to that pit, I am here to ' hollo ' you back, and warn you of your danger. I am here, also, as the chief of sinners, saved by grace, to tell you that the grace that saved me can surely save you."

In the providence of God the ministry of Mr. North thus began at Dallas, which had been for many years the scene where he lived after the course of this world, eagerly following its fashions, frivolities, and sins. It was here that God so ordered it that he gave his first public testimony in the house of God on behalf of the Son of God, whom by his life he so resolutely opposed and persecuted. After his great change, when a friend asked him what he intended to do, his reply was, "I have done all the harm I could in Scotland, and now I intend to remain there and do all the good I can." It is always hard to unlearn evil that has through a course of years been learned, but it is harder still to undo evil that has through a course of years been done. It was touching to those who met him in private after his conversion to see how much his heart was set on this, how earnestly he longed and prayed for it, and it is touching to find to what a very large extent his heavenly Father granted him this desire of his heart, and made him useful to many to whom of old his influence had been hurtful. We have only been able to obtain clues to this interesting feature of his work in a few cases; but from knowing how much his heart was set on it, and from the humanly speaking accidental manner in which these cases have come to our knowledge, we cannot doubt that, could we trace the influence of his two lives, we should find many instances in which his God made him a minister of mercy to those whom formerly he had encouraged on the broad way that leadeth to destruction.

As showing how much he desired and laboured for the conversion of such, we may state that shortly after his awakening, and long before he found peace himself, he undertook a long journey to visit a careless family with whom he had been intimate, to try to arouse them to concern for their souls. While residing in the house of my father, he once confined himself to his room for a great portion of the day, writing a letter with which he seemed much burdened, and he mentioned that the reason why it was costing him so much anxiety and prayer was, that it was addressed to one whom he had known well in the days of his folly and sin, and whom he now earnestly desired to be the means of leading to the Saviour he had found.

A gentleman, who had been a boy at Eton with him, wrote in reply to a letter asking for information about his Eton days, that all his school recollections of North were painful and saddening; and yet, in God's all-wise providence, Brownlow North was made a means of blessing to his old schoolfellow's son, who is now a minister in the Church of England.

Naturally many of his old acquaintances dropped in to hear him preach, men who had been his associates on the moors, at the billiard-table, or at the hunt. An officer addressing him one day, said " The last time I saw you, you were lying on

your back in the hunting-field, your horse rolling over you."
One day in Edinburgh a Christian lady, who has long since
entered into the joy of her Lord, wrote to ask him to visit her
brother-in-law, who had been one of the friends of his godless
days. He shrank greatly from it, but intended to do so, when
he mislaid the gentleman's address, and could not find it. He
was in a cab on his way to the station, starting for Glasgow,
when on putting his hand into one of his pockets he found the
lost address. How many would in the circumstances have
taken not altogether reluctant advantage of the temporary loss
of the address to salve their consciences for the postponement
of an unpleasant duty   But Mr. North at once, at considerable
inconvenience to himself, put off his departure from town,
drove straight to the residence of his former acquaintance, and
spoke to him most faithfully and seriously about the concerns
of his soul.

That much honoured and experienced minister, the late Rev.
Samuel Miller, D.D., of Glasgow, mentioned to us that once
he happened to be on a visit at the shooting-quarters of a friend
in the Western Highlands, in a district where Brownlow North
had lived a good deal in his godless days. When there, he
was asked to see a lady who was on her deathbed, and who,
along with her husband, had been an intimate friend of Mr.
North's, and on whom he was conscious that his example and
friendship had exercised a deleterious influence. After his
conversion he had returned to this locality for the express purpose of trying to undo some of the evil he had done, and to
testify for Christ where he had openly served the devil; and
among others in this district to whom he was blessed was this
lady. When Dr. Miller visited her, not long before her death,
she was full of adoring praise to that God who had saved her
as a brand from the burning, and who had done it through the
instrumentality of one whose influence with her had formerly
been all for evil. Thus it was that God gave him back, as
saved souls for his reward, one and another and another of
those with whom he had travelled on the broad way; and in
his conduct in this has not this servant of God left us an example that we should follow in his steps?

From the date of his conversion, Mr. North carried the conscientiousness we see displayed in these instances of seeking to save the souls of his friends into everything that he viewed in the light of duty. He was in the habit of impressing upon young converts the duty of setting before themselves a high ideal of the Christian life from the outset of the heavenly race, and trying steadfastly to act up to it, to ask God's guidance in all matters, and to seek to do all to His glory.

An incident illustrating this point happened when he was staying at the hospitable home of his dear friend Mr. Grant, late of Arndilly. Arndilly is one of the most beautifully situated mansions in Strathspey, where that fair Northern river, the joy of the angler and the artist, with lordly flow sweeps round the house beyond the sloping lawn with its hoary timber, that stretches from the Hall door down to the river bank. Mr. North had been laid aside by the doctor's orders from active work for a little, and had gone down to Arndilly to recruit his strength. A lady, who was a guest in the house at the time along with him, sends us her recollection of the incident. " Those who were acquainted with Mr. North's counsels to converts will remember how constantly he held up Col. iii. 17, as the proper touchstone by which to prove every action : " Whatsoever ye do in word or deed, do all in the name of the Lord Jesus." ' If you can do it in the name of Jesus,' was Mr. North's advice, ' *do it*; if not, *don't*.' He had a strong desire to try the effect of a little amusement at his favourite pastime of fishing. His conscience was very tender on the subject, and just because he was so fond of it, and never had handled a fishing-rod since his conversion up to that time (this was in August 1860), he asked Mr. Grant's advice on the subject before a large party at luncheon. ' Arndilly, tell me, do you think I should fish this afternoon?' The reply in substance was, ' If you are not able to *fish for men,* and if you think it would make you sooner able to do that, I don't see why you should not. But let every man be fully persuaded in his own mind.' Mr. North said, ' Well, I will go into my room and ask the Lord Jesus Christ to come with me, and unless I feel

persuaded that he will go with me, I will not go.' The sequel
is told in a letter to my father;

"ARNDILLY, *August 9th*, 1860.

"MY VERY DEAR BROTHER,—I have just got your dear
kind letter, and will not go to bed without writing a line. You
remember our conversation about 'fishing.' Well, after
much thought and some prayer, I felt it was bondage not to
go. I felt sure it would do me good, and out I went.
With every cast of my rod I seemed to improve in
health. The first day I killed a fish—second day none—
third day, engaged a man to come with me, and going out
about four in the afternoon we killed six, (I four and he two),
and walked and felt a new man in mind and body for vigour
and spirits. Fourth day, started after dinner, about four.
[The lady whose letter was quoted above, says she was with
him that day, and that they had hardly been a quarter of an
hour on the river before he had landed two grilse.] Going
down a steep bank, I slipped, and broke a sinew in my leg,
and was brought up the brae on a man's back, and home in a
donkey chair! From the first moment I was able to say, It
is the Lord, and to praise, and I am sure it was His hand in
love. I *could not* fall to the ground without His will, and I
felt it was His will to stop the fishing, *perhaps*; but of this I
am not clear. I have now been laid up a week, with my leg
in a thing that keeps it bent, and in a few days I hope, with
the help of a high-heeled shoe, to hobble about. Oh, do pray
for me, that whatever the Lord would have me to learn, He
will send His Holy Spirit to teach me for Christ's sake; for if
He does not, though the book is put before me in the shape
of 'accident' or what not, I shall learn nothing aright. I got
much pleasure out of Romans viii. 28 and 32 the other day:
'We know that all things work together for good to them that
love God,' etc. These things are all so literally true and real,
or else there is no truth in any part of God's Word, and as
that is not true, it follows *all* is true. And oh what joy and
peace thus to receive it! A principal, and in your letter a
dashed, word defies me to read. I wish you would learn to
write better; but don't put off writing to me till you do; for,
hard as they are to read, I can say, 'without dissimulation,'
I love to hear from you, and almost always get some good

from your letters. Reid wrote to ask permission to print my last tract in the 'Stirling Messenger,' which of course I gave him. This gives it a large circulation at once, praise the Lord. Most who will read it will be persons more or less concerned about religion. Who can tell the good that may not be done! But would I rejoice as much if it were somebody else's tract? Alas, no. Oh to be unselfish and single-eyed! Pray for me.

"B. N."

What with his previous overwork and breakdown in health, and the accident in fishing, he was laid aside for a good many months. Most of his Christian friends who are in the habit of observing the Lord's dealings will probably think that the illness and subsequent accident were both sent in a never-erring Providence for one purpose, to take him apart by himself with his Lord "into a desert place, that he might rest awhile." The soul is apt to receive injury by constant and excessive and exciting work in the Lord's vineyard, and many have had cause to say, "they made me keeper of the vineyards; but mine own vineyard have I not kept." The God of all grace was pleased thus to hedge up his way with thorns for a season, that he might be preserved from the snares which beset one who is very successful and immensely popular, and that the work of grace might be advanced in his own heart, that thus he might be made still more useful to others.

A few months afterwards, and while still forbidden to resume work, he writes to my father: "Need I say how *very, very* much I should have liked to have been able to come to Edinburgh? And I *could* do it, but I cannot see that I could ask God's blessing on going. It would look in my own eyes as if I thought He could not do so well without me, when He can, as He has shown; and may He do so in your midst yet more, and that exceeding abundantly above all that I can ask or think. May the Lord be with you in public and in private."

When Mr. North came before the public as a preacher of Christ crucified, there were not a few even of earnest-minded Christians who thought that he ought to have lived in seclusion for some years, or confined himself wholly to such private efforts to do good as have been recorded in this chapter. Although a whole year had elapsed since he became a reformed man, before he ventured to open his lips in public, still a year was nothing to a lifetime spent in serving another master. Opinions differed as to whether he should have remained silent for a longer period after his conversion; but looking back upon his ministry, it will be manifest that he entered upon it just at the right time, so far as man can judge, with regard to the Lord's gracious purposes concerning our beloved land. He was sent, a preacher of the stamp of John the Baptist, to awaken dormant souls, to break up the fallow ground, and by ploughing deep into men's consciences to prepare them for that flood of blessing which was to follow in the course of two or three years in the Revival of 1859-60. Still the fact that his life was publicly known to have been in opposition to the law of God, if it attracted many from curiosity to hear him, awakened bitter opposition in others; but the Lord so overruled it as to bring good out of this evil.

Mr. Grant, of Arndilly, has recorded an incident bearing on this point.

One evening Mr. North was about to enter the vestry of a church in one of our Northern towns in which he was going to preach, when a stranger came up to him in a hurried manner, and said, " Here is a letter for you of great importance, and you are requested to read it before you preach to-night." Thinking it might be a request for prayer from some awakened soul, he immediately opened it, and found that it contained a detail of some of his former irregularities of conduct, concluding with words to this effect: " How dare you, being conscious of the truth of all the above, pray and speak to the people this evening, when you are such a vile sinner? " The preacher put the letter into his pocket, entered the pulpit, and after prayer and praise, commenced his address to a very crowded congregation; but before speaking on his text he produced the letter, and informed the people of its contents, and then added, " All that is here said is true, and it is a correct picture of the degraded sinner that I once was; and oh how wonderful must the grace be that could quicken and raise me up from such a death in trespasses and sins, and make me what I appear before you to-night, a vessel of mercy, one who knows that all his past sins have been cleansed away through the atoning blood of the Lamb of God. It is of His redeeming love that I have now to tell you, and to entreat any here who are not yet reconciled to God to come this night in faith to Jesus, that He may take their sins away and heal them." His hearers were deeply impressed by the words he spoke, and that which was intended to close his lips was overruled to open the hearts of the congregation to receive his message.

The way in which the startling news that Brownlow North had become a preacher of the gospel of Jesus Christ struck his old friends may be gathered from a single instance of one who knew him well, and who was as rejoiced as he was amazed to hear it. The Rev. William Robertson, D.D., thus writes: " My acquaintance with Brownlow North reaches back to the days of our youth, when in the year 1826 we met on the Continent and travelled for a short time in company. I will say nothing about his early life, as he has frequently in the pulpit taken the public into his confidence in reference to his character and habits in those days, and all who heard him know that in his confessions he did not spare himself, uniformly holding himself up as a remarkable example of the forbearing mercy of God, and the mighty power of His grace. A truly astonishing example he was! The first time I heard of his change of character and life was from a copy of the ' British Messenger ' which I found by accident in the coffee-room of an hotel in Hull, where I had just arrived from Rotterdam. Brownlow North preaching the gospel of Jesus Christ! Did my eyes deceive me? Could it be the same Brownlow North with whom I was so well acquainted? What could be the meaning of his preaching? Was it some mad or impious jest? What could have tempted him to this? Very naturally I had no belief in his sincerity until shortly afterwards we met in Edinburgh, when he recounted to me the remarkable history of his conversion. From that moment I never entertained a doubt that he was a truly converted man. I shall never forget an observation of his when he perceived the astonishment, perhaps mingled with doubt, with which I listened to his narrative of his conversion. ' I see you are filled with wonder, William,' he said to me, ' you are filled with wonder. But why should He not? *why should He not* lift the vile thing out of the dung-hill? ' The rest is well known, and one who has marked with a very attentive eye the progress of late revivals has declared that the ministrations of no revivalist preacher in our days have ever been crowned with such success as those of Brown-low North."

CHAPTER IV

Early Evangelistic Labours

WE have seen how Brownlow North was led to the entrance of what proved to be a long and eminently useful course of public evangelistic labours. He felt that the providential indications that this was the path in which the Lord would have him walk were so clear to his own mind, that to have refused to undertake the work would have been to decline the call of God. Most of those who knew him felt, as strongly as he himself did, that the Lord had need of him to publish the gospel of His grace in the country districts and the towns and cities of Scotland; and the Lord so manifestly accompanied the preaching of the word with signs following, that all doubt was gradually removed from the minds of most of those who had at heart the advancement of the kingdom of Christ in our beloved land. With characteristic energy and thoroughness, whenever he was assured in his own mind that the Lord had called him to pass through the towns and villages of the land, proclaiming the gospel which had gladdened his soul and renewed his life, he threw himself enthusiastically into the work, giving up without hesitation his stated home. What to a gentleman of fully middle life was the undoubted trial of having no settled residence was gladly met by him, and as gladly and cheerfully shared by Mrs. North.

The late Sir George Sinclair, Bart., of Ulbster, in a letter to the Rev. Dr. Guthrie, of Edinburgh, which was published at the time, after giving a brief sketch of Mr. North's conversion, and his commencement first of private, and then of more public efforts to save souls, said: " The foregoing unvarnished and interesting narrative presents, I humbly think, a complete

49

vindication of our respected and indefatigable friend from the charge of having intruded himself into the functions of the ministry, and usurping a position to which he had neither claim nor calling. It must be evident, even to the most prejudiced caviller, that he was led on, not only gradually, but reluctantly and unexpectedly, to become a preacher of the everlasting gospel in truth and verity. When he first obeyed the summons to attend the death-bed of a dying Christian, it no more entered into his contemplation that the time was at hand when congregated thousands would assemble from all quarters to hear him, than the prophet imagined, when he entered the shallow stream, that the waters which were only to the ankles would ere long be to the knees, and ultimately reach to the loins. Retaining as I still do my objection to lay-preaching in general, ' what am I that I could withstand God ' (Acts xi. 17), when in such an exceptional case as that of Mr. North, He is pleased to grant such unequivocal and uninterrupted tokens of His countenance and presence?"

So solemn did he feel the post even of a lay-evangelist to be, that we are sure that all his most intimate friends will bear us out in the assertion that nothing but a convincing and over-powering sense of his having been called or thrust forth by his Lord to " preach the Word " would have induced him to stand up and plead for his God with his fellow-men. For hours before ascending the platform or pulpit he was weighed down with a sense of the greatness of the responsibility of addressing sinners in the name of the Saviour, and none can say that in the discharge of his duties he was ever light-hearted. His abiding impression was that a dispensation of the gospel was committed to him, and that woe would be to him if he did not preach the gospel. He felt he owed a debt, not only to the Saviour who had washed him in His blood and pardoned his many sins, but to sinners around him who had a right and a claim to the sinner's gospel; a claim to have it declared to them and pressed upon them with all fulness, freeness, and forcibleness by one who had himself experienced its saving power. This was the debt which in the strength of God he now set himself with all his energy to discharge, and in the zealous execution of this great trust he continued to his dying hour.

After having begun to preach in the Free Churches of Dallas and Forres in the beginning of July 1856, Mr. North was invited and consented to preach in many of the churches in Morayshire and the adjoining counties. In August of that year he went to Fortwilliam and the district of Lochaber, in which neighbourhood he had held shootings for some years, and preached with much power, creating among the people who had known him in his careless days a deep impression, and awakening among them a serious concern about Divine things. In October of that year he preached in different churches in the town of Inverness, thereafter at Petty, Auldearn, and Nairn, returned again to Inverness in November, and visited the towns of Forfar, Montrose, and Aberdeen, in the last months of the year. Wherever he went, the Lord accompanied His word by awakening the careless and arousing the sleeping. Written statements by ministers of the Established, Free, United Presbyterian, and Independent Churches all testify to the deep impression made upon their congregations by his message.

Nearly twenty years had passed since the last revival in Scotland under William Burns, at a time of deep spiritual thought which may be said to have been a preparation for, and to have culminated in, the ever-memorable Disruption of the National Church in 1843. Strangers from England and America often seem to suppose that there is so much religious knowledge and spiritual life in Scotland as to leave no room for anything like a deep or widespread religious impression. No idea could be more erroneous than this. Religious knowledge is not, alas, at all the same as spiritual life, and is not infrequently found in an unnatural separation from it. Even in regard to the former it is the simple fact that at the time when Mr. North began his evangelistic work, as at the present time, there was a very large amount of ignorance, both of the letter of the Word of God and of the doctrines of grace. This ignorance prevails especially in certain districts of our land, namely, those which were under the deadening influence of Moderatism in the latter part of the eighteenth and the earlier part of the nineteenth century, in some of which there had been no general spiritual movement since the Reformation. Indeed, the state of Scotland in regard to Divine things, over a pretty large extent of her territory, was very lamentable, and two sins, viz., those of drunkenness and immorality, had given her a sorrowful prominence among Christian communities. It is remarkable that the divisions of the country in which the sin of immorality is most flagrant, and in one of which Mr. North began his evangelistic labours, are precisely those which had lain for a very long period under the sway and blight of Moderatism, which was just the Rationalism of a former age. It is noteworthy that this rationalism, which prided itself on confining its preaching to legalism and morality, ignoring faith, free grace, and the work of the Spirit, was not able to produce that virtue which it so extolled, and bent itself wholly to cultivate.

It shows us in a practical instance that the gospel of God's grace is the only way to holiness, as well as the only way of salvation. This grace of God, exhibited in all its fulness by this novel and powerful preacher; this gospel of God, containing the good news of a Divine Redeemer, all-necessary and almighty to save, and of a Divine Spirit, all-necessary and almighty to sanctify, burst upon many individuals, many families, and even many congregations, as an altogether new discovery.

Brownlow North's public ministry, like his private labours, was fruitful from the very first. A gentleman wrote to him, that his visit had produced a deep impression in his own household. " The two nurses, I am happy to see, continue to evince much earnestness, the other two maids are also evidently inquiring, and the men-servants have become greatly sobered down and subdued. On Sabbath, instead of their wonted frolicsome and light habits, they are now found reading the Bible and religious books. This in a ' bothy ' is a step certainly in the right direction. We are making a very feeble effort to foster these sympathies by having a very interesting little prayer-meeting in our house."

From the very first Mr. North was made a means of quickening and reviving to the Lord's children, as well as of awakening to the lost, and was used as an instrument for bringing many into the full assurance of their interest in the Saviour. On the 18th December, 1856, a blacksmith in one of the towns he visited wrote to him : " I am desirous to express the sense of gratitude which I feel for what of the Lord's goodness I have experienced through your instrumentality. I trust it was a day of the Spirit's power to my soul. I have had such clear views of the glory and excellency and suitableness of Christ Jesus to the sinner's case, and of my personal interest in Him as my own Saviour, that I have been enabled to rejoice with joy unspeakable and full of glory, and with the great Apostle of the Gentiles I have sometimes had a desire to depart and to be with Christ, which is far better. I have known more of what it is to have the full assurance of faith for the last four months than I ever did in all my past life. Surely a believing sense of the presence and favour of God enjoyed is heaven begun on earth; and although I have heard you preach in Forres, in Rafford, in Dyke, in Kintessae, in Boghole, in Nairn, and Auldearn, still I want to hear you again, and I know there are hundreds here equally anxious to hear you."

Of his first appearance as an evangelist in Huntly, where he had spent some of his godless years, as already referred to, the Rev. Mr. Williamson wrote : " The first time he spoke at Huntly I well remember. The Duchess of Gordon had asked him to visit her, and he agreed to address my weekly meeting for prayer. The attendance was very large, from anxiety to see one who had been so notable in all the ways of folly in the neighbourhood in other days. When he stood up, he was greatly moved, and said, ' My friends, you all know me; you know how I have lived in other days; but God—— ' Here he was so overcome that he had to sit down, and was overwhelmed with a flood of emotion. After a little he twice again tried to speak, and failed, and indeed was unable to address the meeting. Towards the close of the meeting he led in prayer, thanking God for His wonderful mercy to us all, and especially to himself."

On the occasion of his first visit to Aberdeen at the very outset of his ministry, a lady who had known him well in his thoughtless days went with much prejudice to hear him preach, and through his message was brought to the knowledge of the Lord. It was also on this visit that he was the means of the conversion of two students who afterwards became ministers of Christ, the Rev. James Collie, and a fellow-student who went to labour in the Cape Colony.

On this occasion also his words were made a means of blessing to a young lady whose life has since been devoted to advancing the Saviour's kingdom in the foreign mission-field. Were sufficient space at our disposal, it would not be unprofitable to give her very full notes of Mr. North's dealings with her and two of her young friends at this time. Of these we can only give an abstract. She had reason to believe that she had given herself to the Lord a few weeks before hearing Mr. North in Gilcomston Free Church, Aberdeen, in December 1856; but in her case the work was greatly deepened, while her friends J. and M. F. were then for the first time savingly awakened and led to Christ. She wrote: " I was struck and startled with the faith of his first prayer. I thought, What is my religion worth? I can't say 'Father' to God, as that man does. His text was Acts xvii. 12, 'Therefore many of them believed.' There was much of the power of the Holy Spirit with him that evening; and as he went on it was all to me so tremendously real and present, I felt as if I had never believed before that the Son of God really came down and died for sinners. At the close he entreated us all most earnestly to speak to Jesus there and then. He cried, ' O, speak to Him! If you can say nothing else, tell Him you hate Him, but speak to Him as you are.' I remember well hiding my face in the pew, and saying that to Him in deepest grief, and begging Him to change me. Next Sabbath his text was Proverbs i. 20-33. In opening up the clause, 'Fools hate knowledge,' he brought together one after another of the Bible descriptions of fools, and applied each most impressively; *e.g.*, the atheistic fool of Psalm xiv, the rich fool of Luke xii. 20, the self-confiding fool of Prov. xxviii. 26, and the backsliding fool of 2 Peter ii. 22. As he described the backslider, and said, ' You are only a fool after all, and now Christ is saying to you, " Turn you at my reproof, behold I will pour out my Spirit unto you," ' I broke down, and turned to Christ to beg to be received, and to ask His Spirit. The following evening my two friends and I went to his lodgings at the hour when he intimated he would be at home. He prayed with us first, then spoke pointedly to each, setting Christ before us from Rom. iii. 21-26, in His righteousness and death and power to save. He gave us Christ's invitations and promises but we could not believe. I asked, ' Has one a right to believe that Christ loves one personally?' He answered quickly, ' If you don't believe that, you will go to hell,' and read to us 1 John iv. 16, ' We have known and believed the love that God hath to us.' He asked, ' Are you willing to forsake all for Christ? to give up the world, its pleasures, companionships, etc.,' and rapidly grouping up a list of trials for Christ, he asked me in his own direct, forcible way, ' Could you bear that?' and I said, ' I think I could.' He answered, ' You remember Peter, he thought he could, and what did he do?' He put the same question to J. F. She did not answer at once, and he said, ' Remember, it is not to me that you say it, but as you must answer at the judgment-seat of Christ.' She answered ' Yes,' very solemnly, and Mr. North turned to her younger sister, M. F., with the same question. She answered ' Yes,' and he added, ' Remember the young ruler.' He said, ' Don't expect to be perfect Christians in five minutes : you must be babes first, and then grow, feeding daily on the Word.' He spoke with evident delight of some of the rich portions of the Word, and said, ' Is not that food?' He talked with us of pardon, and acceptance, and victory over sin, and the welcome at last, ' Well done, good and faithful servant,' and bade us meet at least once a week to read and pray together, which we did for some years, till our paths in life separated. The servants came a second time to say that many more were waiting to be spoken with; and warning us not to lose our convictions, he bade us farewell, saying, ' God bless you, my dear sisters!' Next day I called again to see him, when, after further instruction and encouragement, he read Romans x. 1-4 with me, reading my own and my friends' names in place of 'every one' and 'they'; and prayed very earnestly for each of us."

After this the writer of the above sketch went through a period of deep spiritual darkness and conflict, which the Lord graciously dissipated in His own time. Her friends received full peace while conversing with Mr. North on his second visit to Aberdeen, a few months later. At that interview he said, "The Lord has his own way of leading us all; but when He gives you comfort don't be afraid to take it." "He spoke to us," she continues, "like a father, and bade us work for the Saviour, even when we felt unwilling, saying, 'When I first began to visit and speak for Christ, I did not like it. There were nasty smells in poor people's houses, and I hated to go. I thought, I can't make myself like it, but I can make myself do it, and as I went on I grew to like it, and now I am as happy as the day is long.' I met him again afterwards, more than once, and he always had some message that was a help to me. He never lost his warm interest in us; and after I had come abroad, he sent me a copy of each of his works as they were published, inscribed with select verses."

The effect which Brownlow North's appearance on the platform and pulpit produced in Scotland was altogether electric. The striking contrast of the work into which he now threw himself with all his wondrous energy to the pursuits of his youth and manhood was alone sufficient to attract notice. Added to this there was the intense earnestness of the man, the natural eloquence which he possessed, the originality of the mode in which he presented truths which had nothing of novelty in themselves, the response which his appeals elicited from ten thousands of hearts, and the hundreds of cases of awakening and conversion that took place under his ministry, which all combined to turn towards him the eye both of the Church and of the world. We cannot do better than transcribe to our pages descriptions of his preaching and labours given in the newspapers of the day, when the impression was freshly struck upon the hearts and minds of our countrymen.

In an account published in one of the Northern journals of the first sermon which he preached in Banff, the writer says:

" I was prejudiced in the extreme against Mr. North, but I listened with astonishment and pleasure. So many in this locality must remember him leading so different a life, mingling among so opposite a class of associates, that it is strange for them to listen to him now, and believe that all is genuine and real. But we must remember God's ways are not as our ways, and the instruments he uses for the accomplishment of His designs are often the very opposite of those that men would have selected. He spoke as one just escaped from the sacked and burning city, with the roar of the flame and the yell of the dying still fresh in his ear, full of gratitude for his wonderful escape, yet still looking back amazed and fearful. We think it was Garrick who, on being asked how he and his friends kept the listeners in rapt attention, when the preacher with a subject so great, so vast, acted too often more as a soporific than anything else, replied, 'We speak as if our fictions were truth, they as if their truth were fiction.' Here is the secret, and certainly in Mr. North's whole manner and address you see a man thoroughly in earnest."

Another newspaper thus comments on his first address delivered in the town of Stirling : " The intense earnestness of his manner, indicative of the deepest feeling of compassion for the perishing, was obviously the grand secret of his tremendous moral power. The most common truths appear to be unheard-of realities, because they are manifestly the utterance of a mind to which they are real, present, and momentous, and they enter many a startled ear because pronounced with burning lips as a message from the Majesty of heaven, the reception or rejection of which might there and then decide the eternity of those hearing. The great source of all spiritual success is doubtless the Holy Ghost, but, humanly speaking, the delivery of acknowledged and elementary truth in an agony of earnestness will never fail to arouse, rivet, and impress a Scottish congregation."

Another journalist inserts a very discriminating article under the heading of " Great Preachers : Mr. Brownlow North." He classifies the great preachers whom the Lord has from age to age raised up in His Church into three divisions. In the first he places Jeremy Taylor, Massillon, Hall, and Chalmers, men whose original and sublime conceptions fire the train of emotion, who are great thinkers and literary artists. In the second class he ranks those who primarily appeal to the reflective consciousness, and whose power resides in the originality and moral pertinence of the thoughts which they utter. As examples of this class, he cites John Howe and John Foster. In the third class, he places those, the secret of whose power lies in the vividness of their spiritual realizations, and the intensity of their spiritual emotions. In them thought, affection, fancy, all live and play in the burning fervour of the spiritual life. The influence of the last class is the widest and most direct of all, because they address themselves to elements which are found in the universal heart of humanity. The audiences of the first two classes are to a certain extent select, that of the third embraces all men. He gives George Whitefield as the best-known instance of this class of preachers, and says, " The black faces of the Kingswood colliers, furrowed with the tears of a pungent spiritual emotion, bore testimony to Whitefield's power at one extreme, and the pockets of Benjamin Franklin, emptied at his resistless appeal, bore testimony as striking at the other. Within the last few days large numbers of our citizens have had opportunity of hearing a preacher of the same order as Whitefield. All the distinctive elements of Whitefield's power, as we are led to infer them from the effects of his preaching, are found in Mr. Brownlow North. The prime characteristic of such men is a simple, direct, realizing, all-absorbent faith. They believe, and therefore speak. They live in as close relation to the spiritual world as the mass of men do to the sensible. Blind must be the eye that does not recognize the Divine hand in a man so transformed and inspired. In an age of prevailing pharisaism, spiritual stupor, and practical infidelity, we hail in his mission a fresh proof that God has not forsaken the earth. Our gratitude need not be the less, but the greater, that we recognize the adaptation of the human medium to the Divine power. The earthen vessel is not picked up at random that is charged with so precious a treasure, and let us feel assured that it is by no accident, and through no random craze of enthusiasm, that Brownlow North, whom hundreds amongst us knew but yesterday as at once the genius of sport, the charm of drawing-rooms, is now the great preacher of the cross of Jesus Christ, on whose lips thousands hang, and to hear whom more struggle in vain for admittance." It may be noted that he attracted and interested these multitudes without ever uttering a sentence intended or fitted to amuse them, or to distract their attention even for a moment from the absorbing theme of his message.

Brownlow North's personal appearance was one that was likely to imprint itself on the memory of all who ever heard him preach. Somewhat under middle height, he was of portly form, deep-chested, broad-shouldered: his address was gentlemanly, and his bearing aristocratic. His manner in private as well as in public was marked by dignity and gravity. Though he dressed in dark clothes, generally in black, his attire was that of a country gentleman, and was not in any way ministerial or professional. He used an eyeglass in reading. His lower jaw was square and heavy, and his forehead, lighted up by the glancing eye, was well developed and thoughtful. He had a massive head covered with curling locks of very dark hair, afterwards tinged with grey; the cast of his countenance, which was well seen from the absence of any hair on his face, was also massive, and his features, though by no means handsome, were striking and impressive, and in his dark and sparkling eye there dwelt earnestness, penetration, and gentleness. The physiognomy is considered by good judges to bear the impress of the history and the character of the man; and while those who trusted to their powers of thus reading character could doubtless detect in his features and expression the stamp of an average lifetime spent in the fashionable world, and in the service of self and sin, they could hardly avoid also seeing clear traces of the great change which at the age of forty-five was wrought upon him, and of the Divine life and the new nature which, then implanted within him, maintained a lifelong and successful conflict with the old. A minister, who had known him before his conversion, when he heard that he was a changed man, and had begun to preach to sinners, said to a friend, "Well, if he is to do any good, he will require a reformed face as well as a reformed life," and we are told by some who knew him previously that after his conversion the whole expression of his face became changed in a very striking degree.

The general cast of his countenance strikingly recalled the pictures of the great Luther, to whom in his energy, his faith, his boldness, his views of Divine truth, and even in the dogmatical cast of his mind, he bore a very marked resemblance.

One day the late Professor John Duncan, D.D., remarked to a friend, as he looked at a good photographic likeness of Brownlow North that was hanging in her drawing-room, "There is intellect in the brow, genius in the eye, and eloquence in the mouth."

His opening prayer always had a solemnizing effect on the congregation, and though the language was unconventional, it had no lack of real reverence and holy awe, and was the expression often of Jacob-like wrestling with the great God for a blessing upon the souls of men. We here insert one of those prayers, which was taken down in Elgin (in 1862): "Lord God Almighty, Thou who dwellest in the heaven of heavens, Thou who revealest to us that 'Wherever two or three are gathered together in Thy name, there Thou are in their midst,' O God, help us to pray! We have stood up before Thee in the attitude of prayer; we have ourselves invited Thine attention by our own act and deed in coming unto Thee; we have called upon Thee specially to regard us at this moment; and O God forbid that, when Thine eye is turned upon us, Thou shouldest see a single heart amongst us that is not endeavouring to pray. It is so hard a thing to pray, that, except Thou pour upon us the spirit of grace and supplication, we never shall pray. O God, before we can pray we must feel want; we must feel that we are poor and needy; O grant us then to feel our need! grant us that hungering and thirsting which Thou hast promised to satisfy. O God, unless Thou create the desire, there will be no desire, for the natural man desireth not God. Is it witnessed of us all in heaven, 'Behold he prayeth'? Thou knowest, Thou knowest. O God, if there be one here who is not praying, we,

Thy praying people, remembering Thy commandment to love our neighbour as ourselves, would join as one man and pray for the prayerless. We pray to Thee, O God, we who do pray, pray to Thee to make the prayerless pray. May the prayerless be compelled to smite upon their breasts, and cry, 'O God be merciful to me.' May they join now, O God, with the praying ones, and may there not be one here of whom it is not witnessed, 'Behold, he prayeth.'

Now, Father, we want everything; we want Thee to take away from us all our own things—everything we have got, so that we may have nothing we can call our own, that all those things which we have by nature may pass away. Then we pray that all things may become new, and that all these new things may be of Thee. And then we pray to Thee, Father, that, being led by Thy Holy Spirit, we may sacrifice to Thee all Thine own. We pray that we may have faith that we may have true love shed abroad in our hearts by the Holy Ghost. We pray Thee that we may have joy and peace in believing. We pray Thee that we may be filled with the Holy Ghost, that the fruit of the Spirit may be manifest in us—love, joy, peace, longsuffering, gentleness, goodness, faith, meekness, temperance—so that men shall be obliged to take notice of us, that the Spirit that is within us is not the spirit of the world, but is a new spirit, even the Holy Spirit, and that we have been with Jesus.

Now, Father, we do not ask this of Thee as a mere form. We believe that Thou art. We believe that we have access to Thee by one Spirit, through Jesus Christ, and we come through that new and living way; and though we cannot use proper words to express our need when we pray to Thee, O forgive us what we are, and make us what we ought to be. It is not for much speaking that we ask Thee to hear us. We do not feel our need, neither know we how to ask for anything, as we ought; but what we ask Thee to do in the name of Jesus is to supply our need, to make us living members of the Lord Jesus Christ, producing very much fruit to Thy honour and glory, and to make us blessings to the land in which we live. We need Thy blessing, Father—Thy blessing and the light of Thy countenance,—that Thou teach the speaker to speak—that he speak by the power of the Holy Ghost, not in word only, but in the power of the Holy Ghost, not in word only, but in demonstration of the Spirit and of power. O may the dead be awakened this night by the entrance of Thy word which giveth light, and may those who have it, have it more abundantly; and may it be evident that Thou canst take the weak things and the base things, and make them instruments in Thy hands, when it so pleaseth Thee, to do good. O may good be done, and no evil, and good above all we can ask or think. Accept us, not for our prayers, but because we ask it, most merciful Father in the name of Jesus Christ, our Lord and Saviour. Amen."

His speech on first rising to address an audience was diffident and laboured, but gradually became more fluent, except towards the climax of his appeals, when words seemed sometimes wholly to fail him. His language was always simple, natural, scriptural, and was used for the sole purpose of conveying his meaning in the clearest manner to his hearers, without any thought of either rules or flowers of rhetoric, although he was a natural orator, a gift which he probably inherited. He always threw his whole soul into the subject he was treating of, and was so evidently interested, impressed, and moved by it that he could not but communicate some of the impression on his own spirit to his hearers. Having read his text, or the passage he was about to lecture from, several times very slowly and solemnly, emphasizing almost every word, he entered at once into his subject, gaining the attention of his audience at the outset, and retaining it in an ever intensified degree to the close.

After his first essays his sermons or addresses were all carefully studied and prepared, but were not written out—far less committed to memory. Some of his sermons were frequently delivered and seemed engraved upon his very soul. His thoughts were written on the margin of his Bible, or on blank pages of interleaving, while the heads and leading ideas of each lecture or address were jotted down on small slips of paper.

Of these pithy, thoughtful, and practical annotations, we may present the reader with a few specimens. Others will occasionally be found quoted in different portions of the volume.

"The precise moment will come when you will have been five minutes in eternity.

"The devil has gained the whole world, and lost his own soul. Who would change places with him?

"Trying without praying, and praying without trying, both are a mockery. Let your motto be, Pray and try, pray and try.

"If a place is lukewarm, be sure the Christians in it are lukewarm. What do you do to prevent this lukewarmness? How much do you pray? How much do you labour? Lukewarm people make lukewarm ministers.

"'Ye cannot serve God and mammon.' It is not said 'do not,' but 'cannot.'

"Those on the left hand are condemned for duties left undone and for negative religion.

"We speak of killing time: we expect a resurrection, but when will there be a resurrection of dead time?

"The smallest allowed sin is far more to be feared than the greatest evil that 'we would not.'

"If you are not sure whether a thing is wrong or not, and do it, it is *wrong in you*.

"As long as a man lets God alone, the devil will let him alone.

"Next to losing your soul, fear losing your convictions.

"A Christian is not afraid of death, but of sin; an unconverted man is not afraid of sin, but of death.

"Ignorance in religion won't save a man.

"God never says more than he means.

"There will be twenty knocks on visits of pleasure, even at a minister's door, for one of an anxious inquirer.

"Christians doubt because they are walking dubiously.

"Get your doctrine from the Bible. Get your example from Christ. A day will not pass after you have closed with

Christ's promise, ere He will meet you with a counsel. Embrace both.

"Begin with sin pardoned and the law kept. What a beginning!

"No one can prevent your being saved but yourself. If you die the second death, you must be a suicide. God will say to you in the judgment, 'Thou hast destroyed thyself.'

"Every man's life is a prayer.

"Seek the wealthiest man in every city, and the holiest man in every city, and let their other circumstances be what they may, in every instance you will find that the holiest is the happiest.

"The sinner in Christ is his justification; Christ in the sinner is his sanctification. The two invariably go together.

"The whole question is not whether sin tempts or not, but whether it reigns or not.

"Are we speaking for Christ as we have opportunity? If not we are still in possession of a dumb devil.

"Godliness with contentment is great gain, but contentment without godliness is the greatest curse.

"If a man receives the Bible, he has to receive a great many things he can't understand, as well as a great many he does not like.

"Let the question of eternity have a monopoly in you. It is an intensely personal question, but instead of making you selfish, it will expand your heart. He who has never felt for his own soul cannot feel for another's.

"If Paul had not had the thorn in the flesh, we should not have had the blessed text, 'My grace is sufficient for thee.'

"God has no power to save sinners but by Christ : Christ is His Power."

The form of Mr. North's discourse was objected to by some critics at first as not being run in the conventional mould of the "sermon." A minister who had given him the use of his church and often listened to him with pleasure, once remarked, "Oh, Mr. North, if you would only study more, you would do still more good." "What sort of study do you mean?" was the reply; "for I devote three hours every morning, before leaving my room to reading the Bible and to meditation and prayer, and during the day I think of Divine truths as much as possible." "Oh," said the minister, "that is all well; but if you would arrange your addresses with more method, they would be more instructive." "Well, as you advise it so strongly, I will try what I can do before next Sunday." And accordingly, after this prudent manse-drilling, he did try much to put his next address into a more "connected form." Sunday arrived, and a great crowd of hearers assembled, so that every space for standing as well as sitting room was occupied; and after praise and prayer he commenced his address. For the first five minutes the ideas that he had arranged came out in nice order, when suddenly his chain of thought was broken, and all he had intended to say passed entirely from him, and a dead silence ensued. It was a trying moment, and most men would have found it overpowering. Not so Mr. North. He knew that his mission was not of man, and did not depend on the method in which his discourses were arranged, but on the power of the Holy Spirit. He therefore frankly told the congregation of the advice he had received, of his endeavour to follow it, and its signal collapse, as the whole train of thought had passed away from his mind! "But," he added, "there is one subject that has not passed away, and that is that many of you are sinners ready to perish, and I know the way whereby you may be saved, and it is the true way, because it is God's way." He then delivered a most powerful address as the Spirit gave him utterance, which was much blessed to several of those who heard him. Probably his command of his subject and method of orderly arrangement of the topics increased rapidly with constant practice; for we cannot say that when he first visited Edinburgh in 1857 we observed any lack in these respects, although he did not formally announce divisions but took naturally the points that successively presented themselves to his mind as being taught in the scripture he was expounding, confining himself usually to the leading topics, and hardly touching upon those that were subordinate.

But if Brownlow North's addresses were not presented in the form of sermons, they were conceived and delivered in the

C

form of the "lecture" or exposition, which has always held a leading place in the Scottish churches as one of the most popular and most useful forms of pulpit discourse. They were indeed much fuller of doctrine than the "lecture" or exposition usually is, and this was no doubt the reason why some persons would have expected to find them exhaustively arranged into "heads" and sub-divisions. He chiefly addressed himself to the unconverted, whether openly godless or self-righteous, and to slumbering Christians; and so little did he beat about the bush in his exhortations, that a lady once remarked that "he spoke as if people never said their prayers or read their Bibles."

The truths he expounded were usually the leading doctrines of Scripture. These he apprehended very vividly in his own mind, handled with a master's force, and presented to the intellect, conscience, and will of his hearers in a way that was always striking, and often had the charm of originality as well as power. He quoted Scripture with great aptness and effect, appealing to its testimony in every argument and exhortation.

When preaching in Aberdeenshire, Mr. North met Mr. Gordon Furlong, who, seeing how the Lord was blessing his message, induced him to come South; and the Rev. William Reid, then editor of the *British Messenger,* hearing him in Forfar, also urged him to extend the area of his labours, and gave a notice of his work in that periodical, which had the effect of drawing the attention of the general Christian community to this new evangelist.

CHAPTER V

Work in Edinburgh and Glasgow: and Recognition as an Evangelist by the Free Church of Scotland

ON his arrival in Edinburgh, in the early spring of 1857, Mr. North at once called on my father, who thus relates his impressions on first meeting him:—

" 'You are not the kind of man I'm in the habit of seeing,' was the thought that rose in my mind and almost to my lips, as my study door opened and a visitor was announced under the name of 'Mr. Brown.' 'Who is Mr. Brown?' was not just the thought that next occurred to me, for that was a question I had no hope of answering to myself, but what is Mr. Brown's occupation? what may be his character? and what can be his object in calling on me? 'A man of the world, yet not a man of the world,' was the nearest guess I could make, when the mystery was solved by Mr. Brownlow North giving his own name, for he saw that I was puzzled; and the man before me did most exactly fit the associations I had attached to the name, as none else in the world could have done. Having heard that he was to be in Edinburgh, I had written to him, asking him to call on me; but I was not expecting him at the time, and I welcomed him with equal surprise and delight.

" At that first visit in Edinburgh we both engaged in prayer, and alike in prayer and in conversation it was impossible not to be deeply impressed with his reverential awe, his earnestness, and his tenderness of spirit. To myself it was unspeakably refreshing to find a man with such a fear of the living God, such brokenness of spirit, and such faith in the everlast-

67

ing Word. It was a great acquisition, and reminded me of the
saying of the first convert under Dr. Kalley's teaching in the
island of Madeira,—where so many hundreds afterwards for-
sook all for the sake of the gospel, but where for a long time
there was only one man converted,—who after much patience
came with a companion to his teacher, and said, ' I have found
a man!' And on that day it seemed to me that I had found a
man whom God was redeeming to Himself, was leading and
instructing, and was sending as a skilful and faithful labourer
into His harvest. From that day forward we were knit together
in the bonds of a life-long friendship and affection."

I can never forget my astonishment when my father told me
that the fashionable-looking gentleman whom I had seen in
conversation with him was to preach in our church on the
evening of the following Lord's Day, and it took some time
before I was convinced that there was not some mistake about
the matter. It seemed as if things were being turned upside
down.

In Edinburgh he preached, if we mistake not, first in the
church of his old friend Dr. William Robertson, of New Greyfriars, who asked his congregation to assemble half an hour
before the usual time to secure their places, and who says that
when he entered the church and looked round, he found that
his precautionary advice to his flock had proved of no avail,
as he could only observe some half dozen of them who had
been able to gain admittance, so great was the crowd, and so
early had all the available space in his church been filled. He
next preached in my father's church, Free St. Luke's, and a
lady who went to hear him, from having had her curiosity
excited by the accounts of his wonderful popularity in the
North, gives her recollections of this sermon :—

" Well do I remember that day when in the morning your
father read Acts ix. 20-29 (the first preaching of the converted
Saul of Tarsus), with the remark, ' How soon God can make a
preacher!' and prayed that this newly raised-up preacher might
have depths of repentance, as a safeguard against his great
popularity. Mr. North preached in the evening with a power
and originality which riveted all, even although such a state-

ment as ' This church is full of devils ' provoked in some a half-smile. Hundreds of times since that evening I have thanked him for his exhortation, ' You say that you pray; but when you kneel down with closed doors, will you believe that Jesus is actually at your side, desiring to bless you?' The incidents of his wonderful conversion were constantly reproduced, not through egotism, but to warn against slighting the motions of the Holy Spirit, or grieving Him away from us. Numbers of his gay friends came to hear him, and even if not converted, were forced to own that it was the finger of God. All who heard him felt that his power did not consist in the words of man's wisdom, but that he spoke what he had learned directly from God through the Word. How often I still turn over in my mind the exhortation so difficult to follow, ' Give self to Christ, and take Christ instead,' and this other constantly repeated text ' *God is,*' which might be called his motto."

The late Francis Brown Douglas, Esq., ever afterwards through life his attached friend, gives the following recollections of the beginning of his work in that city: —

" His one object was preaching the Word and gaining souls to the Master. Many a week-evening did we go with him to Free St. Luke's and join the large congregation; and many a Lord's Day when he was to preach did we see that division of Queen Street, where the church is, literally crowded an hour before the time with expectant hearers, many of whom, after long waiting, had to go away disappointed, not being able to get admission.

" Each morning, during that time, our house had many visitors, Mr. North, who was our guest, meeting them by appointment made on the previous evening, and seeing them in succession. We did not know, nor do we know now, who these visitors were, but learned afterwards that several of our own acquaintances and friends had then come to see and converse with him, having received through him, as the instrument, divine teaching and impression which remain to this day.

" It was not always that what he thought his best sermons were his most successful ones. Many godly ministers have stated their experience to be the same. One evening he preached from the text, 'Turn ye to the stronghold, ye prisoners of hope,' dwelling on each expression. When he came home, he said he had never felt more unfit to preach than that Sabbath evening; it was as if his thoughts were gone and his mind weak—no power at all in him; words would not come. Often he had more to say that he could get out, and was obliged to stop from exhaustion, but that night he stopped early, not because he was tired, but because he had nothing more to say. Yet he seldom had so many inquirers coming to speak to him as after that address. One young woman, he told us, burst into tears and said, 'O, sir, when you said the devil was blinding our eyes and holding us down fast in chains, it went through me like an arrow; it was just my case.' On this occasion he showed us the following letter received the next day: "Sir, excuse the liberty taken by a stranger in thus addressing you, and trespassing on your precious time; but you love to do good to the souls of your fellow-creatures. You requested the prayers of a praying people: may I, who have no one to pray for me, request your special prayer on my behalf, that God for Christ's sake would enlighten my darkened soul, take from me the hard and stony heart, give me a new heart and right spirit, and loose the chains that bind me to Satan? While listening to your solemn, beseeching address, the most fearful thoughts took possession of my soul, which if clothed in words would make the most hardened shudder. Oh, pray, pray that I may be converted, sanctified, saved. I am an orphan, and almost alone, with none to whom I can tell my sorrow of heart, and must still remain a stranger even while making this urgent request."

Among other subjects which Brownlow North constantly alluded to in his sermons, was the great controversy whether we are to believe God or our own heart. "Unconverted people," he would say, "follow their own hearts. They do what their own hearts, not what the Word of God tells them. They read, 'Lay not up for yourselves treasures on earth,' but their hearts say, 'Take thine ease, eat, drink, and be merry.' Now what I want God's people to do is just this, to put God's

Word where their own heart used to be, and their heart where God's Word was; to believe God's Word, and to do what it bids them; to disbelieve their own heart, and not to follow its teachings and suggestions. Many never begin at the beginning; they work, and pray, and read, and perhaps make a god of their Bible, but they are never brought down to that great truth, I know God as a personal God, and I believe this message, 'By grace ye are saved through faith, and that not of yourselves, it is the gift of God.'" Then urging this humility of spirit, he would say, "'God resisteth the proud, but giveth grace to the humble'; and see how different the treatment is of the king and of the poor. The king must fall down before Him, but 'He will deliver the needy when he crieth, the poor also, and him that hath no helper.'"

From Edinburgh he wrote to Miss Gordon, of Wardhouse, his impressions of the door that was opened to him in the Scottish capital.

"EDINBURGH, *Saturday*.

"MY BELOVED AUNTIE,—I really feel ashamed at not having written for so long, but indeed you would excuse me if you saw how I am pressed. I hardly know what to begin to tell you, but I *do* hope the Lord is with me. I have had to do with many awakened and anxious souls. May *He* own the work, and make the end to be true conversion of the heart to Him, for Jesus Christ's sake! Doors upon doors have been opened upon me, and the interest to hear seems on the increase still. Last Sabbath I was in Dr. Candlish's; Monday, Charles Brown's; Thursday, Moody-Stuart's; tomorrow, if God wills (and if He does, may He *exceedingly bless*), Haldane's old church at half-past two, and Moody-Stuart's at night; Friday, Dr. Brown's, the original U.P. On Sabbath, the 19th, by his own personal request, couched in language I should not like to repeat, at half-past two (his own usual service) I preach in Dr. Guthrie's Church. The wise, the mighty, the learned will all be there: may God be pleased to perfect his praise out of the mouth of me, a very babe in Christ, that am not worthy to be called a babe; but by the grace of God I am what I am, and I hope *by the will of God* I am *where* I am. Oh what a glorious honour! May I just do so much, and no more than He chooses! Letters have come up from Thurso to Sir George Sinclair, asking him to get me to go over there for the herring-fishing time, when thousands are gathered, and he has earnestly pressed it on me, so that I think it seems a duty to go. Believe me, with much Christian love,

"Your truly affectionate, B. NORTH."

As the complement of the descriptions of his work on his first visit to Edinburgh thus given by himself and by Christian friends, we may quote a journalist's impressions of the same visit, published in March 1857:—

"Brownlow North, Esq., a connection of the great Lord North, and hitherto a gay and careless 'man about town,' has been preaching in various Free Church and Baptist pulpits during the week. On Sunday evening he held forth in Dr. Candlish's church to one of the largest audiences it ever contained. He is a man apparently about forty years of age, as destitute of pulpit airs as when he was a leader of fashion and a keen hand for the turf: but in spite of his short shooting-coat, and the negligent tie, and the gold eye-glass dangling on the breast of his tightly-buttoned coat, there is tremendous energy and force in his preaching. There is something contagious in a man who is terribly in earnest. North begins his service with a low faltering voice; but before he has got half through the opening prayer, his breast begins to heave with a convulsive sobbing, his whole frame is agitated, and the tears stream over his cheeks. There is then no faltering. The words come quickly, and all the graces of a natural orator are developed. He becomes a great example of the truth that there is no teacher of elocution like the heart. When he implores his audience, with tears, to forget all about the messenger in the message; when he graphically sketches the position of the gay worldling, evidently picturing from experience, but scarcely ever alluding to his own past career; when he breaks out abruptly, in the middle of a sentence, with a radiant smile, and states the happy conviction that some souls are being saved; and when, with unaffected simplicity, he asks the prayers of the congregation on his own behalf, that he may be supported in the extraordinary position in which he finds himself, no unprejudiced spectator can doubt that he is a man in earnest, and that we may yet expect to hear great things of the work which he has begun. There is a significance in his appearance at this time which affects the future of the Church. As a spur to the regularly educated and regularly appointed ministers, and as a powerful living commentary on some of their most prevalent and fatal defects, Brownlow North seems destined to exercise a wide influence as a reformer."

One night, in preaching to young men in St. Luke's Church, he had spoken with more than usual power from Matt. vi. 6, and solemnly charged them all to go straight home and pray to Him "who is in secret," with the undoubting assurance of His presence in their closets, and of the certainty of His listening to their prayer. A few days afterwards a young man of perhaps twenty-two years of age called on Dr. Moody-Stuart to express his gratitude for that sermon as the means of his salvation. Under the impression of Mr. North's closing words, and with a deep sense of the nearness of the living God, he left the Church with the fixed resolution of casting himself down on his knees as soon as he reached his room. But the house was at some distance, and as he walked through the silent and lonely streets in the dark night, he said within himself, "Why need I delay so long? Why need I go to my closet to find my Father who is in secret? Is He not here in this solitude, as much as there? and may I not find Him now as well as then?" And with the sense of God all around him he knelt down quickly on the cold and hard pavement, and did not rise from his knees till he found that God is near to all that call upon Him; and like the publican of old, " he went down to his house justified " through faith in Christ Jesus.

After Brownlow North had left Edinburgh we find a letter to him from the late Mrs. Stuart, of Annat, dated 24th April, 1857, in which she wrote:—

" Your visit to Edinburgh has been a season of refreshing to many, and I trust *that* day will declare that not a few have in consequence been translated out of darkness into marvellous light. How gracious is our God in having made you a savour of Christ here! Oh, may He keep you humble and watchful, and feeling continually that your sufficiency is of God! We had a visit from Mrs. H.'s little governess. Her face was so bright, that I greeted her by saying, ' I don't need to ask how you feel, for your countenance bespeaks peace.' She called, poor thing, to thank us for our kind reception that day when she was in deep waters. I do think she has got a lesson from you to cease from poring over self, and rather to keep gazing on Him who is made unto His people righteousness, and sanctification, and redemption. Commending you to the God of all grace, and praying that He may bless you and keep you, and cause the light of His countenance to shine upon you,

" I am, ever yours in the Lord,

" JESSIE STUART."

It was probably of the young lady here referred to that Mr. North remarked to a friend at this time, " Her face is just like April, sunshine after showers," so sweetly had the shining of the Sun of Righteousness dispelled the cloud of her weeping.

The Hon. Miss Mackenzie, of Seaforth, in a few lines written in her old age and blindness, on 1st May, 1857, sent him the Levitical benediction of Numbers vi. 24-26: " The Lord bless thee and keep thee," etc., " I wished to send these sweet words of blessing to dear Mr. Brownlow North, with a few words of grateful remembrance, but my blind eyes will not serve. Is not that a sweet word?—

" The Lord will light my candle, so that it shall shine full bright,
The Lord my God will also make my darkness to be light."

Psalm xviii. 28.

May it be yours, and many, many souls be given you. Pray for me, dear friend!

" Yours affectionately in the Lord,

" CHARLOTTE MACKENZIE."

Before leaving Edinburgh he thought it right to make an

insurance on his life in favour of his wife, for whom, in the days of his dissipation and worldliness, he had made no provision. Accordingly he went to an Insurance Office, and considerably startled the officials when they put to him the usual question, whether he knew of anything that might shorten his life, by the prompt and naive reply, " Oh yes, I feel that I may not live for an hour!" Ever since his awakening, he was under the impression that his life would be very short. However, after being examined, the medical man certified that his fears were groundless; and on his return he said to my father, " Only think, Moody-Stuart, the doctor says that I may live till I am seventy, that is twenty years; and how many souls I may be the means of saving in that time!" In God's providence he was spared exactly twenty years to preach the gospel.

After finishing a season of fruitful evangelistic labour in the Scottish metropolis, he was invited to Glasgow, and was as highly appreciated and blessed among the teeming population of that great commercial and industrial city. The general effects of his preaching may be gathered from the notices in the city newspapers, which are in the same strain as the journals already quoted.

In one of them a full report is given of his discourse upon the Parable of the Sower. The report continues : " The discourse occupied above an hour. After giving out the intimations of his further services, he for some fifteen minutes most solemnly and urgently addressed the audience, especially those who had never thought seriously of their salvation. He advised them to favour him thus far, to give ten minutes daily to prayer and to reading God's Word, and to remember that when they read the Bible God was speaking to them, and that when they prayed they were speaking to God." The article further draws attention, and rightly, to the great strength and shrewdness of mind that were apparent in his discourses, to the correctness and aptness of his quotation of Scripture, and to his use of popular language, and a style which was pointed, vigorous, and telling.

The work appears to have been as full of permanence as of promise : indeed, the stability of those converted under his instrumentality was everywhere very marked. His preaching was much blessed in the Rev. Alexander Cumming's congregation. The results of his first visits to Paisley, Greenock, Rothesay, and other towns in the Western district of Scotland were of a similar encouraging and impressive character. From one of these towns he wrote to an old and much interested friend describing the work in which he was engaged.

34, UNION STREET, GREENOCK, Monday.

"I received your letter, my dearest auntie, with much pleasure, and though I have a very large correspondence, and headache to boot, will, God willing, send you a few lines.

"You will be glad to hear that I have every reason to hope that my more than merciful God and Saviour is daily forgiving me all my blunders and wickedness, and blessing the words of His truth that He enables me to speak. It would take sheets and days to write you anything like a detailed account of the appearances of good in Glasgow; and since I have left they have been, I think, fully proportionate in other places. In S., where I was staying for a week, preaching in the neighbourhood, the six-foot-two London butler was two mornings in my bedroom, before I was up, on his knees in prayer, and has been over here to-day to see me, still in the same mind; and the same spirit appears to have aroused that house, from the mistress to the dairy-maid, which latter sent for me after I had retired to my room for the night, to come to speak with her, on the evening preceding my leaving. I am much pleased with all the letters I get from C. D.; still I feel very anxious about her. I wish the dear Duchess would ask her to Huntly Lodge. I trust her cold is better. Give her my warmest Christian regards.

"Dearest Auntie, I have much to write and think about. All the doctors are crying, 'Rest, rest.' May the Lord Jesus Christ keep us, soul and body, to His own glory and the good of our fellows! We are <i>not</i> our own. Love.

"Your affectionate, BROWNLOW NORTH."

His ministry in the West proved as popular and attractive as it had been in the North. In Lochwinnoch, where, in consequence of heavy rains, the road connecting the village with

the district lying on the south side of Castle Semple Loch and
Barr Loch was covered for some hundred yards with several
feet of water, two hundred persons from that quarter appeared
at the meeting notwithstanding this obstacle, having got across
the flood by walking along the top of the wall on the roadside.
The singularity of this long procession of serious and solemnized worshippers going homewards in the still, gloomy night,
marching in single file and with cautious steps along the narrow path of stone, on either side of which lay a wide waste of
waters, is well remembered by many in the parish to this day.
The impressions produced here also on many hearers were
profound and permanent.

Mr. North owed a great deal to the friendships which he
formed with many of the most honoured and most deeply
experienced of the Lord's dear children throughout the length
of Scotland, who gave him a most hearty welcome from the
very outset of his ministry, and threw open to him both their
hearts and their homes. The most honoured and blest ministers, alike in town and country, invited him to their pulpits,
and guided him by their experienced counsel; while others, like
the saintly Duchess of Gordon and the beloved Christian ladies
whose letters have just been quoted, gave him direction in a
more private manner,—and no man was more willing to learn
from the very humblest of the Lord's chosen ones than was
Brownlow North. But besides these, at this time he formed
acquaintance and friendship with a number of devoted Christian gentlemen, with time and means at their disposal, who
became his cordial fellow-labourers in the work of the Lord.
He owed much to them, and they in turn owed much to him.

This band of evangelizing Elders was a distinguished one,
and its members did not belong exclusively to any one of the
branches into which, by the progress of events, the Scottish
Church had unhappily been divided.

Mr. North's work had now attained such proportions as to
claim some public recognition at the hands of the Church in
Scotland. Within little more than a year from the time when,
as he once said in his own pithy language to a little gathering
of young men, the Lord " took Brownlow North from his com-

fortable seat beside the fire, where he was reading some religious book, and crucified him at the bedside of some poor
bed-ridden women," he found himself overwhelmed with invitations to give addresses as the most popular preacher in
Scotland.

A Christian relative of his, foreseeing such an issue as possible, and dreading the effects of success upon his spirituality
of mind, had rather dissuaded him at the outset from preaching, reminding him that when he used to frequent the hunt,
it was " first North, and then the hounds," and that while he
might similarly excel as a preacher, it might prove injurious to
him. But by God's grace he was to a marked extent preserved
from the snare of pride, and while he was not without faults,
he was characterized to an unusual degree by the grace of
humility.

Several circumstances combined, in the providence of God,
to render the position which Mr. North occupied before the
Christian public, for nearly twenty years, unique in its influence
upon the community.

The fact that he was a layman, and not a minister, was one
of these. Before his day laymen had done invaluable service
to the Church of Christ, and the advancement of His cause in
Scotland. Not a few very distinguished laymen had been
raised up by the great Head of the Church in our beloved land,
men who occupied as high a position in society, who were as
truly devoted to the Master, who gave up much that they might
obey that Master's call, men of higher intellectual acquire-
ments, if not of as high mental force and calibre. But there
were none of these, except the brothers Haldane, whose influence upon the spiritual state of the community as a whole
was for a moment to be compared with that of Mr. North.
Their influence was confined, at least during their lives, almost
wholly within the bounds of the denominations to which they
severally belonged, and their efforts were directed mainly to
the defence and propagation of such great truths and principles
as were identified with the public testimony of the Church to
which they adhered. From the fact that he was trained in
none of the sections of the Scottish Church, but as an English-

man, and the son of an English rector, in the Church of England, Brownlow North obtained and held a position which gave him access to the congregations of each of the Scottish Presbyterian Churches. His membership in his own Church he never relinquished, although in his work in Scotland he became thoroughly associated with Presbyterians, whose form of worship, and Church government, and doctrinal views, he greatly admired and loved. His position gave him a powerful vantage-ground for good, and was recognized by him most thankfully as a talent entrusted to his care by his great Master, and used most humbly and most prudently.

Mr. North's views on the right and duty of laymen, possessed of the needful gifts and grace, to proclaim to their fellow-men in public address, as well as in private conversation, the glad tidings of salvation through the Great Redeemer, were clear and decided. In his annotated Bible he draws attention to Acts viii. 1, where it is written that after Stephen's death through stress of persecution, the disciples " were all scattered abroad throughout the regions of Judea and Samaria, *except the apostles,*" and verse 4, " They that were scattered abroad went everywhere preaching the Word;" and he adds, " Surely this is in itself sufficient warrant for lay-preaching. What the Christians spoken of in the fourth verse did is clearly the duty of every Christian. The Apostles were not even among the preachers; every member of the Church was a preacher in those days." He refers to the same subject continued in Acts xi. 19-21, where it is stated, that " they that were scattered abroad upon the persecution that arose about Stephen, travelled as far as Antioch, preaching the Word, and preaching the Lord Jesus; and the hand of the Lord was with them, so that a great number believed;" and notes, " The success of all work for God depends on this, the hand of the Lord being with us. These preachers had no ordination from man; because the hand of the Lord was with them, these lay-preachers turned many."

But, on the other hand, his views as to the value and the divine institution and authority of a regularly-ordained ministry were no less clear and no less strong. He writes : " Let no one for a moment suppose that I in the least intend to teach that a stated ministry is unnecessary. God forbid. I believe that, next to His Word and His Spirit, a minister taught by the Holy Ghost is the best gift God has to give us." He upheld the ordained ministry with all his power, honouring them on account of the honour of their Master and the honourable nature of their work. While, of course, he could not co-operate with worldly and godless ministers, and used in private often to warn his converts of the danger and the damage to their souls of sitting under an unconverted minister, or one who did not feed their souls with any spiritual food, he never indulged in those general and sweeping denunciations of ministers, or of large classes of ministers, which have too often been uttered by many devoted and useful lay-evangelists, and which have irritated congregations and ministers who, by a more wise and forbearing conduct, might have been conciliated, and not improbably benefited, through their zeal-inspiring services. Mr. North always remembered that the wrath of man cannot work the righteousness of God, and he never allowed private slights, or even personal opposition, to dictate or to tincture any of his public utterances. The grace of God, along with natural prudence, and an overpowering sense of his own responsibility for every word uttered in His name to saints or sinners to that Master who is the Judge of all His servants, and to whom alone they stand or fall, kept him from forming hasty judgments in this matter, and from giving rash expression to them even when they were formed deliberately. But as a general rule for all, he used very solemnly both in public and private to say, " Do not sit under a lifeless ministry."

Frank outspokenness could not demand more, and fidelity to souls, and to the God of souls, could demand no less. Ministers have no reason to be jealous of laymen who share his spirit, even though they may not share his talent.

At the same time, while Mr. North began his labours simply as a lay-evangelist, his university education for the Church of England, his ability as a theologian, and his power as a preacher made him occupy quite a unique position, while in some other respects also his qualifications were exceptional.

A strong desire now began to be felt in various quarters that Mr. North should receive formal Church recognition as an evangelist. Nor is this to be wondered at, especially in view of the parentage of Scottish Presbyterianism.

All the Scottish Churches were scions of the old Reformation Church of Scotland, which in her order of " Exhorters " and " Readers " had embedded in her very constitution a recognition of the right of unordained men who were called and fitted by God's Spirit, to preach the gospel and to exhort the people in an orderly method. Their mother-Church in this had moulded the outlines of her polity in harmony with apostolic practice and precept; and the Church of the Apostles had recognized the right of laymen to preach the Word, as the older Jewish Church of the synagogue had assigned to it a definite place many generations before.

The desire to recognize Mr. North as a preacher took definite form within the Free Church. It was both fitting and advantageous that this should be the case, for not only had this Church thrown herself with enormous energy, from the very period of her separation from the State in 1843, into the work of evangelizing the country, and from his first appearance had given a very cordial and general, though unofficial, welcome to this distinguished preacher, whom her exalted Head was so greatly owning in the spiritual harvest-field, but at this period she embraced within her pale many of the most widely known, most learned, and most acute divines in Scotland. Having then in her Church councils such master-theologians as Principal Cunningham, Dr. Duncan, Dr. Candlish, Principal Fairbairn, all now removed to the general assembly of the first-born above, but whose praise will long remain in all the churches, and such experienced Church jurists as Sir Henry Wellwood Moncrieff, and Mr. Murray-Dunlop, and holding a conservative position in the eyes of Presbyterian Christendom, it was clear that whatever action she might take in this matter would bid fair to meet with the approbation of all the English-speaking Presbyterian Churches in the world.

The General Assembly of the Free Church of Scotland met in Edinburgh in May 1859, under the moderatorship of the revered Principal Cunningham, and an "overture" was prepared to be submitted to it for the recognition of Mr. North as an Evangelist. By this ecclesiastical action Mr. North was taken out of the category of lay-preachers strictly so called. He jocularly said immediately after to a youthful member of my father's family, who happened to smile at some remark he had made, "Why, sir, are you laughing at me? Do you not know that I am now a probationer of the Free Church of Scotland?" His studies at Oxford enabled the Church, without scruple, now formally to admit him to her pulpits. But while this was the case, the words "welcome him as an evangelist," in the resolution of the Assembly recognized his right to engage in evangelistic labours previously to his having received this formal recognition.

Although my father was not himself a member of the Assembly of 1859, the burden of taking the necessary steps to procure an object which he, along with many others, felt to be eminently desirable, fell mainly upon him. The result of his conferences with the brethren was that on the 25th of May, 1859, there was laid upon the table of the Supreme Court, what is termed in Scottish ecclesiastical phraseology, an "overture," asking the Assembly to appoint a committee to meet with Mr. North, and to report as to his views on the great essential truths of salvation, and, should they be satisfied with these, that the Assembly should formally welcome and sanction him in the labours which he had been carrying on in the land for the three previous years with manifold tokens of the Divine blessing.

The overture was signed by sixty-eight ministers and thirty-eight elders.

The Assembly Hall of the Free Church of Scotland, at the head of The Mound in Edinburgh, has been the scene of many intensely interesting deliberations and decisions, which have influenced the progress of the church of Christ alike in Scotland and in distant lands. Those who have been present on any of the occasions when momentous issues were at stake, whether in regard to the defence or the propagation of the truth, will carry with them through life impressions that can never be effaced from the tablet of remembrance. And the day on which the General Assembly deliberated as to its course with regard to the recognition of this evangelist, whom the Head of the Church was so extensively blessing to the awakening of souls, will rank, in the recollection of all who witnessed it, among the memorable scenes that have taken place in a Hall consecrated by many sacred and inspiring memories.

A Committee, consisting of all the Theological Professors, along with Drs. Beith, Candlish, and Wood, was appointed to converse with Mr. North and to report as to the soundness of his doctrinal views.

On Friday the 27th May, the Report of this Committee was given in, which stated that having met with Mr. North they had heard from him a clear and detailed account of his views of the great essential truths of salvation, as well as a narrative of the way in which he was led to engage in evangelistic work, and of the steps of his subsequent progress therein, and embodied a unanimous and cordial recommendation that the Assembly should welcome him as a friend of the Saviour, who had been in a remarkable way conducted into his present course by the hand of God, and whom He had eminently qualified for addressing his fellow-sinners on the things which belong to their everlasting peace.

Professor Gibson, D.D., whose conscientious jealousy for soundness in the faith was proverbial, stated that he had never on any occasion heard a more distinct, simple, and lucid statement of the great doctrines of grace, first, in relation to the condition of man as a sinner in the sight of God, dead in trespasses and sins, and as to the sovereignty of God in the election of grace; and secondly, as to the method of a sinner's justification, solely and entirely through the imputed righteousness of the Lord Jesus Christ; and thirdly, in reference to the perpetual obligation lying even upon the sinner to obey the law of God, and the binding and unchangeable nature of that obligation upon the believer, and the duty of the believer, in gratitude and love to God, to show it forth in his life and conduct. Nor had he ever heard a more clear statement of the work of the Holy Spirit in relation to the condition of man as a sinner, utterly unable and indisposed to anything good till renewed by the Spirit of God.

During the interesting proceedings the proposal formally to recognize Mr. North was warmly advocated by many of the most distinguished ministers of the Church, such as Dr. Candlish, Dr. Beith, Dr. Begg, as well as by representative men among her Elders, such as Professor Miller, Mr. Balfour and Mr. Brown-Douglas.

The motion was unanimously agreed to, and Mr. North came forward to the table of the House amidst loud and general applause.

The Moderator, Principal Cunningham, then addressed Mr. North in the name of the Assembly,—and it was most fitting that this important duty should devolve on one whose vast erudition, mastery of theological controversies and clear judgment gave peculiar significance and weight to all his utterances. He said—" Mr. North, I have great pleasure and heartfelt satisfaction in announcing to you that I have been called, by the unanimous decision of this House, to recognize and welcome you as a servant of Jesus Christ who has received unusual gifts for preaching the glad tidings of great joy, and whose work in this department the Lord has greatly honoured. The General Assembly has come to this decision, I believe, in full knowledge, and on deliberate consideration. I concur heartily with the grounds on which this judgment has been adopted. I never could see the warrantableness of any Church of Christ venturing to lay down as a resolution that she would not see, and would not recognize, gifts for preaching or for the ministry, except in men who had gone through the whole of the ordinary curriculum. No Church has a right to lay down that rule. This Church has not laid down that rule, and I trust never will. The Church must lay herself open to consider exceptional cases, to mark God's hand, and to make a fair use and application of what He has been doing. I believe, if we leave an opening for occasional exceptions, it will be of more importance in enabling us to maintain a high standard and full compliance with our strict regulations in regard to nineteen-twentieths of our students, than by attempting to carry out the same rule to the whole twenty-twentieths, and thereby running the risk of lowering the standard of the whole body, and losing, besides, the benefit of the exceptions. I have very great pleasure, Mr. North, in tendering you the right hand of fellowship, and in recognizing and welcoming you as a servant of the Lord Jesus Christ, and as highly honoured by your Master in your work. And perhaps you will allow me to say that your position is a somewhat peculiar one,—that while you have eminent gifts, there are, of course, difficulties and temptations to which, in your position, you are exposed. I have no doubt you will feel that you stand deeply in need of wisdom and guidance and discretion; and I have no doubt you will feel that, amid all the encouragement you have had, you have still much cause to wait upon God, and walk humbly with Him."

The Moderator, on concluding his speech, gave Mr. North the right hand of fellowship, amid loud and general applause. This was also done by Sir Henry Moncrieff, Drs. Beith, Grierson, Wood, and others.

Mr. North, who appeared deeply affected, and spoke with difficulty at the outset of his remarks, then addressed the House as follows:—" The Lord says, ' How can ye believe, which receive honour one of another, and seek not the honour that cometh from God only?' Now, I think that at this moment I have received an honour such as it is impossible to exceed. For me to have been sitting in this House, and listening to the language I have been hearing, and to have been welcomed as I have been welcomed,—nothing can exceed the weight of all these things,—language cannot express that which I feel put upon me at this moment. And I do earnestly request the prayers of this Assembly, that what the Moderator so kindly and affectionately put me in mind that I require, may be granted to me. One of my own prayers has been, from almost the first day that I prayed at all, that I might receive marvellous grace, and marvellous grace to bear the marvellous grace. To find myself where I am at this moment, I can only say I trust and believe it is the Lord's doing, but it is marvellous in our eyes. Dr. Candlish told me yesterday, that I would probably be asked to say a few words to-day and that it would be on the subject of the state of religion in Scotland. I have had an opportunity during the last three years, of seeing much of the religious state of the country; and I have come to this conclusion, that although we are by God's grace gathering many prisoners out of the chains of sin and Satan, still it is but one of a city and two of a family, and that the whole world is no better now than in the days of the apostle, when he said it was *lying in wickedness*. Now, dear friends, by the help of God's Spirit how much might not you, who are now before me, effect in leavening this putrid mass of iniquity?

" I believe there are *four special things* for which God is very angry with the land, and for which His Holy Spirit is so little among us. *First,* the neglect of united prayer—*the appointed means of bringing down the Holy Spirit*. I say it, because I believe it, that the Scotch, with all their morality so-called, and their outward decency, respectability, and love of preaching, are not a praying people. Sirs, is not this the truth? The neglect of prayer proves, to my mind, that there is a large amount of *practical infidelity*. If people believed that there was a real, existing, personal God, they would ask Him for what they wanted, and they would get what they asked. But they do not ask, because they do not believe or expect to receive. Why do I say this? Because I want to get Christians to remember that, though preaching is one of the great means appointed by God for the conversion of sinners, yet, unless God give the increase, Paul may plant and Apollos may water in vain; and God says He will be inquired of. O ministers! excuse me,—you gave me this chance of speaking,—urge upon your people to come to the prayer-meeting. O Christians! go more to prayer-meetings than you do. And when you go to the prayer-meeting, try and realize more that there is *use in prayer*.

"*Secondly,* I do not believe that there is a more effective system in Christendom for the promotion of true religion than the Presbyterian system, *if it was carried out*. But the machinery is not worked. Look at the mass of elders there are in the Presbyterian Church. But what are these elders doing as a body? Blessed be God, there are many holy, self-denying, godly men, who seek not their own things, but the things which are Jesus Christ's, and who go into the lanes and alleys of the cities, and pray, and speak, and try to lead people to God. But do the elders, *as a body,* do that? I believe there are elders—it is possible there may be such in this very Assembly—who know that God, who searcheth their hearts, sees that from week to week, and from month to month, they never make a single attempt to do anything for the glory of Jesus Christ, and such must give an account to God at the last day.

" The *third* point I have seldom or never heard touched upon, because, perhaps, men hardly know how to alter it, but I believe it lies at the very heart's core of the irreligion of the land; and it is this,—in the Church of England, and in all the Presbyterian Churches of Scotland, and I doubt not, in all other bodies, men are brought up from childhood to say that they are going into the Church—men are put to college and educated for the Church, and men in England are brought before their bishops, and in Scotland before their Presbyteries, and without any fear of being struck dead for committing the blasphemy against the Holy Ghost, they swear in my Church, they state in yours, that they believe they are called by the Holy Ghost to the ministry, and that they enter it out of a desire to promote the salvation of the souls of their fellow-creatures; *and they know when they say it they tell a lie.* I say there are multitudes of instances of this: even in this Assembly there may be those who know that they have been guilty of this fearful sin—for even among the twelve apostles there was a Judas—even in this Assembly there may be those who have even now no reason to believe that they have been born again of the Spirit, and who are nothing but hireling shepherds. Oh, if there be, I implore you to conceive your position! If it was a dreadful thing for the rich man to think of the entrance of his five brethren into hell, knowing how their reproaches would increase his torments, what will the entrance of your congregations into hell be to you? How will you bear their reproaches? Think of it! The day of judgment will come, and if you know in your hearts that you are not yet converted, and are not really labouring for souls, as those called of God to labour, ah, follow the advice that Peter gave to Simon Magus—confess your sins to God, pray for pardon and the Holy Spirit, and for the baptism of that fire which can yet enable you to awake the dead around you; and then, instead of being lost for ever, you may yet appear before God in glory with many children which may still be given you. Brethren, bear with me. I do not presume upon my position : but if I lose this opportunity of speaking, no man can tell if I will ever have the like again. I asked God this morning to bless me, and to give me a word that should be blessed to you.

" *Lastly,* the very best amongst us are exceedingly guilty in neglecting the apostolic injunction to be instant ' *out of season.*' How solemn is the introduction to the command, ' *I charge thee therefore before God, and the Lord Jesus Christ, who shall judge the quick and the dead at His appearing,*'—' I charge thee '—what? ' *Be instant in season, out of season.*' Now, we can all speak when we are expected in the pulpit, in the prayer-meeting, or at the family altar, but are we faithful *out of season*? I feel convinced if the godly minister would prayerfully commence a system of individual, faithful, personal dealing with his people in their own houses, speaking as one who was in earnest, and beseeching men not to rest in a mere form of godliness, but to be content with nothing short of God's Spirit witnessing with their spirit that they were born again, that he would very soon see of the fruit of his labour, and have reason to bless God and take courage. We need more *out-of-season work,* more talking to people apart in private as to the state of their souls."

Mr. North concluded, amidst applause, by thanking the Assembly for the honour done him, and expressing his hope that he might never give them any reason to regret it.

The Assembly then engaged in prayer, that the Divine blessing might rest upon his labours.

What was in one sense the climax of Mr. North's success was now reached when he gained for lay-effort a place and an express recognition such as it had not obtained since the period immediately succeeding the Reformation. This alone would secure for his name a lasting place in the religious history of our country. He takes rank not merely as a very successful evangelist, but as the father of evangelists in our day, as the leader and pioneer of what has proved a very notable movement.

CHAPTER VI

Brownlow North's Post Bag

THIS chapter may probably prove to some readers one of the most profitable, and we hope it will also prove not the least interesting in the volume. The variety of spiritual experience that is here recorded in the writers' own words is as great as the diversity of position in life, occupation, and circumstances of the correspondents, and may perhaps strike a chord of sympathy in the bosom of some reader, who may in one or other of these heart effusions find a picture that is not very far from being a portrait of himself.

We think they may prove helpful to persons under spiritual anxiety, or at the outset of their Christian course, by showing them that their state of mind in its general features, whatever its special details may be, is not peculiar to themselves, but that others have suffered as they do, and have been succoured. It is right to call the reader's attention to the fact that, in the greater part of the letters here selected for transcription, the letter was written after the lapse of several years since the professed experience of a saving change. This affords a pretty good guarantee, not only of the writer's sincerity, but of the reality of the change that had taken place. In some of the cases here recorded, as well as in many others which might have been narrated, we can ourselves vouch for the fact that the conversion, however sudden, has been attested by a long course of consistent Christian life and, in several instances, of successful public work in the Lord's vineyard.

The letters which came to Mr. North in such numbers are

from persons in all ranks and positions of life. Here are letters from peers and peeresses, Indian rajahs and German princesses, professional men, busy merchants, acute lawyers, soldiers and sailors, squatters in the lonely Australian bush, from young ladies, from boys, from governesses, students, footmen, letter-carriers, domestic servants, farm servants, etc., etc., all bearing on the one great question. A few are from Christians encouraging him in his work, but the great mass come from those who had been awakened, or converted, or delivered from spiritual distress through his preaching. Some are from persons who had never known what sin is according to the world's estimation, but had been deeply convinced of it by the Divine Spirit; a few from those who had been guilty of the blackest sins, all preserved with equal care, and docketed methodically by this indefatigable evangelist. Of hundreds of such letters we can only give here a very short selection.

The first letter is from a sailor; and if we could have peeped in on the writer we should have found him penning his epistle to his spiritual father in one of Her Majesty's ships of war lying in the beautiful estuary of the Firth of Forth, above the point where the northern and southern shores curve inwards as if to embrace each other, but suddenly retire, leaving between them that fair stretch of deep, calm, and almost landlocked water known by the historical name of St. Margaret's Hope. The writer is not a lad, but a married man and the father of a family, and had returned half a dozen years before from foreign service.

A Sailor's Letter.

H.M.S. ——, *April 5th*, 1860.

"My dear Sir,—I take the pleasure of writing to thank you for the great blessing you have been the means of bringing on a most hardened and wicked sinner. You may remember coming to preach one Sunday on board of this ship. Your prayer was heard that day. The Lord sent your words home to the heart of one of the greatest sinners who was listening to you, and who thought he had been so vilely used that there was no truth in religion or in the Bible; one who reviled God's truth, and argued against it, and many times said man had no pre-eminence above a beast, and brought the Bible to prove it, and in fact had almost become an infidel. But you stopped me: I heard you say you had been guilty of almost every crime, you thought, but murder; so thinks I, 'That's a plain-speaking man, I'll just pay attention to him,' not thinking to do much good by it; but when you asked if we ever thought upon God, it went like a shot through me. I had forgotten Him altogether.

"Family distress in fifty-four, when I came home in the Frigate ——, had driven God out of my thoughts, and the devil took the advantage, and goaded me on to drink, and ran me into all sorts of evil. Your coming on board that day just saved my soul from his snare; but I have had to struggle hard, as you told us. I prayed to the Lord Jesus to assist me, and He has done so, and has beaten him; and I am happy to inform you the good Spirit is master within, and shall never more be drowned by an evil one. And now, instead of reviling God's truth, I adore it, and read it earnestly, and pray while reading for the Lord to open my eyes to see the hid treasures therein contained; and I think He grants my prayer; and instead of not being able to think of Him a minute without some worldly thought coming in, I think of Him long and often. I found all you said true. I was eating husks all my life till now. I never was so happy before. I often think of you, sir, and pray the Lord to prosper all your efforts, and may His blessing ever attend you for the blessing you have brought on me. My heart is full.

"From yours ever thankful,

"A——B——,

"H.M.S. ——.

"P.S.—There is a prayer-meeting on board this ship every night. It was held in a cabin, but they are obliged to go into the stoke-room, the cabin was not large enough. Mr. Palmer (the Lieutenant) attends with the men."

The same address which was blessed to this sailor had been carried home to the heart of one of the officers in the ship, who soon afterwards became, as he has ever since continued, an active worker for that Lord whom he then chose as his portion.

About a dozen years after that memorable day he thus writes to his spiritual father:—

A NAVAL OFFICER'S LETTER.

"*January* 15*th*, 1871.

"DEAR MR. NORTH,—Do you remember, now nearly twelve years ago, your preaching on board H.M.S. —— from the Prodigal Son? It was that little sentence, ' when he was yet a great way off,' that the Holy Spirit blessed to my soul. How wonderful it all was, and still is! One hour amongst the tombs, mad; the next, sitting at the feet of Jesus, in one's right mind. What a comforting text that is, ' kept by the power of God through faith unto salvation.' What should we be without the Lord's protecting care? How soon would Satan be in possession of us again! I am so sorry to be off early to-morrow to London, but I trust we may meet again; at any rate, we shall meet before very long with our robes washed and made white in the blood of the Lamb. The conflict will be over then for good and all. God grant that an abundant blessing may have accompanied your words to-night.

"Believe me, ever yours in Christ,
"GEORGE PALMER."

We shall now give an extract from a letter this officer wrote to Mr. North six months after his conversion, which shows how active he was from the first in seeking to stand up for Jesus and win souls to Him.

"*November* 7*th*, 1860.

"I am happy and thankful to be able to tell you of fresh instances of God's mercy to sailors, as during the last month the chaplain and myself have had a school in the evening, composed entirely of our own men, quite independent of the fishermen, who also meet every night for prayer. Fifty-two men have been attending for the purpose of learning to read and write, and the last half-hour we devote to the service of God. I had between seventy and eighty fishermen in the engine room last night, and last Sunday I could not go up to the ' E '; but to make up for my disappointment God enabled me to speak His word to fifteen of our own men between two guns on the main deck: and truly I was never more proud and delighted in my whole life; it was such a direct answer to prayer, as I had so longed to get our own blue jackets together by themselves. It is a glorious privilege to be permitted to be an instrument in His hands for good, and to endeavour in our poor way to show our gratitude for all He has done for us. Our chaplain is away on leave, so I am quite by myself now at the school and meeting."

Let none suppose that all the correspondence came from persons able to analyse and express their feelings, and trace their spiritual history.

There is many a short, ill-spelt, ill-written note, expressing in a few lines the anxiety of the writer's soul, yet as carefully preserved and docketed by this skilful soul-gatherer.

It was in reading, studying and replying to such letters as these, which came to him morning by morning in great numbers, that Mr. North spent the forenoon at least of each day, after the large portion he reserved for private devotion, and diligent perusal and study of the Word of life; which occupations together always confined him to his own room till one o'clock. It was through the post office, as well as through the inquiry-room, that the book of the human heart was laid open to him, which with the book of revelation, formed the volumes he studied, and studied all the day. These two books, the Bible and the human heart, were his theological library, and perhaps some of us in the ministry would find greater help and success in our work, if we studied these two volumes far more intently than we do. To answer such letters, each with some distinctive feature in the case, he had to look much up to God for wisdom, and much into His Word for direction, that he might minister the suitable instruction, warning, counsel, and encouragement to every soul. The work is one of the most exhausting that a man can engage in, and it is a matter of thankfulness that, with a frame somewhat weakened, he was enabled for so many years to bear the great fatigues providentially laid upon him in private teaching and dealing with cases of spiritual distress, as well as in public preaching.

The writer of the next letter was a student in the grey granite capital of Northern Scotland, a city that has always been celebrated for the acuteness and intellectual power of its divines.

A STUDENT'S LETTER.

ABERDEEN, *March 2nd*, 1863.

" MY DEAR SIR,—I regret much that I have been deprived of a personal interview with you, though I have been privileged to hear you every time you have preached in Aberdeen. I therefore take the liberty of sending you this note to tell you that I have never repented the choice I made some seven years ago, when, in Albion Street Chapel, you pointed me to a personal Saviour. Very often, to my shame and confusion, have I proved unfaithful and treacherous; but so great has been His love to me, that He has not cast me off, but has again and again gone after His lost sheep in the wilderness, folding me in His bosom, and speaking words of cheer and comfort. I have been frequently in the depths, often in the hot furnace, and of late in the wilderness; but wherever I am, there He is; and in the very wilderness He has given me songs, vineyards, choice dainties. Oh His love, His forbearance, His tender mercies! Would I could praise Him more, and were moulded into His glorious image! In a few months I expect, D.V., to be licensed, but I shrink back from the work when I think of its awful nature and responsibility. Oh! try sometimes and remind Jesus of me, that I may be an able minister of the New Testament, one dead to self and to the opinion of the world. The Lord has had much to do with me, a proud, stubborn, wayward child; but He sees my heart, and knows that it is my earnest desire and prayer that I may sit at His feet and learn of Him!

" Yours very truly, J. H. C."

The next letter is from a German lady sojourning in London, and has no signature or address by which the writer could be traced; but it shows us how uniform, under a vast variety of outward conditions, are the ways of Divine grace, and proves that the Lord will gather in His own chosen ones by some instrumentality or other, in ways that are as beautifully wise as mysterious.

A GERMAN LADY'S LETTER.

LONDON, *April 7th*, 1860.

"MY DEAR SIR,—Suffer me to express to you from my deepest soul my thanks for all which, next to God, I owe you. I am a poor German sinner, who left her country three years ago; I do not know why, my heart yearned for England; and oh, how wondrous are the ways of the Lord! it was here that I should recognise the truth, and gradually be penetrated of it. I never shall forget the 18th of March, when, under your pulpit, I listened to your precious message; my stony heart was melted, and all hesitation vanished, and, like Rebecca, my decision was taken. How happy and rejoicing I went home that night, thanking the Lord for what He had done for me, and praying Him not to leave me for a minute! Joyfully I looked forward to Good Friday, when I should hear you again, and most fervently I thank you for expounding, as through the inspiration of the Spirit, this psalm so mightily and beautifully. Earnestly I read and prayed the words of David in the evening. But how busy the devil is just when we feel the most sincere! He would not let me pray, 'Lead me and guide me,' but showed me how hard and unpleasant the ways of the Lord often would be. Your warning, 'The Lord expects you not only to be a joyful Christian, but a *hell-shaking* Christian,' came not out of my mind, and I trembled at the responsibility of my new office. Oh, how can I be faithful to the end, which perhaps may be very far? But the Lord heard my cries, and comforted me; for it is written, 'As thy day so shall thy strength be '; and Jesus said, 'I will be with you always.' Oh that I could remember all that you say, dear Mr. North! because I need it all for the dear people of my country: nay, that you rather would go yourself, and tell them the gospel, as they have never heard it before. Surely the Lord has not sent me here without purpose: oh that I might be enabled to do His work, always trusting in Him as my strength! I am only an infant in Christ, and feel weak as such, but will you pray for me that I grow in grace and in the power of His might?

"From one of your devoted sisters in Christ Jesus."

Strange to say, the sermon which awoke such a strain of thanksgiving in the bosom of this poor stranger lady, and brought her sweet note of gratitude, awoke bitter opposition in another breast, and brought an angry and rude letter, also anonymous, from one holding that redemption was universal, and casting back into the preacher's face the gospel, as proclaimed by him that day, as being no " good news " for any sinner. Mr. North could afford patiently to bear such taunts when the Lord so graciously accompanied his words with signs following. "Perhaps," this writer says, "(indeed, I should say *certainly*) if you had been ' sent,' you would have had a pleasanter message than the one you gave us out of your own head on Friday night." But it had proved very pleasant to at least one wounded heart.

The next letter is from a young lady in Edinburgh, who, though not awakened, or brought to seek and find the Saviour by Mr. North (as was her only sister), was led by him to entire separation from the world, and consecration to Christ, and into clear views of the Gospel, which filled her with light and peace. The writer of this letter was well known to the author, and after many years of a consistent and useful life she fell asleep in Jesus in February, 1872.

A YOUNG LADY'S LETTER.

" EDINBURGH, *September 28th*, 1859.

" DEAR MR. NORTH,—As you know so little of my past history, perhaps you will allow me to say a few words about it, to show how wonderful God's dealings towards me have been; for I may truly say, I was brought by ' a way I knew not.' I believe the Holy Spirit has striven with me since my childhood, though I often, often resisted him. Until I became Christ's, my life was one long course of disappointments (how different *now* !). Gradually I was convinced of the sin of novel-reading and waltzing, and felt compelled, by a power I could not resist, to give up these snares of Satan. Still I was without Jesus. It proves how dark and blind the natural heart is. The preaching of Mr. Caird [Principal Caird] used to affect me powerfully. It was in January, 1853, after a very awakening sermon by him in Greenside

D

Church, that on Monday I was led to ask myself what I was to do. A voice within urged me to read James's *Anxious Inquirer*; Satan tried hard to prevent my doing so, but the Holy Spirit prevailed. I found in this little book a simple explanation of the way of salvation. I saw that faith was necessary to justify the sinner; and knowing that I had no faith, I prayed to God to give me faith in Jesus, and received an answer within that week. I can remember the moment when light came into my soul, and I knew I was accepted in the Beloved. My heart now turned from the world, and longed for Christian friends; but I knew none to whom I could open my mind. I was very ignorant then. I knew little or nothing of the work of the Holy Spirit in the heart, or the necessity to watch and pray against the temptations of Satan, whose personality I did not realize. I gradually lost the tenderness of conscience I had at first, and became worldly-minded again.

" This state of things went on till God in His long-suffering love sent me to hear you preach. It was more from curiosity than any other feeling that I went. I was told by one lady that she would on no account go to hear you again, as she shook all over, and would have given anything to get out of church, only she found that impossible, owing to the crowd. I asked my sister to accompany me, but she declined, so I went to hear you alone one forenoon. You preached from Titus ii. 11-14. You said a good deal about lukewarm Christians, and their ungrateful return for all the love of Jesus, and all He suffered on earth for them. I felt that sermon come home to my soul with a power I had never experienced before. I felt I was a lukewarm Christian, and resolved and wished that I could give myself entirely to Jesus; but still there was a mist within. I got my sister and father after that to go to hear you at the Greyfriars. Your preaching was to me different from anything I had ever heard before. You made religion a thing of happiness and beauty, and I felt irresistibly drawn again and again to hear you. Your last sermon in Edinburgh at that time, in Free St. Luke's, was blessed as the means of my dear sister's awakening. How we ever went to see you is a wonder to us now, but our heavenly Father did it all. I know I have been a new creature since that interview. Light dawned into my soul when you were talking of the promises being ours independently of feelings, and I saw a beauty in Jesus I had never seen before. My heart was so full of gratitude for Jane's conversion, that I gave myself all away to Jesus for the rest of my life; and though I know now, better than ever I did before, how wicked and deceitful my heart is, yet it is my earnest desire to live to His glory, and to do His will in all things. Our ambition now is to gain *jewelled* crowns. Do pray for us, that we may win many souls to Jesus, and never be ashamed to confess Him before men.

"Praying that God may bless you and your labours most abundantly, believe me,

"Yours most gratefully in Jesus, C. O."

Six months later, another long and interesting letter from the same correspondent came to Mr. North, giving an account of the progress of the work of grace in herself and her sister, and goes on to say:—

"My sister and I and two other friends hold a little prayer-meeting once a week, to plead for our unconverted friends. We paid two visits to Newhaven, with dear Miss W——. It was delightful to see the eagerness and pleasure with which the converts talked of being brought out of darkness into light. One young fish-woman told us that when anxious and told to 'believe,' she said to those about her, 'I believe everything,' but she could get no peace till, as she said, 'I saw I must *trust* in what I believe.' I mention this, as at that time we thought it a very simple definition of faith. I have not forgotten what you said about striving against that fear which is so apt to come over one when trying to pray before others; and though it was sometimes very hard, yet the Lord has enabled me to overcome it in great measure. I believe there is as much pride as timidity in this. I know with myself it is so, the fear of not being able to make a good prayer; so when I found this out, I saw it was sinful to yield to this wicked pride.

"Ever yours most gratefully, C. O."

Two letters from Mr. North to this lady, in reply, will be found at the commencement of the next chapter.

In the latter part of the year 1862, Mr. North paid a visit

to Haddo House, the seat of the Earl of Aberdeen, and a sermon which he then preached, along with private personal conversation, was made a means of blessing to two of the sons of that highly esteemed nobleman, both of whom were carried by sudden death into the presence of the Saviour whom they had learned so ardently to love and manfully to serve.

The bereaved mother thus wrote to Mr. North :—

"HADDO HOUSE, *January 3rd*, 1872.

"DEAR MR. NORTH, . . . This season of the year brings back very vividly to my mind the remembrance of that never-to-be-forgotten time when you were here. Do you recollect reading the fifty-fifth chapter of Isaiah, and the short prayer afterwards? My darling George asked that they might not be as the thorns, but like young fir-trees, bearing fruit to God. Often afterwards, when I saw those two boys growing such fine-looking men, and being what they were, I remembered that day, and I thought of that verse in the Psalms, 'The righteous shall flourish like a palm tree, and grow like the cedar in Lebanon.' Now the following verse is appropriate, 'Those that be planted in the house of the Lord shall flourish in the courts of our God.' He has taken them out of this world, but they are transplanted, I firmly trust, into the courts of our God. I hope you are well in health, and much encouraged in your work. . . .

"Believe me, yours very truly and gratefully,

"M. ABERDEEN."

A sketch of the short life of the younger of these two brothers, the Hon. James Gordon, in memory of whom the Dowager-Countess of Aberdeen founded the Gordon Memorial Mission, in connection with the Free Church Missions in South Africa, was written by Dr. Alexander Duff. The following extracts from letters which he wrote, in the year after his conversion although not addressed to Mr. North, but to a young friend, contain clear evidence of the abundant fruit of his message as received into this prepared soil, and show us how very rapidly the work of grace had matured in the heart of one who was then only nineteen years of age.

A CAMBRIDGE STUDENT'S LETTER.

" DEAR ——,—As for yourself, do not be afraid. You say you are not sure that you are safe. If you are *saved*, then you are *safe*. 'Fear not, for I have redeemed thee. Fear not, for I am with thee. Fear not, for I will help thee.' But you must give your whole heart to Jesus; keep nothing back. Remember, He gave up all for us, and we must give up all for Him, if we would be His; and how little that is in comparison with what He gave up for us! For His were no common sufferings. The very fact of being clogged and held down by a body like ours must have been torment to the King of Glory, who had been Lord of all from eternity. He, too, had bitter struggles with the devil, and therefore He is able to succour us when we are tempted, and to sympathise with us. I am sure you must have a hard fight: but if you confess Christ openly, and come boldly out to take up your position under His banner in answer to His call, ' Who is on the Lord's side?' then He will give you strength. I am sure, when we look back on the time of our warfare on earth, we shall wonder why we were so faint-hearted and so cold, when we had such a glorious reward before us. We shall wonder how it was that we were not willing rather to go through fire and sword, through flood and flame, to prove our love to Him who loved us with such exceeding love.

" The old year will soon be gone. It is a solemn thing to look back on a whole year, and to think how much of it we have wasted, and worse than wasted. Truly the Lord is long-suffering and gracious, or He would long ago have cut us off for ever. There are many thoughts which come into my mind at such a time. Last New Year's Eve I went to bed with scarce a thought about my soul,

> ' I knew not my danger, I felt not my load,
>   Jehovah-Tsidkenu was nothing to me.'

But the very next day, by the grace of God, I was brought to know the love of Christ which passeth knowledge. Yes, New Year's Day, the birthday of the year, is the birthday of my soul, and ten million years from this time I shall be singing the praises of Him who on that day called me into His marvellous light. ' Hallelujah, hallelujah! salvation to our God!' And there, too, will be the harpers harping with their harps, and the angels, ten thousand times ten thousand and thousands of thousands, their voices as the sound of many waters, all singing the praises of the King. And the ransomed of the Lord shall be there, arrayed in white robes, and palms in their hands, and crowns on their heads singing, 'Worthy is the Lamb that was slain'; and you and I shall be among that number; for Jesus has said that if we come to Him, He will receive us; and when He has received us, no man shall pluck us out of His hand: we are safe for time and for eternity; we are His, and He is ours. Let us then be mindful of the great reward. Let us run with patience the race that is set before us looking right to Jesus, and through Him to glory, honour, and immortality.

"Try to confess Christ openly before men, and to speak often of His name, and the Lord will hearken and hear, and will write it in a book of remembrance, and you shall be His in that day when He makes up His jewels (Mal. iii. 17).

"Yours affectionately, J. H. GORDON."

The next letter is from a lady residing in the North of England, who has ever since been actively engaged in the work of the Lord, in which she has been largely owned, having been the means through her classes, and otherwise, of bringing not a few to the knowledge and love of the Saviour.

AN ENGLISH LADY'S LETTER.

"*March 3rd*, 1862.

"MY DEAR SIR,—I desire to express my warm gratitude, first to God, and then to you, who were the means to me of enlightening and quickening in the way of grace. I attended every one of your public weekday addresses during my visit to Edinburgh, and was led by them to regard religion as a more real, personal thing than before. I have known these things as long as I can remember, with the head, perfectly, but my heart had become so accustomed to them, that I took them all as a matter of course, and thought for years that I was a Christian. On hearing you, however, I doubted it, and was very unhappy for some weeks, going about to establish my own righteousness, trying to make myself better before I came to Christ and miserable because I could not '*feel*' good, nor sorry, nor anything that I ought to feel; and this remained up to the middle of your last address, Thursday, Feb. 27th, on Romans x. 1-4. Then I saw by God's Spirit, that I must not consult my ' feelings ' any longer, but give up all my own righteousness, the good as well as the bad: and I was the more ready to do this, having proved that my righteousness was as filthy rags; and that I must take Christ's righteousness as my own, a free gift imputed to me. And I have been joyful in Him ever since. Now I know what faith means, and why it is ' precious faith.' I could not before understand those words, ' Believe on the Lord Jesus Christ,' for I did not know what to believe about Him. But now all things are new: the Bible has depths I never saw before; Jesus Christ is to me ' wisdom, and righteousness, and sanctification, and redemption.' I cannot praise Him enough for revealing Himself to me; and I am most grateful to you, dear sir, as having been the means of showing me this new life. I thank you especially for having shown it so clearly in the Bible; for now, if any doubts arise, I can turn at once to those passages, Romans iii. 20-24 and x. 1-4, which brought me, through the grace of God, life and salvation. . . .

" I remain, with deep gratitude, yours sincerely,
" M. J. F."

In the next chapter the reader will find Mr. North's replies to some of these letters, and to others of a similar character, from persons asking to be shown the way of life, or to be guided in that way.

CHAPTER VII

Brownlow North's Letters

MR. NORTH seldom if ever wrote even a short note without mentioning the name of the Master whom he served and loved, and referring to the progress of His work or the teaching of His word. The abundance of the heart sought utterance in his most familiar intercourse with his friends, whether by speech or pen. We have found it, however, difficult to procure letters written wholly upon religious topics, as these were generally directed to strangers, and sometimes in distinct letters the same line of thought is followed. We hope that those contained in this chapter may prove as useful to others as to those to whom they were originally addressed. The first letters are addressed to Miss O——, Edinburgh, extracts from whose letters to Mr. North were given in chapter vi.

LETTER TO A YOUNG DISCIPLE.

"NEWCASTLE-ON-TYNE, *Thursday, May* 13*th,* 1858.

"Your last letter has been forwarded to me to this place, and I received it and your former one with much pleasure. May you seek and obtain strength from the Lord Jesus Christ to perform the covenant you have entered into; for remember His own words, 'Without me ye can do nothing;' and let your present feelings and confidences be what they may, be sure of this, that unless you abide in Him, and His words abide in you, you will perish at the last, like the stony-ground hearers, who, when tribulation ariseth for the word's sake, are offended and fall away. I write not these things to trouble you, but as my beloved child I warn you; for you have a terrible conflict before you, and have need of the whole armour of God on the right hand and the left. Your enemies are *exactly* described, and not one jot or tittle exaggerated, in Eph. vi. 12; therefore, as a good soldier of Jesus Christ, buckle on what God has provided for you; and *never* counting yourself to have attained, but ever coveting earnestly more and more of Christ's true riches, that you may lavish them as fast as you receive them on those who have need, go boldly forward, strong in the Lord and in the power of His might, looking unto Jesus, who, for the joy set before Him, endured the cross, despising the shame. Remember, *looking unto Jesus* is the great safety. Perpetually endeavour to realize His real personal presence and existence, and then what this real Person has done and suffered for you, and so you will catch something of His Spirit, and will be willing to do or suffer for Him. Do not take your Christianity from the example of those around you, however excellent they may be, but study the life of Jesus, how He acted and how He spoke, and strive to speak and act as He did. Above all, be constant in private prayer. Beware of the first beginnings of shortening private prayer. Be you hot, cold, or lukewarm, still pray; and going as you are to God, ask Him for *Christ's sake* to make you what you should be. May the Lord make you a burning and shining light, remembering that humility is the first of the Christian graces, and may He give you to win many souls by your chaste conversation and meek and quiet spirit. (*See* 1 Peter iii. 3, 4.) I have written more than I intended when I commenced. May God bless it to you. And ever remember there is *no truth in us in our hearts*; that the *only truth* is in the *Word of God*. He that trusteth in his heart is a fool, but he that believeth in the Lord Jesus Christ *shall be saved*, saved not only from the punishment of sin, but from the power of it. So when your heart says one thing, and the Lord another, believe Him whom you have now, in the presence of God, of men, of angels, of devils, taken for better, for worse, to love, honour, and obey, as your Lord and your God."

A letter written on the same day in very similar terms to another young convert was found long afterwards, after her death, by her husband, bearing marks of constant perusal.

To THE SAME.

"DUNDEE, *Nov. 12th*, 1859.

"MY DEAR MISS O——,—May the Lord bless you and keep you, and make you an honoured instrument in His hands to bring Him much glory; but remember that you must let *nothing* lead you to neglect your own soul. Private prayer and private reading are absolutely necessary for spiritual health and life, and it is in the closet that we must seek for the Holy Spirit to tell us that in the ear which we may after proclaim to the benefit of our fellow-sinners. Give my Christian love to your dear sister, and tell her that I can say with John, that I have no greater pleasure than to hear that my children walk in the truth. May the Lord minister bread to both your souls, multiply your seed sown, and increase the fruits of your righteousness. Now is the time to be always abounding in the work of the Lord—*in due time* we shall reap, *if we faint not*. I trust A. B. is well, soul and body. Give her my Christian regards, and tell her to be watchful against the *pride* and naughtiness of her heart. How much need the very best of us have of this caution, lest we should think ourselves somebody when we are *nothing*! I am delighted to hear what you tell me about Miss C——. I saw her for a minute the last time I was in Edinburgh, and was much pleased. May the Lord Jesus, that good Shepherd, watch over us all. Be sure and pray for me, and alway expect to do me good. I hope to be in Edinburgh for a few days before going to London, where I expect to preach about the 18th of December. Believe me, with much interest in you and your sister,

" Yours in the very best of bonds,
" BROWNLOW NORTH."

The next letter is from Mr. North, in reply to a gentleman who was troubled with rationalistic difficulties and was apparently rejecting the gospel on their account. In his letter he had stated two difficulties, the first relating to the Divinity of the Lord Jesus, and the second to the equitableness of God's having attached a penalty to man's fall, seeing that fall was fore-known by Him, and therefore fore-ordained. Mr.

North very wisely deals with his correspondent's conscience as well as intellect.

LETTER TO A RATIONALISTIC OBJECTOR.

"*March 24th*, 1859.

"SIR,—You may easily imagine I have little time for letter-writing. I return your letter, that you may, by having it by you, better understand my answer. Until you are willing to condescend and humble yourself to *every one* who is likely to be better instructed than yourself in divine things you cannot enter into the kingdom of heaven.[1] Secondly, *man* is *not* to *ask*, but *believe*. The natural man has *no reason* that can help him, no spiritual discernment. Read (first going on your knees, and asking in Christ's name for God's Spirit to lead you) the first three chapters of 1st Corinthians, beginning at the eighteenth verse of the first chapter; read two or three times carefully, and may you be taught to cease from your own wisdom, and to seek the 'Spirit which is of God, that you may know the things which are freely given to you of God' (ii. 1, 2). *It is written*, 'The just shall live by faith'; and, God helping me, I have made up my mind to stand or fall with Jesus Christ. If He is the *truth*, I am saved; if He is the truth, the man who leans to his own understanding is *damned*! Awful position! No safety except Christ. Christ tells me in the fifth of John, verses 19, 23, 'that whatsoever things the Father doeth, the same doeth the Son, that all men should honour the Son, even as they honour the Father.' *I do so;* therefore, if I do wrong, I plead His own word; I can't do more. The Bible is full of that which can only be received by faith. I never try to reconcile. It is certain damnation if we refuse to receive what we cannot reconcile. See the irreconcilable yet heavenly thing, 'And no man hath ascended up to heaven but He that came down from heaven, even the Son of man which is in heaven' (John iii. 12, 13). Your second question I answer as Paul did the blasphemer's in Romans ix. 18, 19, *Because God chose it*, and it will not lessen the agony of the penalty, that through the countless ages of eternity you continue asking, why? why?

[1] His correspondent had said it was only from a few in this world that one could *condescend* to ask instruction.

Let it be sufficient for you—*It is so*. Shall not the Judge of all the earth do right? and though the answer to your question is not revealed, it is revealed that if you will *do* His *will*, you shall know of the doctrine, whether Christ spoke of Himself, or whether it be of God. Crucify therefore your own pride and carnal inclinations, as one who feels eternity to be at stake. I would wrestle with you in the name of Jesus for the Holy Spirit to lead you. Diligently shape your life as He directs you. May He bless you! I send you the 5th, 6th, 7th, 8th verses of the third of Proverbs: ' Trust in the Lord with all thine heart, and lean not unto thine own understanding. In all thy way acknowledge Him, and He shall direct thy paths. Be not wise in thine own eyes: fear the Lord, and depart from evil. It shall be health to thy navel, and marrow to thy bones.' Take the counsel there contained, and the promise in the last verse *shall be fulfilled* in *you*.

"Yours with much interest, BROWNLOW NORTH."

TO ONE WHO HAD BENEFITED BY HIS PREACHING.

"STRATHLEVEN, DUMBARTON, *Dec*. 30*th*, 1858.

"MY DEAR FRIEND,—I must send you a line to say how heartily I congratulate you on the news you are able to give me about A——. May the Lord bless him and keep him, and He most surely will if he will only believe God's word, and not his own lying heart and feelings. Nothing can prevent God's doing the mightiest of works in and for a poor sinner that goes to Him, but unbelief. You pray, and the answer too often is, ' I can do no mighty work because of your unbelief.' The command is, ' Whatever you ask, believe that you receive.' It would be good for us all if we would look at God more as ' the God of truth,' and whenever anything is suggested to our belief, to ask ourselves, ' Can this that I feel or think be true if God is true?' and if it *cannot*, then make God *truth*, and your own heart the liar. All sin has its origin in making the devil the God of truth, and God the Father of lies. This is the cause why the careless man continues in sin, and the anxious man in unbelief. They believe the statement of their own spirit, and disbelieve the words of God's spirit. Give my kindest Christian love to your dear husband, and ask him to read the enclosed, a copy of which I purpose to send to every minister in Scotland.   "B. N."

The enclosure here referred to was a copy of that very useful leaflet which Mr. North published under the title of " Six Short Rules for Young Christians," and which is worthy of being preserved in this volume.

Six Short Rules for Young Christians.

I.

Never neglect daily private prayer; and when you pray, remember that God is present, and that He hears your prayers. (Heb. xi. 6.)

II.

Never neglect daily private Bible-reading; and when you read, remember that God is speaking to you, and that you are to believe and act upon what He says. I believe all backsliding begins with the neglect of these two rules. (John v. 39.)

III.

Never let a day pass without trying to do something for Jesus. Every night reflect on what Jesus has done for you, and then ask yourself, What am I doing for Him? (Matt. v. 13—16.)

IV.

If ever you are in doubt as to a thing being right or wrong, go to your room, and kneel down and ask God's blessing upon it. (Col. iii. 17.) If you cannot do this, it is wrong. (Rom. xvi. 23.)

V.

Never take your Christianity from Christians, or argue that because such and such people do so and so, that therefore you may. (2 Cor. x. 12.) You are to ask yourself, How would Christ act in my place? and strive to follow Him. (John x. 27.)

VI.

Never believe what you feel, if it contradicts God's Word. Ask yourself, Can what I feel be true, if God's Word is true? and if *both* cannot be true, believe God, and make your own heart the liar. (Rom. iii. 4.; 1 John v. 10, 11.)

A few days after the date of the above letter the Duchess of Gordon wrote :—

"THE LODGE, HUNTLY, *Jan. 3rd*, 1859.

"MY DEAR MR. NORTH,—I thank you much for your letter, and do most cordially desire for you the richest blessings of Christ's own covenant, all sure in Him, sealed by His blood, administered by His Holy Spirit, acted on by His grace. Truly everlasting praise is due to the Father, Son, and Spirit for all He has done in you and by you. Oh, how much I have to thank and praise for all His many mercies and love during the past year! I like your tract very much, and thank you for allowing me the privilege of helping to send it (to every minister in Scotland). With much sincere and affectionate Christian regard,

"I am, yours very truly, E. GORDON."

The Duchess of Gordon had been the means of his previous awakening, and must have deeply sorrowed when the fair blossom went up as dust, and yielded no fruit; and now she rejoiced that the tree, which had borne nothing but leaves, was bringing forth a plentiful harvest of fruit to the glory of God the great husbandman, who had spared it in mercy, and digged about it, and watered it by His grace.

Only a few weeks after this the Duchess's heart was filled to overflowing with gratitude for a remarkable work of the Lord in Huntly, in her own house and in her schools. She wrote to my father, "A baby of four was sobbing, so that Mr. Radcliffe [who was then greatly blessed in Aberdeenshire] took her in his arms to find out if she were hurt. 'Oh, no, only while you were praying I felt my heart so hard I could not love Jesus.' Jesus is all their cry. Mrs. A. says, 'Siccan a bargain as the Lord has made wi' me. He's ta'en my son, and He's gi'en me His ain Son. Blessed Jesus.'"

The next letters have a somewhat interesting history connected with them. The gentleman to whom they were addressed (Mr. W. T. McAuslane of Glasgow) was in 1863 on the staff of the *Glasgow Morning Journal* newspaper, and went in that capacity to report one of Mr. North's services which was held in the Queen's Rooms, Glasgow, in that year.

Not only, as one has said, was the sermon (from Psalm cxix. 26), transcribed by flying pencil on his note-book, but by the Divine Spirit upon the fleshy tablet of his heart, to be published not only in the morning's news, but in the more permanent record of his consecrated life. Some months afterwards he wrote to Mr. North, wishing still clearer light, especially on the subject of assurance that our prayers are answered, and that pardon has been bestowed. Mr. North wrote in reply :—

ON THE ASSURANCE OF FORGIVENESS.

"DEAR SIR,—I have received your most interesting letter, and regret that I have not found time to answer it sooner. I have now great pleasure in answering the questions you propose to me, as far as my own light and knowledge enable me. May God the Holy Spirit, for Jesus Christ's sake, teach us both.

"1. You are to believe God's word without any other warrant whatever, simply because it is God's word; but doing so will necessarily produce peace and joy. Feelings are to flow out of faith, not faith out of feelings. If you *really* desire the pardon of God, and His favour, I believe you have it, because *He says* He will give it you if you ask it for Christ's sake; you *must be* glad.

"2. Yes, if what God says and what you feel cannot both be true, let God be true, and your own heart the liar.

"3. The feelings which faith should produce are love, joy, peace, a hatred of sin, and a desire after holiness. No doubt they will vary, because our faith varies, and all in us is variable; but we should ever remember that He *never* varies, but is always the same to us (Mal. iii. 6). Satan's great object is to get us not to trust God, but God's command is, ' Trust in Him at all times ' (Ps. lxxii. 8).

"4. When you can see Christ, you may look at your sins, your frames, or anything else you please; but when in darkness or doubt, or fancying yourself without Christ, you must look at nothing but Him. You must leave every other object of contemplation, and gaze at what He is, what He says, and what He has done. For He says, ' I am the Beginning,' ' the Alpha,' ' the Foundation '; and we must begin with and also build all on Him.

"May God make clear to you what you desire to understand. Endeavour to obey the injunction contained in the
first eleven verses of 2 Peter i, and try and DO righteousness,
whether you *like it* or not. It is never said *like it*, but *do it.*
And recollect God's definition of love in 1 Cor. xiii. 6, John
xiv, 21, 'He that hath my commandments, and keepeth
them, he it is that loveth me.' With much interest,

"Yours sincerely, BROWNLOW NORTH."

This letter afforded much comfort; but this was interrupted
by a minister observing that 1 John i. 9, "If we confess our
sins, God is faithful and just to forgive us our sins," was a
promise for Christians, and that a sinner was not entitled to
appropriate it. Mr. McAuslane again wrote to Mr. North in
his difficulty, and his reply gave him comfort and peace.

"MY DEAR SIR,—In regard to your friend's statement, that
1 John i. 9 was written for Christians, I answer, that a
Christian is a man who believes what God says in the gospel
of His Son, and that a man becomes a Christian the moment
he believes. Scripture cannot contradict itself, and no confession of sin is considered as such by God, where there is not
an intention to resist it and forsake it; but the man who goes
to God by Jesus Christ, and asks for pardon for His sake,
and does not believe he gets it, makes God a liar, as much as
does the man who says he has no sin. See 1 John i. 10, in
connection with the previous verse. If we confess our sins,
and say we do not know whether He has forgiven us or not,
when He says His faithfulness and justice are pledged for our
pardon, we make Him a liar. . . . I believe faith to be a
thing of degrees, and that a person may be in a state of salvation, and yet be very hopeless and desponding. Such a state,
however, is quite foreign to the intention of the gospel. There
is a great difference between faith and fellowship, or communion. This is promised to a certain line of conduct pursued after faith. Believe me, with much interest,

"Yours in Jesus, BROWNLOW NORTH."

The next letter was written to a lady, one of whose letters
is given in chapter vi, who was brought to the Saviour through

his ministry. It is a reply to a letter telling of her work for her Lord.

TO A CHRISTIAN WORKER.

"PLYMOUTH, *Feb.* 16*th*, 1871.

"I do so thank God for all He has done for you, and in you and by you. I rejoice over my 'grandchildren' [so called because they were the spiritual children of one of whom he was the father in Christ], and firmly believe that through your conversion children's children yet unborn shall praise the Lord. To Him be the praise, for no one knows better than yourself that it is only when *He* gives it that there is any blessing. I am sorry in a natural sense that you are not in better health, but I am so persuaded that God is dealing with you as a child whom He loveth, and that all things are working together for your good, that I am unable to wish anything altered, or rather to ask Him to alter anything, only to keep you abiding in Him and He in you in a continually growing and closer union. How I do rejoice with you in what God has permitted you to see of the fruit of your work for Him! and by this time I trust you have seen some more."

At another time he wrote to the same correspondent:—

"I think it is decidedly unscriptural to fix any time with God for His doing anything. The times and seasons the Father hath put in His own hand. The man Christ Jesus has asked for the heathen, and He *will* get them, but He has waited eighteen hundred years already, and has told us that as man He knows nothing of the 'when.' Pray on, and believe; you *shall* reap."

TO A FRIEND, ACCOMPANYING THE GIFT OF A BIBLE.

"MY DEAR ——,—Accept from me this copy of God's Holy Word, as a small mark of very much regard and affection. I thank God for the good work which I trust He has begun in you; but I would take this opportunity of urging on you not to count yourself to have attained, but to study with all diligence to go on unto perfection, remembering that *perfection is the likeness of God*. This perfection is only to be obtained by a spiritual knowledge and a spiritual practice of the truths contained in this Book. Therefore, not only read, but *search* the Scriptures daily, and be sure that there is no source from which so much useful knowledge is to be obtained as from the Bible. But remember that its words are *spirit* (John vi. 63), and can only be profitably received by the teaching of the Spirit; therefore be much in prayer *for the teaching of the Spirit*. Thus reading, and thus praying, you have a scriptural warrant to expect that He who wrote the Bible will tell you words in secret, which shall not only be life to your own soul, but which, when you proclaim as you have opportunity to others, shall be to the glory of God and the good of men.

"That God for Jesus Christ may bless you and keep you, multiply your seed sown, and increase the fruits of your righteousness, is the earnest and heartfelt prayer of,

"Yours very affectionately, Brownlow North."

"James iv. 7, 8; 1 Cor. iii. 19; Col. iii. 11; 1 Cor. i. 30."

The next letter is one written at a considerably later date than those already quoted, having been sent very shortly after her being brought to Christ, to a young lady who was one of the fruits of his ministry in London, at the Rev. Adolph Saphir's church, in 1873.

Letter to a Young Disciple.

"34, Sussex Place, Kensington, W., *May 26th*, 1873.

"My dear Miss E——,—I sit down with the full intention of writing to you, as you ask me to do, a very long letter; that is, of getting to the end of this big sheet of paper, which, if I do, will be as long a letter as I have written for years. I naturally feel a great interest in you as my child in the Lord, and have great pleasure in writing to you. May the Lord enable me to say a word or two worth reading. What a marvellous blessing your visit to London has been to you! what a treasure God has given you to carry home with you! not merely 'the unsearchable riches of Christ,' so that you not only have abundance of all really good things for yourself, but *to spare*, so that you can give to others, and make them as rich as yourself; but He has given you *Christ Himself*! *He* is yours, and you are his, and you may boldly say so. He is *in you*, your Lord, your Husband, your Brother, your Friend, your Counsellor, your Saviour, your God. Oh, be faithful! *He* is faithful who hath called you; and through Him, and by His strength, you can do all things; and He has said He will never leave you nor forsake you. Therefore fear not, dear Miss E., no matter what may be the cross He may see fit to call on you to bear. Learn Isaiah li. 12, 13, by heart, and pray God to bless the word to you, and then, looking unto Jesus, ' be ye stedfast, unmoveable, always abounding in the work of the Lord.'

" I cannot tell you how delighted I was to find you occupied as I did the last time I saw you. It strengthened my heart, and gave me courage to hope that through your instrumentality I shall be found the father of many grandchildren. May it please God to make Mrs. A. one of them. I hope you will not lose sight of her, and if you have any news to tell me of her, please let me know it. I have had much to encourage me ever since I saw you. God is so good to me. Yesterday I preached at the Agricultural Hall. After the service one tall old gentleman on the platform came up to me with tears in his eyes, and thanked me for what he had heard, and before I got off the platform another came in the same way. Two on that small platform! There were about 3,000 hearers. Oh, may the blessing over the whole have been at least in the like proportion! On Sunday next I preach, God willing, in a church near here, and on Monday go to stay with Lord Cavan for a few days at Weston-super-Mare, returning to preach for Mr. Saphir on the evening of the 8th. Remember me in prayer especially that night.

" Yours with true Christian interest and affection,

" BROWNLOW NORTH."

A year later he wrote to the same lady a letter from which we extract a few sentences.

" GLASGOW, *April 8th,* 1874.

" MY DEAR MISS E——,—I am filled with shame at myself when I look at the date of your kind and most interesting letter, which was sent to me here, and is now before me; but the truth is, that I am so overworked, that I look with dread at letter-writing. I thank God, who has enabled you in spite of crosses to persevere in His ways. Go on, dear child, in nothing terrified by your adversaries, and in due season you shall reap.

"What you tell about my tract, and your tract distribution, is most interesting, and I will order a quantity of different ones I have written to be sent to you, carriage free, on hearing that you are still at home, and would like to have them. You speak of 'complete sanctification.' I do *not* believe that any one will ever attain to it *here*; but for all that, we are to strive after it, because *He* tells us to. In so doing we may get near it, but the man who is nearest it will be the last to say he has it. I shall be so glad to accept your drawing, but keep it till about Christmas, and then send it to me at 34, Sussex Place, Kensington. Send me a line, and never think I am not interested in you because I do not write; for I am always, though very busy,

"Very heartily yours in Jesus,

"BROWNLOW NORTH."

CHAPTER VIII

Brownlow North's Theology and Preaching

"MR. NORTH," said the late erudite and distinguished divine, Dr. John Duncan of Edinburgh, one day, in the house of Dr. Moody-Stuart, "you are an untrained theologue." "Very untrained," was the reply. "You mistake me, sir," was Dr. Duncan's rejoinder; "I laid the emphasis not on 'untrained,' but on 'theologue.'" He sometimes spoke of Mr. North, whose addresses he often listened to with the humility of a little child, as a "born theologian." The celebrated Dr. Cook, of the Irish Presbyterian Church, gave a similar testimony to that of the Free Church Professor, saying to a number of his ministerial brethren who had been listening to Mr. North, that "he was one of the best theologians among them all, and that his preaching of Christ for Christ's own sake, accompanied by the Spirit's power, led those who hung upon his lips to open their whole hearts for a whole Christ." To give one more testimony of a different sort, we may mention that Mr. Jenkinson, in the Free Assembly Hall, Edinburgh, remarked one day, after having secured Mr. North's services, "Now my mind is at rest for a week. Mr. North is the only lay-preacher who has preached in this Hall, whom no one has ever come to me to object to, on the ground of some real or supposed misstatement of doctrine."

We have narrated his conversion, the marvellous success of his ministry, and the influence it has had on our country, and we naturally enquire next, What was the cause of this success? Some will say, it was because he was a layman. But though he started alone as a lay-preacher, he was followed by multitudes of others, none of whom achieved anything like his

success, except Mr. D. L. Moody. Others have said, it was
curiosity that drew such crowds to see one who had been
known as a man of the world, living a fast life, now standing
up as a preacher of the gospel. This might have drawn
crowds for the first year, or at most two; but it cannot account
for the fact, that to the end of his life, through twenty years
of labour, the audiences that flocked to listen to him were
limited only by the capacity of the church or hall in which he
was advertised to preach.

The great secret of his success, coupled with the fact that he
possessed natural eloquence, and subject to the sovereignty
of the Divine Spirit, who uses whom He will, undoubtedly
lay in his doctrine commending itself to the intellects and
hearts of men. For Brownlow North was a great doctrinal
preacher. He was eloquent, but his eloquence consisted in
the clear, powerful and earnest statement, exposition, and
application of great doctrines. He had not the thrilling pictorial power of Dr. Thomas Guthrie, the marvellous fecundity
of illustration and the musical voice of Charles Spurgeon, the
telling command of simile and analogy of William Arnot, or
the exhaustless fund of anecdote of D. L. Moody. With
Brownlow North doctrine was everything. His style was terse
and plain, but unadorned. He had no rounded periods, no
graceful similes, no oratorical peroration. Often voice and
words both failed him in the climax of his most earnest
appeals. His power lay in the solemn and forcible statement
of his doctrines, in his convincing proof, and in his thrilling
application of them. And what is remarkable is that he derived his theology mainly for himself from a study of the Holy
Scriptures.

If the mariner finds it needful, from time to time, to correct
the results of his dead-reckoning by direct observations of the
heavens, it is as needful for those who navigate the bark of the
Church, throughout the angry and treacherous seas of life, to
correct the dead-reckoning of their log-books by new observations of the sure words of prophecy, the heaven-hung lights
that shine in the firmament of our night. It will satisfy some,
and provoke others, to find that the result of this fresh set of

careful and prayerful observations made by a hard logical head and a clear eye, is almost an exact photograph of what is known as the theology of the Reformation.

In preaching, Mr. North very much confined himself to the leading landmarks of theology. Although he had a competent knowledge of Greek, and occasionally refers in his annotated Bible to the original reading, his mind was of a dogmatic rather than critical cast and he commonly studied the Bible in English. He seized and preached the leading aspects of each doctrine rather than those that are subordinate, and avoided the handling of secondary points as being more suitable to the pastor than the evangelist.

His preaching gave a fresh impetus and influence to old truth in our churches. One of our theological professors has remarked, that there was a wave of divinity students who came under the spiritual power of Mr. North's teaching, were impressed by it at the time, and bore the impress afterwards. Let us examine what this teaching was. It can be summarized under a few leading heads, which were his favourite and characteristic topics.

I

" GOD IS "

THE EXISTENCE, PERSONALITY, AND PRESENCE OF GOD

" THE subject of ' God ' is lacking in reality," was the remark of the editor of a leading French publication, when an article was offered him by Paul Leroux, on " God." Brownlow North invested the question of God's existence with the most intense actuality. This grand essential truth he made the foundation of all his discourses. In the prominence which he gave to it, his preaching differed as much from the ordinary run of preaching as the vividness with which he presented it differs from the mode of its presentation in most discourses and treatises on this subject.

In his hands the truth of God's existence became a tremendous and burning reality, borne in upon the convictions and consciousness of his hearers with terrific force. When once the hearer was convinced of the existence of God, he pressed upon him the fact that that existence involved most momentous consequences to himself; that it was a personal God of whose existence the soul was convinced, even the God and Father of our Lord Jesus Christ; the God who formed us for His glory; the God against whom we have sinned, who is to be our Judge at the last day, and is our Judge even to-day; the God with whom we, one and all of us, have to do.

The God whose existence he thus felt himself called upon to preach was not presented as the God of the man of science, the Great First Cause, or the God of the student of philosophy, the great subject of speculation and of contemplation; but as the God of the Bible, the God of the patriarchs, prophets, and apostles, the God of the spirits of all flesh, and the God whose claim to be his God the rebellious sinner is daily rejecting; a God who is a Person, the Hearer of prayer, possessed of free-will, love, and other personal attributes.

In his last published work he writes: " I believe there are numbers of what are called learned and deep-thinking people, who profess to believe in God, and who would be troubled in their minds if they thought they were not honouring God, whose God in reality is no better than an idol of their own creation. They believe the revelations of their own intellect, rather than the revelations of Scripture; and while they acknowledge a God of the universe, a God of nature, a God of creation, they know nothing of the only living and true God, the God of the Bible."[1] His teaching was that the God of nature is the God of Revelation also. *God is,* were two words which he used to announce with most solemn emphasis in his oral addresses, and which he not infrequently prints in capital letters in his published works. They formed the basis of all his preaching, the foundation of all his theology, and that, not in the way of a postulate taken for granted by the preacher, but as the first great doctrine which the human heart naturally was prone to call in question, which required to be intelligently

[1] " Christ the Saviour and Christ the Judge."

believed by every true and acceptable worshipper, and not only believed, but realized.

The evidence on which he mainly rested this truth was the internal evidence, that the mind of man craves for a god, and is so constituted that it cannot do without a god of some kind; that we have an inborn, intuitive consciousness of the existence of an Almighty, All-wise, Omnipresent, and altogether Holy God; that our conscience tells us of a God who is a righteous Lawgiver and Judge; that the God revealed in the Bible exactly meets these cravings and intuitions, and this testimony of our nature; that His words appeal to our hearts as the voice of the great God; that the blindness which leads many men to doubt or deny His existence is engendered by sin, and is both a willing and a sinful ignorance,—a darkness loved by the blind man. In the fourteenth Psalm, which Mr. North was continually quoting, the fool's denial of the existence of God is shown to be the result more of his moral than his mental obliquity. God's existence is an indisputable corollary from man's sense of guilt.

The fact that Brownlow North gave such prominence in his preaching to this doctrine, may be naturally traced to his own spiritual experience at the time of his conversion, which we have already narrated. The intensity and protracted character of the temptation to embrace atheism as a refuge from conviction and alarm were singular, but the temptation itself is by no means uncommon, and, alas, in many cases not unsuccessful; and other eminent men of God there have been, who have gone through as deep and painful a spiritual conflict on this very doctrine. Especially has this been the case with those who were being fitted by the Divine Spirit for awakening others, or for dealing with other awakened consciences.

Mr. North regarded atheism as the capital sin, and brought the charge of it home with convincing power to many hearts which had been in the habit of considering themselves very far removed from it. He showed that the man who took for granted God's existence, and imagined he assented to it, was really denying it, unless his intellectual assent to the doctrine carried with it the practical consequences of submission and obedience to that God in whom he professed to believe. Few who heard his striking appeals can forget the impressiveness with which he depicted the " folly " of the atheist, whether he belonged to the speculative or the practical class, showing that he was a " fool " in God's sight to-day, and would one day be exposed as a " fool " in the sight of the whole universe, whatever his reputed wisdom or acquired human knowledge might be.

The fact that a preacher who had the ear of Scotland as no other had it at the time, having access to churches of almost all denominations, having the power of attracting crowded audiences wherever he went, moving from town to town and district to district, and awakening the interest and attention of almost every class of society in these districts, should have been led to press so powerfully upon the multitudes whom his voice reached, the existence of a Personal God, was surely a providential preparation of large numbers of the Scottish people for withstanding those assaults upon this fundamental doctrine, both covert and avowed, which were made by Sceptics, Materialists, and Positivists during the later years of this evangelist's work, and are likely to be made for years to come, as persistently, by many of our leading literary and scientific men. This doctrine stands on the forefront of the Decalogue, and the histories of the ethical systems of the world from which it is absent prove, by their very failure, that it is the necessary basis both of religion and morality.

The Materialism or Nature-worship of our leaders of science of to-day appears to be a return to the earliest and one of the subtlest forms of heathenism, viz., the Baal-worship which arose soon after the Deluge, and spread from Assyria well-nigh throughout the whole human race, consisting in a worship of law, light, and life. The earliest and the latest religion of man's unaided intellect are essentially the same, almost the only difference being that it is taught to-day in university class-rooms and public lecture halls, in place of temples, high places, and stone circles; and should it, by allying itself with Rome, become once again a religion as well as a philosophy, the worship of the creature will, through Christendom, be once more substituted for that of the Creator, who is over all, God blessed for ever.[1]

Of this scientific Pantheism Mr. North says, "If a man elects to place his hope of salvation on the doctrines of research or science, on the teaching of his own or any other human wisdom, and refuses to receive the Bible in the spirit of a little child, he must stand or fall by his own election, but let such a man remember, *if the Bible is true he is lost.* A God who did not so love the world as to give His only begotten Son to be a propitiation for man's sins, is a God that has no more existence than 'Ashtoreth the abomination of the Sidonians,' or 'Melcom the abomination of the children of Ammon.'"

This is not written to glorify man, but to magnify the Spirit, who called him to this work, and taught and fitted him for it. In the clear exposition and urgent pressing of the way of salvation for the sinner in Jesus Christ, he did not differ from the other lay evangelists who succeeded him, although he was their leader and to a certain extent moulded their preaching on those points, but in preaching the doctrine of the Divine existence he stood alone.

Again Mr. North writes: "I believe there is nothing more necessary to salvation in the whole Scripture than the reception of this name of God, I AM. So important do I feel it to be, that I think I have alluded to it in every tract that I have written, and very, very often in my sermons and addresses. Whenever God has a purpose of mercy either to an individual or to a nation, His first teaching is, I AM. Surely then I cannot do wrong in making it my first teaching.

When God was about to deliver the children of Israel out of their bondage, the lesson that He tells the minister by whose hand He will deliver them is, "Say unto the children of Israel, I AM. Do not tell them at present to lay hold of any of my attributes; do not call their attention to my power or my

---

[1] We must remember that at an early period it inoculated the Christian Church with priestly celibacy and tonsure, altar-lights, and probably also virgin-worship, and the sunward position in devotion.

mercy, to my justice or my holiness; but set them as the first thing they have to do to grapple with this one great truth, I AM. The natural eye cannot see me; the natural ear cannot hear me; the natural heart cannot receive me; but for all that, say unto the children of Israel, I AM, and tell them to believe it."

In a sermon preached at Elgin in November, 1862, from the text, " The things which are seen are temporal, but the things which are not seen are eternal " (2 Cor. iv. 18), he said, " The Bible tells us that the just shall live by faith, that faith is a condition of salvation. Believe in God. In the eleventh of Hebrews, at the sixth verse, we have the definition given us of the smallest degree of faith with which it is possible to please God. ' He that cometh to God must believe that *He is*.' I believe that that verse is the *first verse* in the whole Bible that a man or woman requires to get into the heart. Till you have got the substance of that verse into your hearts you are without saving religion in the sight of God. Now if I could give to every one in this large congregation a practical belief that GOD IS, that the God and Father of our Lord Jesus Christ is really a God that sees us, and hears us, and will save us if we come to Him, I would be glad to shut this Bible and go home and bless God for it to all eternity; for I believe that this is the grain of mustard seed which will grow into the great tree in the end."

" It is not more true that every man by nature is born a fool, than that by nature he is born an infidel, an unbeliever in the very existence of the God of the Bible."

The real and immediate Presence of God with the true worshipper, was a truth which Mr. North was in the habit uniformly, in almost all his discourses and published works, of building upon; the solid foundation which he had laid in the doctrine we have examined. It is in itself a direct corollary of the truth of the Divine Existence—God is, therefore God is here beside me, and hears me,—omnipresence being one of the necessary attributes of the Divine Being. His favourite text, Heb. xi. 6, brackets the two truths as necessary to be believed in by every accepted worshipper. No ministering priest of old could have appeared to realize more vividly the immediate presence of the great unseen God, hid from him only by the thin veil of sense that obstructed his bodily vision of the most Holy, but could not obstruct the vision of faith penetrating within the veil. His sense of the Divine Presence was so manifest, not only in his discourse, but in the solemn awe of his eye, his gestures, and his whole bearing, that even one who had entered the house of God in a light spirit was often constrained to exclaim, " Surely the Lord is in this place, and I knew it not!"; he felt himself in the presence-chamber of the King of kings. Those who left the place of worship unimpressed with the sense of God's immediate presence, could not possibly leave it without the persuasion that the preacher at least was possessed by this belief, or delusion if such it were, and were constrained to acknowledge that others were dealing, or imagined they were dealing, not only with abstract doctrine, but with a real and most august Person unperceived by the outward eye, or even by the eye of reason.

This belief in the Divine Omnipresence may be compelled by logical argument, but it is by faith alone, and under the teaching of the Word and Spirit, that it becomes a saving truth. This was what Mr. North taught.

Speaking of the period of his conversion, he says he was led to the conviction that God had seen him during his long course of sin, and therefore saw him now when he was on his knees before Him:—" I took the answer to my prayer from what He said who was in the room with me. My burden fell off, and I rejoiced in a pardon according to the word of the Lord."

" No man can really be said to believe that ' God is,' who does not believe that He is present when he prays to Him, and hears and sees him." " God always is present with us. To realize this, to believe it, and to act as if it were a truth, is what we should seek for before all things. That it is so, is our only safety. ' In Thy presence is fulness of joy.' This is simple truth. Let us ask ourselves if we would and do feel it joy to be in the Lord's presence. To many the very idea of being in God's presence is horror of horrors. This is because they are unconverted. Never rest till you are enabled to desire God's presence, and to rejoice in it."

II

" IT IS WRITTEN "

THE INSPIRATION AND DIVINE AUTHORITY OF HOLY SCRIPTURE

BROWNLOW NORTH had an intense veneration and love for the Bible, as the word of the living God. It was inwoven with his whole spiritual experience. From that day in Elgin, when striking his hand upon his open Bible, as his eye rested on the text Rom. iii. 22, he exclaimed, starting to his feet, " If that scripture is true I am a saved man," till the day twenty years afterwards, when on his dying bed in the house of a stranger he turned to a young officer, and said, with his fast-ebbing breath, " You are young, in good health, and with the prospect of rising in the army : I am dying; but if the Bible is true, and I know it is, I would not change places with you for the whole world," that Bible was the daily food of his soul, his lamp in the night, his teacher, his counsellor, his trust, and his treasure. Never for an hour did he swerve from his childlike faith in these Scriptures of truth, or from his manly allegiance to all the doctrines, precepts, and promises of the Divine Word. And he spent his whole time, talents, and toil in preaching to the people, wherever they would come to listen, all the words of this life.

No listless listener could see him open the sacred volume, and hear him read even the introductory psalm of the service, without being sensible that the preacher was thoroughly convinced that this volume was indeed the very word proceeding out of the mouth of God, and was of Divine origin from its beginning to its close. And the impression made upon the hearer by his opening and reading of the Bible was not effaced, but was steadily increased, by his handling and expounding of it throughout his whole discourse. So far was there from ever being any lightness in his handling of the Scripture, that many times in every service the sense that he was reading and preaching the living word of the living God seemed to be almost overpowering. No high priest in the Holy Place could have handled the Urim and Thummim with greater awe and reverence than this preacher treated the Divine oracles. He believed that the Word of God was the sword of the Spirit; and the very remarkable effects upon the consciences, understandings, and lives of men, wrought through him by this instrument, fully bore out his belief. With many others, he could say, " experto crede;" and the argument from experience and experiment, which is now appealed to as the surest test in many of the sciences, must be allowed its rightful place in the science of theology.

The title, " the Word of God," was to him no empty phrase, no euphemism for the " word of good men," as it is with many. It meant simply what it expresses, that it is the utterance of the mind and will of God. He never looked upon the Bible as containing the words of God hid among the words of His servants, nor preached that Word as one who was searching for grains of Divine truth buried in the sands of human opinion, for nuggets of gold hid in mounds of ore. He preached the Word as precious gold already examined, tested, and guaranteed by its Author. His creed was the creed of Protestantism.

He riveted every argument with, " *It is written;*" he barbed every arrow of appeal with, " *What saith the Scripture?* " and ever seemed to tremble lest he should be found diminishing aught from that Word, or adding aught to it.

Regarding Scripture from the Reformers' point of view, as a full Divine revelation of the rule of faith and duty, and an inspired record of the history of God's dealings with our race, and declining to discuss debatable details, he placed it in a position of absolute and infallible supremacy; and though his mind was not of a poetical cast, he loved, according to the use and wont of the Scottish pulpit, to spiritualize the histories of the Old Testament. Attacks upon the inspiration of the Scripture had begun even at the commencement of his ministry, but it was only towards its close that the Church became so painfully familiar with them. Of those views which subvert the full divinity of the Word he had the greatest horror, and once in a public address in Edinburgh he stated that before coming to town he had conducted a large Bible-class for a popular and esteemed minister, and had been both grieved and alarmed by the views on inspiration which were expressed by the young men attending it.

A military officer writes thus, and his experience was that of multitudes : " Brownlow North was of great service to me in leading me to pay particular attention to each verse of Scripture, and to take more notice of the meaning of each word in it. He was most helpful to me *on* the Word, though not the first to point me to it." He taught the doctrine of inspiration not scholastically or controversially, but dogmatically and experimentally, and as a question of life and death to the individual rather than to the Church. The former, however, includes the latter.

While not claiming for him any originality in his teaching on this point, we must recognize his claim (along with that of the other lay preachers who followed him) to the gratitude of the Church of Christ in this land, for his clear, bold, and unwearied proclamation and enforcing of the grand foundation truth of living Protestantism, viz., the full divinity of the Holy Scriptures, and consequently their supreme authority as the only ground of faith, rule of life, and judge of religious controversies, in opposition to all human tribunals whether of traditions and Church authority, as set up by Romanism, or of human reason as set up by Rationalism. In the face of current tendencies in religious as well as in worldly circles such teaching was of the utmost importance.

We have only space further to note on this great doctrine that Mr. North always regarded the written Word not only in an historical light, but as containing the direct answer of a present God to our petitions. The order of his teaching was, God is,—God is a person,—God is present,—God has spoken, —or rather God speaks, in the revelation He has given us. His position was, that a silent God is a God unrevealed, that a God unrevealed is a God unknown, and he shrank from such a thought with all the intensity of his nature, as did the Psalmist of old when he cried, " Be not silent unto me, O God; lest, if Thou be silent unto me, I become like them that go down into the pit " (Psalm xxviii. 1). He emphatically taught that the answer to prayer is to be sought, not in any mystical internal idea or feeling, any more than in any external sign, but in the written Word, as well as in the works of providence and grace. This Word is instinct with life, and comes to us as if newly uttered by the mouth of God.

If any other ever earned the title of " the man of the book," assuredly this man did. He spent hours every day in hard and prayerful study of its pages. To anxious inquirers his undeviating counsel was, " Go home and read your Bible." His farewell words before his last illness to an intimate friend were, " Dear—, there is nothing for any of us but the Bible." The words written of another were eminently true of him, " *To him the Bible was alone and altogether the book.*" It was his constant companion and counsellor, his study all the day, and to a large extent his library. One of the favourite resting-places of his soul was the testimony, " Heaven and earth shall pass away, but my words shall not pass away."

III

" YOU ARE IMMORTAL "

THE IMMORTALITY OF THE SOUL, AND THE ETERNAL DURATION OF SPIRITUAL LIFE AND DEATH

THE first tract which (so far as we can recollect) Mr. North published, bore the title " *You are Immortal.*" It has often been reprinted since. It opens with these words, " Reader, you are an immortal being. You have been born, and you will have to leave this world, but you can never cease to exist. You *must* live for ever! It is of no avail to you that you are so debased by sin that you would wish to be like the brutes that perish. I know that all this may seem very dreamy and unreal to you, but it is nevertheless true." The immortality

E

of the human soul, and its endless existence in a state of holiness and blessedness, or of corruption and misery, were statements which were constantly upon his lips.

Many an audience has been startled and riveted by his saying sharply, " I can tell you to a minute how long your life is to be : it is to be as long as the life of God."

Brownlow North with marvellous vividness and dramatic power, as well as with the most intense solemnity and earnestness, used to open up before the crowded audiences, whom he was called on from the very beginning of his ministry to address, the vista of their eternal existence. One might have heard a pin fall on the floor, or the rustle of a ribbon on a thoughtless head, as these immense crowds, thronging aisles, passages, and pulpit-stairs, hung on the preacher's lips as if afraid to draw their breath, drinking in the message with eyes as well as ears, while he told them that they were endowed with immortality, and in his own favourite phrase, " could no more go out of existence than could God."

The annihilationist theory is much more prevalent, and even fashionable, now than when Mr. North began his preaching; but at so early a period as the spring of 1859 a gentleman who had adopted these views wrote to him from Paisley, objecting to his constant and dogmatic statements that the human soul is immortal. His letter which is a long one, filling two very closely written sheets, argues in terms that are gentlemanly and courteous, but very decided, against Mr. North's position that man, as his objector fairly states it, " possesses a part that cannot die, nor be put to death." Mr. North was quite aware that there was a then nascent error to which his teaching was diametrically opposed, and that his preaching was more offensive to the supporters of this tenet than that of most ministers, who, while firmly believing in the soul's immortality, did not give it the same prominence in their preaching. " The second death," Mr. North writes, " is something different from annihilation :" and in his annotated Bible he repeatedly states his belief that it consists in being forsaken by God—the death which, as he held, Adam died on the day that he fell—and the death which the eternal Son of God endured on Calvary, when

He cried " My God, my God, why hast Thou forsaken me?"
The theory that the death of the soul is annihilation thus struck
at Mr. North's view of the Atonement, viz., that Christ saves
sinners by suffering their death, for confessedly His human
nature was not annihilated.

The lines of argument which Mr. North took in defending
what he preached on this subject were two. The first was that
the Creator had communicated to man at his origin a nature
similar to His own, and which therefore was endowed with
immortality as one of its natural and inalienable properties.
So both heathen and Christian teachers have reasoned, " We
are the offspring of God " (Acts xvii. 28): and no advocates
of evolution, whatever be their theory as to man's body, have
a right to dictate to the believer as to the origin, and therefore
the destiny, of that mysterious spirit by which we are allied
much more closely to the God who tells us He breathed it
into our corporeal frame, than by that frame which links us
with the animal creation. His second argument was, that nothing will satisfy the desires and cravings of a man's spirit, but
having the eternal God as his portion : therefore we draw the
conclusion that a man who craves for an eternal satisfaction
must be himself eternal in his nature. Still his main proof was
the teaching of God's Word. He says, " It is from the Bible
we learn that we are immortal, and only from the Bible that
we learn how to escape an immortality of evil and inherit an
immortality of glory."

But Mr. North's teaching was opposed not only to the views
propagated by the annihilationist, but to those held and taught
by the believers in the theory of universal final restoration;
and by this latter class his teaching was bitterly attacked, even
in the columns of some of the most widely circulated religious
periodicals. In one of his letters to the late Lord Kintore, he
said, " The ———, a paper advocating the non-eternity of
punishment, has published a long notice abusing me."

The line of proof he adopted on this subject was the direct
and infallible testimony of Scripture, which he used, not only
to prove the naked immortality of the soul of man, but in
support of his teaching, in accord with that of the Church in

all ages, that while some have the blessed reward of everlasting life, others receive the woeful doom of everlasting death. This truth is a very awful and mysterious one, never to be handled by any without the greatest awe and tenderness; and in dealing with it, those who are teachers and stewards of the mysteries should also surely see that they keep most scrupulously, in all their statements, within the limits and the expressions of the written Word. We have been told by a Christian lady, an intimate friend of the late Principal Candlish, that on one occasion she observed his eyes filled with tears when conversing with her on this very awful subject, and the current views on it.

In the margin of his New Testament, opposite Matt. xxv. 46, the words of which are " These shall go away into everlasting punishment, but the righteous into life eternal," Mr. North notes, " The duration of the punishment of the wicked and the life of the righteous are equal." This fact that the same word is employed in these two clauses, should be enough to satisfy most persons of fair and unprejudiced judgment. The word is 'αιώνιος, and any objection taken to its meaning " everlasting " on the ground of its etymology cannot invalidate Mr. North's common-sense argument, when we consider that the philosophical Greeks and Romans certainly had an idea of eternity, and both used this word to express it. Those who are inclined to criticise Mr. North's doctrine on this subject should remember also that he was not writing a speculative treatise regarding the destiny of such exceptional classes or cases as have not had the full means of grace; but that he was preaching to those who were daily rejecting the Saviour, and resisting the Holy Spirit (on which sins he laid the greatest emphasis in all his preaching), and who by so doing were in imminent danger of sealing themselves up in final impenitence. Of the sin against the Holy Ghost our Lord says (Matt. xii. 32) that " it shall not be forgiven, neither in this world, neither in the world to come;" while the Holy Spirit says in Heb. vi. 4-6, that it is impossible to renew such sinners to repentance, on grounds that are independent of the lapse of time. This is surely " sin unto death."

Of this terrible state of irremediable impenitence Mr. North often spoke, and thus writes, " If we are willing to give up sin and to go to Christ, we cannot have committed this sin;" and again, " The man who has a good thought left is not left of God."

To the Edinburgh University students he said, " I believe that the sin against the Holy Ghost is grieving the Spirit once too often. No man who had a good thought in his heart, the least desire to go to God, let him be a hundred years of age, and his sins what they may be, has committed the unpardonable sin. But though I say that a man eighty or a hundred years old may turn to God, yet I believe there are people, (and who shall say how young the youngest is now in hell, or yet walking on this earth?) against whom God has sworn in His wrath that they shall never enter into His rest. ' Wherefore the Holy Ghost saith,'—He puts His own name to it, and I think in a book written entirely by the Holy Ghost, this is an awful word, as if He would call particular attention to it,— ' To-day if ye will hear His voice, harden not your hearts.' "

CHAPTER IX

Brownlow North's Theology and Preaching Continued

IV

"*BORN AGAIN*"

THE NECESSITY FOR THE SPIRIT'S WORK ON THE INTELLECT, AFFECTIONS, AND WILL

THE doctrines already reviewed as forming the sum and substance of Brownlow North's preaching are doctrines of the Church Catholic. Those which follow, and which, equally with the preceding, were mottoes on his banner and watchwords on his lips, belong more distinctively to the system of theology that is named Calvinistic, or Augustinian, or Pauline. Although their roots ramify through the whole of Revelation, they were first taught in connected form by the inspired Apostle Paul, were recovered from the oblivion and neglect of generations by the mighty sanctified genius of Augustine, and were once more resuscitated from the tomb, in which for well-nigh a millennium of murky years they had lain buried, by the divinely guided and commanding intellects of Martin Luther and John Calvin. In the publication of these doctrines these two great reformers were supported by all their illustrious coadjutors in the Reformation. Their work is graven as with " an iron pen and lead in a rock " in the symbolic books of the Reformed faith, and perpetuated with even greater exactness in the leading Confessions of the succeeding century. The master minds of the English Puritans adopted this system of doctrine with one consent.

It is also not unworthy of being noted that the vast majority of those servants of God who have been honoured by Him in producing revivals on a national scale, from the English Wycliffe and Bohemian Huss to those of the present, have been Augustinian or Calvinistic in their theological views. Thus a system which is by many reckoned narrow and unfitted to move the mass of mankind, however it may suit the logical reasonings of a divine closeted with dusty tomes, has not only had the support of the acutest intellects and most logical reasoners in the Church of Christ, but has stood the test of having moved multitudes and nations more thoroughly than any other system.

Brownlow North's teaching was in all points most pronouncedly Calvinistic. Indeed, so much was this the case that it seems marvellous that it obtained such very wide popularity; and perhaps in no country except Scotland or America could one, laying so marked stress on such doctrines as human inability and the necessity of the Spirit's work, have acquired almost at once such general acceptance. May it not be to this characteristic of his preaching that the stability of those converted under his labours is under God in great part to be attributed?

What makes the adhesion of Brownlow North to the leading doctrines of the so-called Calvinistic system a most valuable testimony to their truth, is not simply the fact that he was a man of a singularly clear judgment, and of very strong reasoning faculties, but still more the fact that he derived his views, not from the Confession of any Church, or the works of any theologian of however great repute, but mainly from a study of Scripture for himself, a study to which he devoted himself from the day of his conversion with the most unwearied and prayerful diligence.

His Calvinism did not in any way hamper him in declaring the freest offer of salvation to all, and pressing its instant acceptance upon every sinner to whom the offer came. The salvation he preached was as free as the sunlight, as authoritatively pressed on every gospel hearer as the august command of God can press it, and as urgent as it can be made by the exactest meaning of the word NOW. Sufficient for all, suitable for all, offered in gift to all, pressed upon the immediate acceptance of all by the invitation, the entreaty, and the command of God, such was his gospel,—and can anything be more free, more full, and more unfettered? No doubt he also insisted on a natural aversion to it, inability to understand it, and incapacity to receive it. But over against this he held out an offer and gift of the Spirit as free as the offer and gift of the Saviour, thoroughly to overcome that aversion, to remove the blindness of the understanding and the alienation of the affections. Human language cannot express a salvation more overflowingly full and more unconditionally free: God offering His Spirit to lost and helpless sinners as freely and unconditionally as He offers His Son.

Mr. North was accustomed with great emphasis, and in no passing way, to dwell upon the fact that man's nature since the fall is utterly depraved and hopelessly corrupt, and that no works wrought in his unrenewed state have any merit or proper holiness. Many will remember the frequency and solemnity with which he used to quote the fourteenth Psalm, ver. 1-3, "They are corrupt, and have done abominable iniquity: there is none that doeth good." Another text which he used to employ as a proof of this doctrine was Heb. xi. 6, "Without faith it is impossible to please God." He showed that the unbeliever, being confessedly destitute of true faith, could not offer any truly acceptable worship or service of God, seeing the main-spring of a right relation to God was wanting.

But Mr. North went further into this subject and used to press the truth that as man cannot be saved by any moral goodness that may be supposed to remain in him, so neither can he be saved by the exercise of his own reason, which the numerous section in most of our churches which has embraced rationalistic views seems to think has escaped the sad ravages of the Fall, which they acknowledge to have spread ruin over the rest of our nature.

Mr. North was extremely jealous of that worship of human reason with which we are threatened in the present day to an extent never known before in our earth's history, and which is in direct opposition to the worship of the Divine Wisdom incarnate in Jesus of Nazareth;—the object of rationalists' worship being human reason in general.

On this subject the margins of his Bibles are often black with annotations such as these: "No man can ever know anything of God or of the things of God, unless they are revealed to him by God's Spirit. Pray for the Spirit. He is promised to all who ask." "If Paul had not received the Spirit of God, he could have known nothing." "Observe why Paul said that all the treasures of wisdom and knowledge were hid in the Father and in Christ, lest any worldly-wise man should say there was knowledge anywhere else. There is no real wisdom or knowledge out of God and of Christ" "In the wisest ages of the world man's religion was the most absurd, yet even now are not the highly esteemed among men in too many instances as literally worshipping the work of their own hands as were the heathen?" "No man can know my secrets unless I am pleased to reveal them, so no man can know the things of God but by the teaching of the Holy Spirit." Man's reason has large and honourable functions, but while we render to reason the things that are reason's, may such teaching as this long prevail which bids us render to God the things that are God's!

Besides dwelling much on human helplessness and human ignorance, Mr. North always taught that the affections had been estranged and debased by the fall, and that therefore the heart required to be changed. He writes: "Even earthly wisdom might discover that unless a man was thoroughly changed, heaven could be no heaven to him. We must have a complete new set of affections and desires, a *new heart* in short, before we can enter into the kingdom of heaven." "When God has a purpose of mercy toward a man, He gives him a new heart. Every saved man and woman on the earth is a new creature, he has experienced the new birth, he has been born again of the Spirit, he has a new heart and a new nature, which produce new affections and new obedience, springing from new motives."[1]

[1] *Ourselves*, p. 52.

But man's fallen state consists also in the determined opposition of his will to the will of God, which can only be removed by the Holy Spirit. Our will must be brought into conformity with the will of God. Salvation is never forced upon an unwilling recipient, but each gospel hearer is called on to exercise his will in an act of choice, and choose for himself the Lord to be his God. But the alteration in our will is wrought by the will of God, as it is said, " Thy people shall be willing in the day of Thy power " (Ps. cx. 3). Very powerfully did Mr. North press the duty of this willing choice upon his hearers. One of his most widely blest discourses was a spiritualized exposition of Genesis xxiv. 28: "Wilt thou go with this man? and she said, I will go." As may be seen even from this volume, soul after soul in different parts of the country was brought to the point of decision, and of closing with Christ, through that sermon, in which he throws the whole responsibility of the choice upon the hearer; yet he states unambiguously at the very outset, that " by the power of the Holy Ghost " his hearers or readers may answer as Rebecca did. On John vi. 37, he notes: " If we are really going to Jesus, this verse assures us of two most comfortable things: one, that Jesus will in no wise, for no reason whatever, cast us out; the other, that we must be among the number given Him, or we would not have gone to Him." And again: " If Christ rejects a coming sinner, He must also reject a drawing Father." Again, on John viii. 43, 44: " ' Ye cannot hear My words; for the lusts of your father ye will do;' the ' will ' explains the ' cannot.' You cannot, because your will is in opposition."

Such was his teaching on these most important points, of which he could say, along with the Apostle of the Gentiles, that " he neither received it of man, neither was taught it, but by the revelation of Jesus Christ;" for he drew it fresh from the great fountain-head of truth contained in Holy Scripture.

Although the doctrine of the Divine sovereignty in predestinating and converting grace is rejected by dogmatic Arminianism, it is accepted very largely, both in their prayers and their praises, by the true children of God who profess that creed. There, where they are free from the war of words and

the din of definitions, they agree with Calvinists in confessing
utter weakness, sinfulness, and corruption before God, and in
supplicating the sovereign grace of His own Spirit; and heart
beats true to heart, even where eye does not see clear to eye
in surveying the field of Divine truth.   Dr. John Duncan,
when a young man in lodgings in Aberdeen, had many a controversy with his landlady, who was a godly woman and a
Wesleyan Methodist.   Admiring her grace, and despairing of
rectifying her theology, we are told that he closed their discussion by saying " Madam, you are like your own clock; it
strikes the wrong hour, but the hands are always right."
Strange to say, no words can better express Brownlow North's
strong Calvinism than Wesley's hymn : —

> " Stay, Thou insulted Spirit, stay,
>   Though I have done Thee such despite,
> Nor cast the sinner quite away,
>   Nor take Thine everlasting flight!
> Though I have steeled my stubborn heart,
>   And still shook off my guilty fears,
> And vexed and urged Thee to depart
>   For many long rebellious years,
> This only woe I deprecate,
>   This only plague I pray remove,
> Nor leave me in my lost estate,
>   Nor curse me with this want of love."

V

FAITH AND FEELING

THE DOCTRINE OF JUSTIFICATION BY FAITH

JUSTIFICATION by faith was the great watchword of the Reformers.   It was their battle-cry, with which they overturned
that justification by works which filled the exchequer of the
Church of Rome, and is precious still to all men of carnal
reason.   If the Word of God was the foundation-stone of the
Reformers, the first doctrine which they built on that foundation was justification by faith.   According to Luther's famous

aphorism, it is the article of a standing or a falling church.

Under the reign of Moderatism in Scotland, ministers and people had to a large extent returned to the exploded doctrine of a righteousness by works, in everything except the name: but with the reviving spiritual life of the last century, this unscriptural dogma had been dislodged once more from the churches, although it lingered in certain districts, and in many congregations, and in numberless hearts and minds over the land. To them the preaching that a sinner is justified by free grace through faith was news indeed, and Mr. North published it boldly and loudly in their hearing, even as Luther and Calvin and Knox had done.

But he found another tendency that had crept in almost unawares in many congregations where the preaching was evangelical, and which was causing much distress and hindrance to sin-burdened souls. It arose from a want of a clear spiritual knowledge that justification is an objective act, external to the man,—that God justifies the ungodly,—that this is the very entrance into the kingdom of grace, and that all evidences of grace in the heart are to be sought after this, and not before it. Mr. North found many, who had been trained and taught by godly ministers, examining their own hearts for tokens of grace, for pious frames and feelings of devotion, or of sadness, or of gladness, as grounds of acceptance, in place of looking simply to the Cross. They knew indeed that that Cross, with its great sin-atoning Sacrifice, is the only ground of reconciliation with the God they had offended, but they did not know that the sole instrument of justification is faith, and in no case feeling, or sensibility, or emotion:

" Oh how unlike the complex works of man,
  Heaven's easy, artless, unencumbered plan !
  *   *   *   *   *
  Inscribed above the portals from afar,
  Conspicuous as the brightness of a star,
  Legible only by the light they give,
  Stand the soul-quickening words, BELIEVE AND LIVE."
                                                    (COWPER.)

We cannot but think that the absence of the emotional element in his teaching, probably caused in part by a lack of it in his own mental character, was a defect, and that his preaching would have been more attractive to many, and still more widely useful, had it allowed a larger and truer place to the religious affections. This element was prominent in the preaching and hymns of the Wesleys in England, and of the great Highland preachers in Scotland, not to speak of such men as Samuel Rutherford and McCheyne, whose deep stirrings of the affections in their writings have filled the Lord's house with the odour of their precious ointment, for long years and generations after the alabaster vessel from which it was poured had been broken, and in the grave had mingled with its kindred dust.

Mr. North's preaching was addressed to the understanding which he sought to enlighten, and to the will, which he sought to persuade, rather than to the tender chords of feeling and affection in the human heart. But while this is the case, there is no doubt that he did inestimable service to many in leading them away from most unhealthy and fruitless introspection to a simple looking to the crucified Saviour, and as great service to many others who were resting on their transient and ever-changing religious sensibility and feeling, in place of Jesus Christ the only Rock.

Repentance he rightly showed not to consist in tears, nor in outward reformation, but in the mental act of change of mind and turning to God, producing reformation. But it must always, if true, be the result of a sense of sin's exceeding sinfulness, which is ever humbling and saddening to convinced sinners, although in various degrees; and often it is only after the soul has repented and believed that the deepest fountains of heart sorrow and the sluices of the weeping eyes are opened. Yet assuredly Mr. North could not too strongly state that the mental emotions are neither the meritorious ground of justification, nor the essence of either repentance or faith, but their accompaniments.

Mr. North often said that every anxious inquirer he ever met with began to converse with him by talking about his own

" feelings." His teaching on this subject is stated in a connected form in the tract published under the title " I feel," and also in one of his earliest tracts, " Trust God," but he enforced it in all his addresses and publications.

We quote the following from his annotated Bible : " Religion is not a thing of mere feeling, but a patient, plodding, perpetual painstaking, persevering life of obedience to the will of God, springing out of an habitual faith that our labour is not in vain in the Lord." " If we would have God to hear us, we must be honest with Him, and confess our sins of thought, word, and deed honestly; and if we do this trusting to the atonement made by Jesus, we may say, ' Thou heardest me,' for God has promised to hear, and we must believe He does, *whether we feel it or not*." " God's word is steadfast rock; rest on it, so in trial, sickness, and death, your soul shall be steadfast, founded on a rock. If you have only feeling, where are you when the feeling is gone? " " Judge yourselves, not by feeling, but by conduct. We know our love to men, not by feeling love, but by doing to them what we would have them do to us." " The proof that any one has received the Holy Spirit is not a sensation, but power over the enemy."

Another doctrine on which he laid great stress was that of the true and proper Divinity of Jesus Christ. In his study Bible we have found every text bearing upon the divinity of the Saviour carefully marked and annotated in his own terse and striking manner, and the last work he printed was an exposition of John v. 16-30, written in defence of this great truth, and published under the title of " Christ the Saviour and Christ the Judge." From this we draw the inference that he expected the next attack upon the faith of God's children to be made upon this doctrine. His judgment was both shrewd and sound in such matters, while, from the very large number of persons who opened their mind to him in private upon their religious difficulties, his opportunities of becoming acquainted with the tendencies of thought in religion were extensive.

In the work referred to he says : " There is at this day, and in this generation, a large body of influential and well-educated people who, professing to believe the Bible, will yet tell you that the Lord Jesus Christ is not, and never professed to be, God. At the same time they will tell you He was the best man that ever lived upon earth, a pattern of every goodness, morality, and virtue, one who has left us an example that we shall do well to follow, but still a man, only a man, and nothing but a man. Verily may we not ask with St. Paul, 'Hath not God made foolish the wisdom of this world?' A man, nothing but a man, and yet the very best man that ever lived upon earth! Away with such rubbish, such soul-destroying rubbish, away with it! Either the Lord Jesus Christ was the greatest impostor, the greatest liar and cheat ever born of woman, and has done more harm on earth than was ever done since the fall of Adam, or He was God. What! a good man, and yet only a man, and claim to do whatever God as God could do! What! a good man, and yet only a man, and claim to raise dead bodies, quicken dead souls, be the Saviour and Judge of the world, and receive as His right the honour that is due to God only! (John v. 19-22.)" Thus scathingly did he expose those who hold

> " The wondrous birth at Bethlehem
> A fiction of the wandering brain."

In addition to these great leading doctrines, Brownlow North's preaching was distinguished by the vivid presentation which he gave of the existence, personality, and power over man of fallen spirits, and of Satan their great head. All who ever heard him must have been struck by this. At present it is fashionable in certain circles, even of religious society, to call these views into question, and to attribute any clear statements regarding the existence of fallen spirits to a superstitious or an over-excited imagination. The same views and statements have characterized some of the very foremost divines, such as Luther and Bunyan, Milton and Dante, as much as Brownlow North. But we are told the idea may be poetical, or may suit a popular preacher, but is not philosophical. Yet if sin does exist at all, if responsible creatures have fallen and rebelled against their Maker, there is no inherent improbability that this rebellion may have extended to other classes of intelligences as well as man. Sin and holiness are moral opposites independent of time and place.

Almost all the religions of the world have recognized the evil influences of fallen spirits; the purest and most philosophical of them all, Zoroastrianism, gives the greatest prominence to this belief, making the god of evil and darkness powerful almost as the God of holiness and light. Scripture itself clearly intimates to us the existence of sinful angels and their power over fallen men, and had this not been practically important for men to know, it had not been revealed. Nor was it merely a part of the pictorial teaching suited for the infancy of the Church; the revelation regarding it is much clearer in the later Old Testament books than in the earlier, and is most fully developed in the New Testament, in the teaching of Christ and His apostles. The glory, the extent, and the power of the Satanic dominion are developed in revelation in parallel columns with the development of the Messianic. Surely then Brownlow North did right in assigning to the god of this world, and the king of fallen spirits, that power and influence over the spirits of men which he is represented in the Divine Word as exercising, and in pressing upon men constantly that there are two kingdoms, two potentates, two gods, one worshipped and obeyed by the children of this world, the other by the children of light.

In a sermon on Proverbs viii, preached at Londonderry, he said that " the man who seeks the things of time and sense more than the things of God prays to the Devil. When man sinned, God left him, and the Devil took possession of him. Every man is inhabited either by the Devil alone, or by God and the Devil, the latter being kept under control. If any were able to be indifferent about eternity, they had received that power from the Devil, a power which he did not possess himself, for he trembled while he believed. Most men believe the Devil, and disbelieve God. The Devil wishes to produce indifference, and to keep people in forgetfulness of God, so that each day they may be nearer hell. It is a want of simple belief in such passages as 1 Peter v. 8 that destroys men. They do not believe in a real Devil. He is a reality, and we are here taught how to resist him."

On the great central doctrine of the Atonement he held the strictly Calvinistic view. Regarding its extent his comment on John 1. 29 is, " 'The Lamb of God which taketh away the sin of the world,' *i.e.*, of all who will give their sins to Him to carry away; His blood is *sufficient* for all, though *efficient* only for those who believe." The fact that he did not preach universal redemption, but regarded Christ as dying as the representative of His covenant people, did not in the least fetter him in making the fullest and freest offer of the great sacrifice to every sinner. He says, " Christ died that He may have a *gift of His death* to give to every lost sinner who will accept it from Him."

From this *resumé* of Mr. North's teaching it will be seen, as was once remarked of him, that the mission given to him was what Coleridge in his " Aids to Reflection " says is one of the most useful a man can be employed in, viz., that of " rescuing admitted truths from the neglect caused by the very circumstance of their universal admission." And the present tendency of theology proves that such neglect ends in doubt and denial of the truths that were formerly unquestioned.

CHAPTER X

Work in Ireland and in London

IN the early part of 1859, that remarkable work of grace broke out in the north of Ireland, which must ever rank as one of the most notable Revivals of modern times. It had been preceded by the great American Revival of 1858, and was succeeded by the Revival in Scotland in 1860. Indeed, the latter awakening may be said to have spread to us from Ulster by a kind of spiritual sympathy or contagion; for, as the late Professor Miller remarked, when he announced in our house the first news of its having touched the Scottish shores, it came just in the track that cholera would have come, crossing the Channel at its narrowest point, and appearing first on the coast of Ayrshire, from which on a clear day a keen eye can descry the outline of the hills of Antrim.

Mr. North's work in Scotland during the previous three years had prepared the way for the general wave of revival which in 1860 burst upon our land. Indeed, the springtide of blessing under his ministry, as attested by the letters of thanksgiving sent to him, reached its highest point in 1858 and 1859, and was therefore independent of the revivals in Ireland and America. It served at the same time as a providential preparation for the advent of that general awakening here, which in all human likelihood might otherwise have had as slight and partial effect upon Scotland as it had upon England and the Scottish Highlands; for in neither of these parts of the land had there been such deep ploughing of the soil of men's hearts which in the Scottish Lowlands had been stirred to its depths with the ploughshare of conviction under this Baptist-like preacher of Repentance.

When the news of the wonderful awakening in Ulster reached this land, many of our most experienced and godly ministers crossed over to witness with their own eyes this remarkable movement among a people sprung from our own, to form a judgment at first-hand as to whether it was genuine or spurious, to render what assistance they could to the over-wrought ministers there, and to seek to receive for themselves, and carry home to their flocks, a new baptism of spiritual life.

The late James Balfour, of Edinburgh writes : —

"It was my privilege to accompany Mr. North to Ireland at the time of the revival of 1859. We sailed from Greenock on a fine summer evening, and paced the deck together most of the night, as we steamed down the Clyde; the water and the surrounding mountains being purpled by the fading light far into the night, and the coast of Ireland brightened, as we approached it, by the early dawn. I remember a little incident that happened at Greenock just before we left. We had gone into a small bookseller's shop to buy a newspaper, and he pointed out to me a copy of the 'Revival' and a cheap irreligious magazine lying side by side, saying, 'What two books to be together!' The shopman interfered, and said, 'You are talking, sir, about what you know nothing of.' 'How so?' said Mr. North. 'Because you never read these books.' 'Yes, I have.' 'Have you read the magazine?' 'Yes, I have; I read it for many years. It is very clever, but very wicked. I am a changed man since then.' 'I know best what will sell,' replied the shopkeeper. 'Oh, yes, if you are living only for this world; but remember you are immortal.' In leaving the shop, he gave him his own tract with that title, 'You are Immortal.'

"After staying a while in Ulster, we went to Dublin, and attended a meeting of the Irish General Assembly, and listened together for some hours to the ministers in private conference, telling the wondrous and thrilling stories of redeeming love in their various parishes, till every eye was moistened and every heart was swelling under the conscious influence of the Holy Ghost. Mr. North on a subsequent day addressed the Assembly, and was received with deep respect, and listened to amid profound silence."

Brownlow North had gone to Ireland as the result of an invitation from William Gibson, moderator of the Irish Presbyterian Church, and in Gibson's standard history of the 1859 revival in Ulster[1] there are many testimonies to the power of North's ministry amidst an awakening which led to the addition of some 100,000 people to the Churches of Northern Ireland. William Gibson writes: " Among those who visited us at this time none were more highly prized, either in Belfast or elsewhere, than Mr. Brownlow North. Mr. North himself, his social status, and the wonderful success attending his labours, especially for the preceding two years in Scotland, all contributed to concentrate public attention on his evangelistic labours. He came to Belfast in the end of June, and did not leave Ulster for two months afterwards. During the intermediate period he was employed incessantly in public ministrations, and had most abundant and sustaining evidence that his labour was not in vain."

Jonathan Simpson, one of the ministers of Portrush, in describing how the revival broke out in that place at the beginning of June, 1859, speaks of Brownlow North as follows: " Brownlow North, Esq., visited most opportunely, and, by his earnest and thrilling appeals, largely contributed to advance the glorious cause. He preached twice in the Presbyterian Church, Portrush, and addressed two open-air meetings, one in the town, and the other at Dunmull. The latter was the noblest meeting ever seen in the neighbourhood; the very sight was grand, apart from its bearings on eternity. Mr. North, accustomed to large audiences, computed it at seven thousand; and so many were stricken that day, that the people in the neighbouring houses never got to bed the entire night. So many hearts were bleeding under a sense of sin, and weeping over a pierced Saviour."

---

[1] *The Year of Grace*. As it was felt that insufficient mention was made by the author to the labours of Brownlow North in Ulster in 1859, this paragraph and others that follow have been added to this reprint of North's life.

" It were worth," concludes Simpson, " living ten thousand ages in obscurity and reproach to be permitted to creep forth at the expiration of that time, and engage in the glorious work of the last six months of 1859."

In the first week of August he preached in Londonderry. The newspapers reported that between 4,000 and 5,000 persons of all classes assembled to hear him in the Victoria Market on Sunday, on which occasion he read and commented on the eighth chapter of Proverbs. He said that " No one would leave that assembly the same person as he entered it. As soon as man sinned he died spiritually. Death was being without God. In God was life, out of Him was no life. All that could guide a man upward left him when he sinned, and the devil took possession of him. The precise moment would come when each would die and stand face to face with Jesus Christ. Jesus is the way through whom we must go back to God. We must go through the rent veil of the flesh of Jesus. Man's wisdom only led him to dishonour God and destroy himself. He was once staying in a house with the high and noble when a scoffer said, ' The instinct of the brute is higher than the reason of man.' He was indignant when he heard the remark, but afterwards he reflected that the brute had the instinct as God gave it, but man had not reason as God gave it. He asked those who followed their own wisdom what hope they had, though they gained the whole world, of escaping hell, unless the Bible were a lie? What was the great conflict between God and man? It was whether man would believe his own heart or the wisdom of God. If they believed that Christ's yoke was easy, they would take it up that night. The speaker in the eighth of Proverbs was the Son of God. It was a call to the foolish and simple to turn at once from their folly. To fear God was to hate sin,—to love God was to keep His commandments. Sinners would be saved by faith, and not by their own feelings. The proof that they had received the Holy Spirit was not a sensation, but power over sin, which was their great enemy. There was one great Gospel commandment, ' Believe on the Lord Jesus Christ.' When his own spirits were low, he often relied on the words, ' Trust in the Lord *at all times.*' He urged

believers to abide in Christ. A sickly-looking branch, by re-
maining in the tree, would become strong and vigorous. The
love of Christ to men was like the Father's love to His own
Son." Such is an outline of his discourse.

In the evening he preached again to an overflowing congregation, from Genesis xxiv. 38: "Wilt thou go with this man?
And she said, I will go." He had given an address from this
text very shortly after he began his work in the autumn of
1856, in Inverness, and he has stated that he did not know that
he had ever preached that sermon without hearing of blessing
resulting from it. He afterwards published it in an amplified
form, under the title of "Yes or No." On Monday evening he
preached again in the first Presbyterian Church, on the Parable
of the Sower (which was also published in the form of a tract),
and on Tuesday evening from Rev. iii. 14-22, the message to
the Laodicean Church; and when he asked the anxious to remain to a second meeting, few left the building.

Another example of the blessing on North's preaching is
given by N. M'A. Brown, a minister of Newtonlimavady.
A movement of the Spirit had commenced there towards the
end of May and "a thrill of solemn dread passed like an electric current, from the one end of the presbytery to the other.
The twelve congregations were all assembled, in crowded
houses, in the course of a few days, and multitudes in each
were crying for mercy."

"A wonderful impetus was given to the good work by the
frequent visits and addresses of friends from Scotland and
elsewhere, but especially of Mr. Guinness and Brownlow
North, Esq. The former addressed some three thousand persons in the open-air with effect and acceptance; but the impression produced by Mr. North was deeper still, and doubtless
will be more lasting.

"He visited this place twice within a week, and preached
once in the open-air and once in a house of worship on each
occasion—four addresses in all. The house he spoke in was
literally crammed on both occasions. The first open-air
address was attended by some four thousand of an audience,
and the second by upwards of seven thousand—the second

largest audience he had in Ireland. These addresses were faithful and true—solemn, searching, and practical—and were highly distinguished for fervour, unction, and power. The REALIZATION of the sinner's lost condition—of the living God just here and looking on—and of a present salvation through faith in God's Son, was the theme upon which he specially dwelt. Want of realization of God and of divine things, he asserted, was practical infidelity, and lay at the root of every sinful, indifferent, and ungodly life. He held a meeting of those who were anxious to ' renounce the devil, the world, and the flesh,' and ' present their bodies living sacrifices to God;' and to these he delivered an address particularly suited to their circumstances. His visit will long be thankfully remembered, and his faithful admonitions produced an effect on many that shall never be altogether known till ' the day shall declare it.' "

After preaching in many other localities, he left for Scotland on the 26th of August.

In Ireland he delivered about fifty addresses, many of them to several thousands of auditors. The tendency of all his teachings and exhortations was to discountenance reliance upon mere feeling, to shut men up into the faith, and to exalt and magnify the written Word. Such ministrations at such a time were eminently seasonable, and were largely blessed.

Several weeks after Brownlow North's visit to Newtonlimavady another minister of the town wrote to him to give an account of the abiding results of the work there :

"N'L'VADY, 17*th August*, 1859.

" MY DEAR MR. NORTH,

"I have waited until I could report respecting the influences of your visit. I have now reason to assure you that God has greatly blessed the word you addressed to us. A number of souls have been converted, and a still greater number are blessing God that their faith in Jesus and His written Word has been greatly confirmed. I bless God that the sickly and unscriptural fervours, that were so widely spreading, have been arrested, and society breathes the purer atmosphere of simple trust in the promises of God. The

Roman Catholic found peace, and has gone home to tell what God has done for his soul. During the prostration a Bible dropped from his pocket, which he afterwards fervently pressed to his heart. A young woman on a visit from Scotland to friends in N'L'vady, began by making light of God's work, but the morning after your last service she found peace in believing. She is praying most anxiously for Scotland, that the Lord may make it like the north of Ireland. A girl in the workhouse was sweeping the door and hearing your voice (the wind blowing that way) she distinctly heard you repeat the invitation, 'Whosoever will, let him come.' She staggered into the house, fell prostrate before God, and found immediate peace. I'll keep a record of cases as they occur, and show them to you when you come back to us. The cry is, When will he come back to us again? The ground has been measured where the people stood at your last open-air service, and it has been calculated that more than 12,000 persons were present. I think we will have 20,000 when you next visit us.

" . . . You will be glad to know that even in the heat and burden of harvest, the work of God goes on with unabated interest. I held eleven public meetings last week, taking the dinner hour, from one till two o'clock, and in the evening from seven till nine, and everywhere I went we had crowded meetings. Our people began last Lord's day at half-past seven in the morning, pleading for the outpouring of God's Spirit upon the Sabbath school; and with the exception of their hours for breakfast, dinner, and tea, the whole day was spent in devotional exercises up to the hour of ten at night. They would not, could not part; it was a blessed season of the sweetest communion. There is hardly a meeting I hold in the country but I hear some sinner telling of mercy received, or some child of God speaking of great enlargement of heart through your services, and I invariably beg of them to prove their love to you by commending you and yours to the oversight of the Saviour. We have had several cases of conversion from Rome. We had two Roman converts with us lately: they are the finest specimens of young Christians I ever met. Oh, how different! One was like John, all love, so sweet and gentle; he had so put on Christ, that you could see nothing but Jesus: the other like Peter, all boldness and fire; he had so put on the armour of light, that he seemed as

one who could venture to do and dare anything in the name
of Jesus. They openly and boldly spoke in many places in
the name of Jesus, and God has blessed their appeals. Many
Roman Catholics have attended, and several have resolved
to leave the Church of Rome. The terrific prostrations that
are weekly occurring in their chapels, and the cries of the
agonized for the blood of Jesus, as they fall beside their
altars, are producing results (as yet) known only to God. One
peculiarity of the present movement is the coming of *poor
simpletons* to Jesus. John ——, a creature who gathered
rags, has been for eight weeks one of the most devout worshippers of the Lord, and although he confesses that he is a
poor sinner, yet his hope is so fixed in Jesus, that he lives in
prayer and praise. In L—— meeting-house a prayer-meeting
was held on Monday evening. After divine service was over,
a Roman Catholic simpleton, who had travelled two miles,
came forward. He was very tall, and clothed in a woman's
dress. He earnestly requested that the minister and people
would pray 'that he might be washed in Christ's precious
blood.' Singular sight, and still more singular request! The
cases of the deaf, dumb, and blind frequently occur, and, so
far as I can judge, the hand of the same God is in this visitation. Doubting souls have come forth revived and comforted. In some cases, like Zacharias, the doubting were
struck dumb; in other cases, like Daniel (ch. x), it seemed to
be the result of a sight of the Divine Majesty presented to the
soul. Several things have been said by them whilst recover-
ing, for which they seem truly ashamed; but Peter on the
mount spoke foolishly. Oh, I wish all our ministers would
give over all their wise solutions of these strange visitations,
and work for God! What we don't know we'll know here-
after. Meantime, we know Jesus is the Physician for all, and
His blood the balm for all.

"Yours in our own loved Lord,

"GEORGE STEEN."

It was in the end of the same year, 1859, that Brownlow
North first visited London on evangelistic work, where he was
honoured to carry a light from the fire which was glowing with
intense heat in Ulster, and had already begun to communicate
its light and warmth to Scotland. His intimate friend, James

E. Mathieson, Esq., thus describes his work in the Metropolis, in the organizing of which he himself took a leading part.

"Mr. North, accompanied by Mr. Reginald Radcliffe, came to London at the close of 1859, to address the Young Men's Christian Association in Exeter Hall; and on 20th December, began a busy season which extended over five months. What had been intended for a brief stay became the first of a succession of prolonged visits to London, and is still felt to be memorable and precious by many grateful hearts. It was a time of blessing. The revival of religion which a year or two before had stirred the churches of America, and had next been manifested in signal awakenings in the north of Ireland, did not leave England and Scotland unmoved.

"The thought happily suggested itself to some of Mr. North's friends, that advantage might be taken of his presence in London to try and reach some of the upper classes during the height of the season of 1860; and for this end, Willis's Rooms were taken for a series of services, at an hour in the afternoon likely to secure the attendance of that capricious class, 'society.' The first of these meetings secured an attendance which encouraged its promoters, and paved the way for gradually increasing audiences during the succeeding weeks; and towards the close of the series, not only was there a crowded gathering, but a riveted attention; it was no longer the curiosity of idlers seeking a new distraction, and asking one another, 'What will this babbler say?' but rather the intense, if often unexpressed, heart-longing for higher and holier life, and the sometimes uttered repetition of the old anxious cry, 'What must I do to be saved?' for some were found to thrust aside conventional reserve, and seek in private conversation afterwards, a solution of soul difficulties, and guidance towards deeper acquaintance with the way of peace. These after-meetings were at that time a novelty, but then, and ever after, they have been found precious seasons of opportunity for personal dealing with souls.[1]

---

[1] At the close of this series of meetings a special service was appointed for anxious inquirers, which was attended by between 500 and 600 persons.

" These meetings naturally brought forth invitations to take part in the services for the people, with which we are now so familiar, but which were still somewhat a novelty, held in theatres and great halls in various parts of London."

" In St. James's Hall, Piccadilly, and in several of the theatres of the east and south of London, North was privileged again and again to deliver his testimony, and with his intense earnestness enforce the necessity of decision for Christ, and preparedness to meet God. He used sometimes to tell his hearers that he believed he was more anxious for their salvation than many among them were for themselves. Regarding the effect of these London services, I may transcribe the following letter from an honoured minister of the gospel, the Rev. Frank H. White, of Chelsea : —

" ' *August 22nd*, 1877.

" ' MY DEAR MR. MATHIESON,—My wife and her two sisters were awakened and brought to Christ, as you know, under Mr. North's preaching during the St. James's Hall services, about 1860. They had gone to hear Morley Punshon, and were told by one assisting at the services that on the following Sunday " a gentleman would preach, whom if they once heard they would never forget." They heard him. His text was, I believe, " Wilt thou go with this man?" They knew little, very little, if any Bible truth, and were utterly destitute of gospel light. They were literally transfixed with terror as they listened to Mr. North's awful description of the sinner's state and danger. " I only remember," says my wife, "that I felt under his preaching that there was really a heaven and hell, and that Mr. North believed in both."

" ' This has always struck me about his preaching—it was so intensely realistic. It was impossible to listen and be in-different, it seemed as if it must either excite the bitterest op-position, or else carry the heart's citadel as by storm, and compel to an immediate and unconditional surrender.

" ' His preaching, however, had in my opinion several ele-ments which much of the preaching of to-day would be the better for. He told people of the wrath to come in language, which, if strong, was not more so than was consistent with that fidelity without which a professed messenger from God can have no true claim upon another's attention, seeing he lacks the very first essential of a herald of truth. Mr. North had what Mr. Harrington Evans avowed to be the greatest need of his time, " a deep sense of the reality of the penal judgment of God."

" ' Another striking feature of his ministry was, that he addressed the *consciences* of his hearers, spoke of sin in plain terms, and insisted upon *repentance towards God*, as equally needful to an entrance into the kingdom with faith in the Lord Jesus. But what, perhaps more than anything else, made his ministry so valuable, and should move us to pray the Lord to raise up more like him, was the fact that he gave no uncertain sound upon the doctrine of the imputed righteousness of Christ. I shall never forget his speaking on this subject in the Stafford Rooms. Taking for his text Rom. x. 4, " Christ is the end (or fulfilment of the law) for righteousness to every one that believeth," he remarked, " Men in their endeavour to work out a righteousness of their own by keeping the law, generally begin *here* (pointing to the elbow of his left arm), and try to work up to the end; but they make no real progress, and only after repeated failures and falls do some see (pointing to the tip of his fingers) that *Christ* is the *end* of the law, and that in His perfect obedience alone they can be justified."

" ' Yours affectionately, FRANK H. WHITE.' "

" Mr. North himself felt that the advantages he possessed as an English gentleman, with access to certain circles of society, formed part of the gift bestowed upon him to be laid out for the Master's glory; nor did he shrink from giving his testimony in season, and out of season, in mixed company as well as amongst Christian friends; at the dinner table and in the railway carriage, not less than in the pulpit or from the platform. Not often, at least in the days now referred to, was there such a fine, daring spirit evinced as when at a large dinner party North would break in upon a worldly conversation with some pointed remark which startled and silenced the majority of the company; or when in some gathering of Christian people, occupied probably with conversation about the externals of their faith, he would thrust in an inquiry which at once put away questions of churches for the more urgent and pressing question of personal salvation, or turned talk about preachers aside to make way for the claims of Christ."

As an example of this, we insert the following instance which was kindly communicated to us by the late Principal Brown, D.D., of Aberdeen. Dr. Brown happened to be paying a visit at Keith Hall along with Mr. North. At dinner a military officer, who was in the neighbourhood officially, was one of the guests.

In the course of the evening, Mr. North seemed to be desirous of entering into serious conversation with him, and at last both got seated on the ottoman together, and talked for a considerable time. Dr. Brown being anxious to know the subject of their talk, asked Mr. North what they had been conversing about. " Oh," he said, " I'll tell you. I got gradually rather closer to his conscience than he seemed to relish when he stopped me with ' Mr. North, do you study prophecy? ' (a thing in which the colonel rather dabbled). ' Oh, well, as part of my Bible I ought to do so, but I have not given it any special study;' whereupon I resumed, and got still closer to him, when the colonel, somewhat wincing, said, ' Mr. North, you *should* study prophecy, you would find it very interesting.' I could stand it no longer, so I said, ' Colonel, you are down at P and Q but I am only at A, B, and C. The first thing with me is to see that I myself am right with God; I must make sure of that, and that has so absorbed me hitherto that I have not yet got past it, and I should advise you, Colonel, to make sure of the A, B, and C of your personal salvation, for only then are you safe to go on to the P and Q of Prophecy or anything else.' "

In society he was fearless as a lion in rebuking any levity on religious subjects or any approach to profanity or scepticism. He did not care who the defender might be, or what his position, he always checked it. In addressing individuals in private about their eternal interests, as well as at social gatherings, he was often called to bear the cross.

On one of his visits to London he received a letter at breakfast from a lady in Torquay, with whom he was only slightly acquainted, telling him that she had a son in London, a colonel in the Guards, and asking him to call on him and speak to him about his soul, giving him his name and address. Mr. North did not at first like this. He did not care to intrude on a colonel in the Guards whom he had never seen, and he knew the writer of the letter so slightly that he hardly felt called on to do so. Still he kept the letter in his pocket, and it was like to burn a hole there. At last he resolved that he would call on him, but he secretly wished that he might not find him at home. On reaching his door he rung the bell, and asked if Colonel A. was at home. "Yes, sir, he is," was the answer, and he walked in and found a tall handsome man with a long beard, very fashionably dressed. He was just about to go out to the Park. His hat was on, and he was pulling on one of his lavender kid gloves. Mr. North began the conversation by saying, "Colonel A., I have come to you on what you will think a strange errand. I am Mr. North. I had a letter from your mother yesterday morning, asking me to call on you and speak to you about your soul." "Oh, you are Mr. North," said the colonel, taking off his hat; "pray sit down on the sofa. I had a letter from my mother, leading me to expect this visit." They conversed for a while together, when Mr. North showed him the danger of being of the world, living with it and perishing with it; and also the only possible way of escape through Jesus Christ as the Saviour provided by God, and he urged him to leave the world and cleave to Christ. "But," said he, "you must do this out and out, and don't be ashamed of it. Go to your club, or to your mess, and tell them that you have changed masters." The colonel indicated that he was not prepared for this. "I daresay," said Mr. North, "you shrink from it. You would rather lead a forlorn hope or brave any military danger. The confession, however, would not be so difficult as it seems at a distance. The lion is a chained one. I am myself a proof of this now. Yesterday morning I got a letter from a lady whom I scarcely knew, asking me to go to a colonel of the Guards whom I had never seen, and speak to him about his soul. If you had got such a message, you would not have liked it." "No," he said.

" I should not." " Neither did I. If any one had come to me on such an errand a few years ago, I should have turned him to the door, and I expected that you would do so to me. But instead of that you have treated me like a gentleman, given me a seat on your sofa, and entered frankly into conversation with me, and I am ashamed of my timidity."

CHAPTER XI

Harvest-work in Various Fields

In the course of this memoir we have already given numerous evidences of the fruits of Mr. North's labours, and the reader will probably have formed a not inaccurate general conception of the widespread results in his ministry during its whole course in widely separated districts and cities of Scotland, England, and Ireland. It may, however, prove both interesting and useful to present distinct testimonies, written by those who were well qualified to form an accurate and sound judgment from their own observation of the effects of his labours in their own neighbourhood. Some of these testimonies were written soon after his visit to the locality, others after an interval of five or six years, while others are reminiscences of his work after an interval of fifteen or twenty years. The first letter is from the late much-respected Free Church minister of the first charge in Thurso, and refers to his visit to that town in 1858, which was one of the years in which he reaped his greatest number of sheaves. He had gone there at the pressing request of his friend, the esteemed Sir George Sinclair.

VISIT TO THURSO IN 1858.

"THURSO, *Dec. 8th*, 1858.

"MY DEAR BROTHER,—Ever since you left I had in view writing to you, and was putting off from time to time that I might be able to speak more decidedly as to the state of matters in this place; and now I am sure you will rejoice to know that the expectations raised at the time of your visit have not been disappointed. Since you left, my time has been chiefly occupied in conversing with individuals on the state of their souls. Of these, many were impressed or brought to the knowledge of the truth when you and Mr. Grant were here. I am thankful to say that the interest in Divine things is not abating. The young converts continue steadfast, and some of them manifest a sweet gospel spirit in a way that interests and refreshes me much. At our communion in the end of October, which was but four months after the preceding one, there were twenty-five new communicants, of whom about half received the truth when you and Mr. Grant were among us. Besides these, several young people who received the truth at the same time did not apply for admission; but I have almost the whole of them, in company with a good many others, under instruction at a Bible-class, and I am thankful to see them holding fast, and, so far as I can learn, walking in the truth. A very pleasing change has taken place in a class that used to be rather a careless one here, that of female house-servants. It is interesting to hear these girls tell in their own way the particular manner in which an impression was first made on them.

"One said, 'I neglected prayer, and I was impressed by hearing Mr. North tell how he got up to pray when his servant was present, and now I pray.'

"Another said to me, 'What impressed me was Mr. North's praying for you the last time he preached in your church, that you might have many seals to your ministry, and so it became a question with me if I was to be one of them.'

"Another was impressed on the communion Sabbath, in church, by her companion rising from her side, and going to the communion table, so that she could not rest till she too became a Christian. And so on. On the whole I do feel deeply grateful to the Lord that He has sent you to us this year again, and also your dear friend Mr. Grant. I earnestly pray that the Lord may continue to bless your labours abundantly, and may cause you in all things to prosper, and be in health, even as your soul prospereth.

"Yours very affectionately in the Lord,

"W. Ross Taylor."

The last two cases particularized in this letter will show that it was a time when the Lord's Spirit was very abundantly poured out, and when souls were, under His sovereign grace,

F

awakened and brought to the Lord by means or words the most simple, and the most unlikely in ordinary seasons to accomplish such great results. As another instance of the same character, we may mention the case of a cabman who came to Mr. North in deep distress. When he asked him what part of the sermon had been the means of arousing him to such concern about his soul, he said that it was no part of the sermon, but a sentence in his prayer; and on his asking what the sentence was, he replied, " Oh, sir, it was when you said, ' We have left undone those things which we ought to have done, and have done those things which we ought not to have done,' and I felt that was just my case."

VISIT TO ROTHESAY IN 1858.

In regard to the results of the evangelist's visit to this busy coast town, we are able to give the valuable testimony of the late Rev. Robert Elder, D.D., which he recorded twenty years later in a letter to the present writer.

"ROTHESAY, *Feb. 7th*, 1878.

" MY DEAR FRIEND,—I have too long delayed writing to you; but I was anxious before writing to see a few of those who were impressed at the time referred to, and who have maintained a consistent profession, and to get some information regarding others who have dropped out of my view. One of those referred to in my old letter died several years ago in great hope, indeed I may say in ' the full assurance of hope,' and her sister has held fast her profession, and is still one of our most earnest and consistent Christian workers.

" Mr. North's visit to this place was at a very early stage of his evangelistic work; he had then no ' inquiry meetings ' in the now ordinary sense of that expression, nor did he separate those whom he counted ' converts ' from the rest. He was here only for four or five days, and on the second occasion of his addressing the people, seeing some apparently impressed, he asked if I would give him leave to ask any who might wish to speak with him to come next day to my house, where he stayed. I think twenty-four came, and after conversing with them, he gave me their names. Both in private and in his public addresses he very earnestly urged all who felt concern to wait on the *regular ministrations* of their pastors, and to attend the *Bible-classes*.

" I remember that a great many came immediately after to my own class, and I believe to the classes of the other congregations interested. There were also several fellowship and prayer-meetings kept up for a considerable time, especially among the young women, one of these having been in existence before Mr. North's visit, but having a larger attendance afterwards.

" Referring to my notes of that period, an interesting and instructive fact has been recalled to my mind. Our Communion came on in June, about four months after Mr. North was here, and while I was frequently conversing with those under concern. The great proportion of those impressed preferred to remain back, and comparatively few on that occasion became communicants, although I would have had great pleasure in admitting them. I found that the *best* of them, after a good deal of emotion and warm feeling, were led after a time to far deeper views of sin and helplessness and a lost condition than they had at first, and were afraid to make a profession of their faith. But the next occasion, in January following, I had, I think, the largest number of young communicants I have ever had here, and many of these I admitted with the greatest comfort. In June of the following year also I had the same experience. I have kept short notes regarding sixty-two persons who conversed with me in 1858, 1859, under more or less concern. Of many of these I can now find no trace. A considerable number, I grieve to say, went back from their impressions, and some lapsed into open wickedness. But a large proportion turned out well, giving hopeful evidence of a saving change. A few I have attended on their death-beds, and have been cheered by the hope that they have gone to be with Christ. A good many are away from this place, and settled elsewhere; but many are still living here, and are earnest and consistent members of my congregation, some of them being active and earnest workers on the Lord's side.

" I remain, yours affectionately, ROBERT ELDER."

Mr. North at different times made special efforts to reach young men, and these efforts were largely blessed. During his ministry, he made it a practice occasionally to intimate a special service for young men, or for men only, and in this way many were induced to go and hear the gospel at his lips who would never have dreamed of attending an ordinary evangelistic service. The writer vividly recalls the deep solemnity that seemed to overhang and overawe the vast crowds of men, principally young men, who thronged to the services specially designed for them in Free St. Luke's, Edinburgh, in the winters of 1858-59-60; and from other parts of this volume it will be seen that to the last, in the great cities of England, he drew thousands of young men to hear him, and that a rich blessing from the great Master of assemblies still accompanied these efforts to arrest and save those who were in the height of their health and youth, and were, like the prodigal, living upon husks fit only for swine, in a country that was far from their heavenly Father's house. Through the earnest and pointed appeals of the preacher, many a spendthrift, fast young man, and lapsing drunkard, was led to exclaim, " I will arise and go to my Father."

The Young Men's Christian Associations in our cities, and even in small towns, were often the agency which invited him to come and hold a series of meetings in their districts, and it is both a touching and a striking proof of the abiding character of his work upon those impressed, that in perusing the letters from the secretaries of these associations, the eye from time to time is attracted to a P.S., marked private, in which, after conveying the official invitation of the society over which he presided, the writer adds some such words as these, " Though I have never met you, it may interest you to know that you were the means of bringing me to the knowledge of Christ in such a place, so many years ago."

ADDRESSES TO STUDENTS OF THE UNIVERSITIES.

It may be interesting to relate something of the addresses which, by special invitation, he delivered to the students of our Universities on more than one occasion. Mr. North is one of the few preachers, whether clerical or lay, who have enjoyed the great opportunity of addressing on the subject of their soul's eternal interests, at the most critical and important period of their lives, the young men who were preparing to fill the various learned professions of the land.

In Glasgow, during the revival of 1859-60, arrangements were made for a series of meetings, specially intended for students; and Mr. North was asked to address several of these. The late Rev. Alexander Andrew kindly communicated to us his recollection of these addresses.

" The meetings were largely attended, and the impressions made upon many were most wholesome. I can recall some of the earnest utterances of the good man at this hour, how he told us to beware of becoming *cumberers of the ground*, for such we would certainly be, if we ventured forward to the holy ministry unconverted. With great vividness he pictured the case of a man occupying some pulpit and some corner of the vineyard, who knew not the Lord, and preached not His gospel, how he not only failed himself to bring light and blessing into the hearts of his people, but prevented, by his presence there, some one from coming in who would be a means of blessing. ' Oh, beware,' he said, ' of being *cumberers of the ground*!'

" Then I think I still see the flashes of indignation that came from him as he spoke of such as only sought to enter the gospel ministry for the sake of social position and a comfortable stipend. He seemed specially anxious that we, as students and aspirants to such a sacred office, should guard against a worldly spirit.

" It was faithful dealing, and when followed and wound up as it generally was with rare touches of pathos, expressed in the yearning and tremulous tones of his voice, and sometimes too in his tears, hardly any one seemed to leave without being more or less impressed with this, that the man was really in downright earnest for the conversion of souls, and particularly for the conversion of those who might largely be the means of converting others.

" The great day alone will fully declare the good that was done among the *alumni* of our Glasgow University by the burning words of Mr. Brownlow North."

It was several years after this that Mr. North was asked to

address the students of the Edinburgh University. During the session already referred to as having been remarkable for a spiritual movement in the Glasgow College, a movement of a similar character, and perhaps still more extensive, had taken place among the students in Aberdeen, under the simple and loving presentation of the gospel by the late Mr. Reginald Radcliffe, of Liverpool. As the result of this awakening, the students there who had been led to Christ formed a prayer-meeting among themselves in the spring of 1859; and at the opening of the following winter session, if we recollect aright, they sent to the students of the Edinburgh University a very winning and faithful brotherly address, which was printed and circulated largely among us, urging those who were undecided to come to the Lamb of God who taketh away the sin of the world, and suggesting to those who were on the Lord's side that they should organize prayer-meetings among themselves for the maintenance of their spiritual life, and for the conversion of their fellow-students. Accordingly, a few of us met together, and resolved at once to begin a meeting strictly for prayer and reading of the Scriptures among ourselves. It was begun with much fear and trembling. Most of us were junior students, and had never spoken to one another on the subject of religion at all, far less had we ever engaged in public prayer. We asked Professor Campbell Swinton for the use of the Civil Law class-room, as it was one of the smallest and most suitable for our purpose, and it was at once granted in the kindest manner. The meeting which was held weekly, on Saturday mornings, became a rallying-place for those who were seeking to follow the Lord, and was very helpful to us in the Christian life. Among those who most regularly attended it, and who have since been called to the church of the firstborn above, were such bright and beautiful Christians as Arthur R. W. Rainey, Andrew Moody-Stuart, and Thomas M. Mure; who were followers of the Lamb, of that pure, healthy, winning, and at the same time decided and manly type of piety which has such a stimulating and helpful influence upon others. Occasionally we asked one of the Professors or one of the ministers in the town to address us.

In the hope of influencing some of the more careless of our fellow-students, Mr. North was asked and agreed to address us on the first Saturday in March, 1862; and as we foresaw that the Civil Law class-room might prove too small, we applied to Professor Miller for the use of his Surgery class-room, which he at once gladly granted to us. Our modest weekly notice of our meeting, this time with the name of Brownlow North on it, attracted attention, and was once or twice torn down. Understanding that opposition was brewing, we sent a deputation to the learned Principal, Sir David Brewster, asking his sanction for the use of the Surgery class-room, which he at once accorded, at the same time warning us that if the matter were brought up in the Senatus, he could not secure us possession of the room, as he had only a casting vote. One or two of the Professors determined to oppose and put down the meeting, and a very hot and acrimonious discussion was held in the Senatus on the subject, some of the members of that grave body being very hostile to the proposed service. The result was, that the defenders of the interests of the students' prayer-meeting were overborne, and the meeting, which had been intimated with Professor Miller's sanction and the Principal's approval, was interdicted. The lecturers of the Royal College of Surgeons, close to the University, hearing of our repulse, sent over on Thursday, and kindly placed their largest class-room at our disposal. Their offer was most thankfully accepted, and accordingly we assembled there at the appointed hour. We had feared that the meeting after all might be a small one, as the number of really earnest students was few, but the opposition had acted as the best of advertisements, and the class-room was choked to its utmost capacity, many students being unable to gain admittance. In consequence of this, we were obliged once more to adjourn to a neighbouring church (Free Roxburgh), which was opened for us. It had been feared that the speaker's voice might be drowned by such unseemly disturbances of cheering, hooting, and pea-throwing, as often interrupted the Principal in delivering the very valuable and interesting addresses which graced the opening and the close of each academical session. But even during the impatient interval of waiting in the class-room, there were only one or two faint attempts made to " ruff in " the speaker, which were promptly suppressed by a general hush, and after the address began in the church, the silence and solemnity were complete.

Professor (afterwards Sir James) Simpson took the chair, and in a few earnest and thoughtful sentences introduced the preacher. " Why have you asked Mr. Brownlow North to address you? I believe the simple answer to that question is this, that many of you are aware that by God's grace, and under God's hand, Mr. North has been the happy instrument of arousing the attention of many to the important matter of religion; and you students must ever remember that of all truths you have to consider that is the most tremendous, because it bears not only on the concerns of this life, but on your joy or misery, your salvation or ruin through eternity. Mr. North has been blessed in an extraordinary manner, in expounding the doctrine of our redemption by Jesus Christ, a doctrine which is perhaps rejected by many because it is in itself so essentially simple."

He then read a passage from Dr. Chalmers' Lectures on Divinity, in which he quoted with assent a remark of his departed friend Robert Hall, that the majority of evangelical ministers do not know how to lay down the gospel so that a man of plain and ordinary understanding should know how to take it up.

After prayer by the Rev. Dr. Guthrie, Mr. North rose and gave an account of his own conversion, in the words in which it has been recorded in our opening chapter, and then delivered a very impressive address from Psalm cxix. 9, " Wherewithal shall a young man cleanse his way? By taking heed thereto according to Thy word." The impression produced was deep and solemn, and we cannot doubt bore lasting fruit. Certainly many students found great help from his clear and decided teaching, during that and other winters in Edinburgh, and could give testimony similar to that of the Rev. Robert Howie, so prominent in the great work of Church extension in Glasgow, who writes, " I remember well how deeply I was impressed when as a student I heard him for the first time.

He made me feel as if I were moving among unseen realities, and on each successive occasion as I listened to his appeals I derived a similar benefit to my own soul."

Ten years later, in May 1873, he addressed the undergraduates of Cambridge University. None but University men were admitted, and it was said that about a fourth of the whole University attended. There was every evidence of a deep impression.

We shall now turn from reviewing his addresses to crowded meetings of University men, and record the results of a visit to one of our most esteemed Scottish noble families, that of the Earl of Aberdeen.

The recollections were kindly given by the Dowager Countess of Aberdeen in a letter to Mr. James Balfour.

VISIT TO HADDO HOUSE IN 1863.
"17 CROMWELL ROAD, S.W., *Jan. 22nd*, 1878.

" Mr. North returned at the end of January, 1863, to be present at the marriage of our eldest daughter and her cousin, Walter Scott, and afterwards visited us again during that year, the last of my husband's life. My husband had a very sincere regard, and I may say a warm affection for him, and, as you know, joined most heartily in the plan for providing him with a place of repose to which he might occasionally retire from his laborious work, which was afterwards carried out in the purchase of the 'Knoll.' At the same time he saw very clearly, and deeply regretted, some weaknesses in his character which he thought injured his usefulness, and did not hesitate to tell him his opinion; but he did this so gently and tenderly that Mr. North, far from taking his faithfulness amiss, expressed his gratitude to him for having spoken so plainly, and their friendship continued unaltered to the last.

" Of late years I saw but little of Mr. North; but on the occasion of his last visit to Haddo House, in the autumn of 1873, I was struck with the mellowed, subdued, and very spiritual tone of his mind. He seemed both more heavenly-minded and more humble than ever before, and though in weak health, and suffering from other causes of depression, he was still full of sympathy for the sorrows and trials of his friends, and I feel sure that he never failed to remember them in prayer. I was deeply impressed by the way in which he turned the subject of common conversation to advantage.

"Believe me, yours very truly, M. ABERDEEN."

Mr. North was in very many cases useful to those who have since in a public capacity proved a means of blessing to others. The Rev. Robert Howie says, " On making inquiry I have been particularly struck by the numbers of those now taking a prominent part in evangelistic work who speak of Mr. North as the means, in the hand of the Divine Spirit, of their conversion."

We have already seen that he was blessed among students, and we may also state that at least in several cases he was made the instrument of the conversion of ministers in the charge of souls, who had been preaching a Saviour of whom personally they had no knowledge.

WORK IN FREE ST. LUKE'S, EDINBURGH.

Winter after winter following on his first visit to Edinburgh in 1857, Mr. North preached in Free St. Luke's Church, and was made the means of blessing to many souls within its walls. Many of those to whom he was blessed were regular adherents of the congregation, but many also belonged to different congregations and denominations in the city. The church, located in a central situation in the new town, and seating, when all the galleries are thrown open, nearly 1,500 people, was peculiarly well adapted for such audiences as Mr. North attracted to it; while the fact that the congregation contained a large number of very devoted and experienced Christian people, who gave themselves to earnest wrestling with the great Master of assemblies for a blessing on the word published by his servant, furnishes a key to explain the abundant blessing which descended upon this place of worship, which had previously, under the rich and searching ministrations of the stated pastor, Dr. Moody-Stuart, been made the birthplace of many souls. A lady, who has long carried on a good work in the Female Industrial Home at Corstorphine, had asked Mr. North to go out and address the inmates in the year 1863, when he was holding services in St. Luke's. On the day and hour fixed, the coachman who had been sent to convey him there at two o'clock one Saturday returned with an empty carriage, and a message to say he was sorry to disappoint his friends, but the Lord had given him work in town, and there were so many anxious souls calling to converse with him, that he dared not come away and leave them. About seventy anxious inquirers had called to see him that Saturday forenoon. Next day he apologized to Miss Maitland for his failure to fulfil his engagement, and said, " I don't know how it was, but it was something I had said on Friday evening about 'grace and peace' that broke them down. I had said, 'You are all wanting peace, but you won't humble yourselves to take grace; but remember, grace and peace are just like the steam-engine and the train; attached the one to the other, the engine *must* go first, and then the train follows: you must have grace, the forgiveness of sin, *or you can never have true peace.*' "

We shall here give in his own words the experience of one who received a blessing from the message of this preacher in this church.

" I was a boy of about sixteen years of age when I heard Mr. North for the first time. Years have passed since then, but I remember distinctly his voice and appearance. His address was the most solemn I had ever heard, and it produced a deep impression upon me. Had he actually been within the pearly gates of the celestial city, had he seen with those solemn eyeballs the dread abode of the doomed, the pictures he drew could not have seemed more real, nor the earnestness of his appeals been greater. The language, which was unmistakably that of conviction, was rendered more forcible by his manner of delivery. Not only his voice, but every feature of his face, revealed the urgency of his message. I had never doubted that there were such places as heaven and hell, yet I had never so far believed in them as to let their existence affect my life. At the conclusion of that address, I believed that hell existed, and I further believed that

I was in danger of going there. An aunt who was with me (she had persuaded me to go that evening) noticed that I did not look quite as usual, and asked if I should like to see Mr. North. I said, ' Yes, I should;' and it was arranged that I should see him the following day. If the evening before I had been awed by his solemnity, this time I was touched by his kindness and his solicitude about my soul. He seemed more anxious about it than I was myself. He spent some little time in explaining my difficulties, then he prayed with me, evincing at every stage such a sense of the preciousness of my soul as was new and striking to me. The apprehension of the dangers and temptations he foresaw I should be exposed to, seemed to affect him much. When we rose from our knees, he embraced me tenderly, and I left him, thanking God for the opportunity He had given me."

This gentleman afterwards engaged abroad in arduous and successful work for the Saviour.

Visits to Durie House, Fifeshire.

Mr. North on several occasions visited the late Charles Christie, Esq., of Durie, and of these visits Miss Christie kindly sent the following recollections :—

" Mr. North on several occasions visited our country home, and preached in various places around. A brother of ours, who had been seeking the Lord for some time, received much blessing, and wrote to a friend that Mr. North ' had helped him to a clear view of the imputed righteousness.' A warm friendship followed between them. In grateful affection he used to call him ' Bishop North.'

" A lady was much struck by his inquiring of her, ' How many have you led to Jesus Christ since you were brought to him yourself?' And another, after hearing him preach, wrote thus, ' I feel like a horse with the spur in his side ever since I heard Mr. North.' More than one of our servants was seriously impressed; and we recall also how earnestly he sought to improve the occasion to us all, when a dear relative of ours was suddenly called away by death.

" His faithfulness and fervour we cannot forget, and with

this is entwined the recollection of a frank and cordial kindliness that must ever endear his memory."

Another correspondent writes:—

" In private life I never saw him ' off duty '; he was always ready to say a word in season. Where his geniality opened the way, his watchful fidelity seized many an opportunity of winning a soul. It may also be mentioned that not only did he never on any occasion omit family worship and exposition in his own house, whatever company he might have at dinner, but that when away from home, staying in hotels or lodgings, he always told the landlord or landlady that he had worship at a certain hour, and that he would be happy if they, their servants, or visitors, would join him in his room at that time. These invitations used to be gratefully accepted, and good was done in several instances through this instrumentality. Only a month or two before his death, his family worship was made a means of blessing to the family of his landlady in a sea-coast town, where he was staying in lodgings."

Multitudes of calls, and crowded halls and churches, never led Mr. North to neglect the simplest means of communicating the knowledge of Christ, such means as are within the reach of the humblest follower of the Lamb.

Regarding his manner of conducting family worship, Mr. Balfour said,—

" There were some who preferred Mr. North's ministrations at family worship even to those in the pulpit. They thought him less excited. And certainly he was often tender, solemn, and striking in these small domestic gatherings. I remember once in a house where several had been asked to meet him, he began by opening the Bible and saying, ' None of you know where I am going to read to-night, do you?' Then he paused. ' No, you don't, and you never will till I tell you. I am going to read in 1 Corinthians. But again you don't know what chapter.' A pause. ' I am going to read the 1st chapter of 1 Corinthians. Now you know, because I have told you. You did not find it out of yourselves. There is not one of you clever enough to do this; you only know because I have told you. And this is the principle upon which the apostle's argument in this chapter proceeds. He says, " The world by wisdom knew not God." None of the princes of this world knew that Jesus was the Lord of glory, or they would not have crucified Him. God was determined that no man should find Him out by his own wisdom. A few, not many, wise men did find Him out, but not by their own wisdom. They had to become babes first, and then it was revealed to them; " but God hath revealed them unto us by His Spirit; for the Spirit searcheth all things, yea, the deep things of God. For what man knoweth the things of a man, save the spirit of man which is in him? even so the things of God knoweth no man but the Spirit of God." ' He then proceeded to expound the first two chapters of the epistle in a very interesting and lucid manner."

Another friend writes : —

" His habit was to conduct our family worship in the evening. This was done in a manner singularly pleasant and profitable. His exposition of Scripture showed he was a man of genius, with deep knowledge of human nature, and who had made a study of the Bible. His application of the truth was remarkably direct, and his prayers were full, though simple; short, so as not to weary; direct, as if speaking to God."

CHAPTER XII

Remarkable Cases of Impression and Conversion

NOT a few of the cases in which Mr. North was made instrumental in awakening sinners to a sense of their danger, in detecting the delusions or errors that were keeping them from the enjoyment of peace, in leading them to the great Saviour, or to entrance into the full light and liberty of the children of God, were of a remarkable character. A narrative of some of these may prove useful to others. Cases, the idiosyncrasy of which appears striking, often turn out on closer study to be typical, and to bear a representative character. Even where this is not so, their recital may serve to exalt our ideas of the attractiveness of Christ, the power of the Holy Spirit, and the fertility of resource employed by Him in arresting and saving those who are going down to destruction.

THE TEACHER'S DAUGHTER.

Mary Ann Whyte was the daughter of a schoolmaster in Inverness-shire, who died before she reached her eighteenth year, rejoicing in the Saviour who had redeemed her by His blood, and enlightened her by His Spirit. She had been religiously trained, and had not been without spiritual impressions, and for nearly a year, ever since the death of her mother, she had been seeking Christ. It was in this state of mind that she heard Mr. North preach on one occasion early in his ministry. Referring to that occasion, she said, " I can tell you the time and place when and where Christ manifested His love to me, and caused me to love Him with an everlasting love; that was the evening on which I heard Mr. North in Inverness; his text was, ' Wilt thou go with this man? ' (Gen. xxiv. 58). I thought when he was, in the course of his sermon, opening up the character of the Man Jesus, and showing forth his matchless love to fallen sinners, that my heart was correspondingly opening; but when, in the application, he called out as with the voice of God, ' Here, here! The Lord of heaven, the wonder of angels, the delight of saints, and the desire of nations is now offering Himself freely to you as your all in all for time and eternity. O will you take Him, *take Him*, TAKE HIM? This may be the last offer you may have of Him. Will you let Him go? O don't! '—I thought my soul was one flame of love to Him. I would not, I could not, I did not let Him go. I know those who were about me were noticing my state; but I could not contain myself. I was overcome with love—love that constrained me to love Him, and since then till now, and, I believe, to all eternity, I can think of none but Himself. Oh, His love is written deep here (laying her hand on her heart), and as a token of His love to me He will soon grant me my desire, and that is, that where He is, there I may be also."

She frequently reverted to that day of her espousals, and wondered if there could be one soul there that could let such a glorious offer pass. The last time she was out at church, that sermon was her theme going and returning. She cherished the most Christian affection for Mr. North, although she never saw nor heard him afterwards.

The late Rev. Andrew A. Bonar, D.D., of Glasgow, kindly communicated to us the following interesting case which came under his notice in his own congregation, and which took place at Mr. North's first visit to Glasgow.

THE SILENT INQUIRER.

Under his preaching in Finnieston Free Church, a young woman was awakened, one who had been well taught and was outwardly blameless. Her conviction of sin was very deep; she was weighed down under the burden. One evening she sought out the house where Mr. North was staying, and asked to see him. She was at once taken to him, and sitting down near him she covered her face with her hand, not uttering one word. Mr. North waited, expecting that she would speak; but all was silence, tears running down her cheeks, and her whole demeanour conveying the impression that she was in profound concern. Still not a word escaped her lips. Mr. North began to try to draw out her mind for her, by such remarks as, "I suppose you are anxious?" "I suppose you have come to speak with me because you are anxious?" But still there was no response. He then said, "You know I can be of no use to you if I do not know your state of mind. Tell me something of what you feel." Even now no reply came, and Mr. North gazed for a minute at the figure before him—a most earnest inquirer, her face buried in her hand, and her frame full of emotion. At length he resumed his attempt to fathom her state of mind. "I need not try to speak to you unless you speak to me. I must just let you go away. But at least answer me this question, *Do you believe there is a God?*" When he had pressed this question, the hand fell from the face, and he got this reply, "Sir, if I did not believe there was a God, I would not be anxious about my soul!" Mr. North at once responded, "Oh, now I understand you. You are troubled because you have to do with God—God, who is a holy and a just God. Let us speak of this." The ice was broken; he had got a look into her heart and conscience, and she was led on to indicate more; nor was it long before she had seen that "God is in Christ, reconciling the world to Himself," and that God accepts the sinner who accepts the Beloved Son in whom He is well pleased.

GIVEN UP BY THE LORD.

Dr. Samuel Miller, to whom we have been already indebted for an account of a striking conversion, has recalled another interesting case. On one occasion when Mr. North was staying in Glasgow, and had been preaching for him in Free St. Matthew's Church, he came one afternoon into Dr. Miller's study, and asked him to go out with him for a walk, as he was very much tired and fagged. On Dr. Miller's inquiring what had worn him out, he said that he had been engaged all day in seeing persons in private who were in a state of spiritual concern, and had just finished a conversation with a lady, which had lasted for an hour and a half. On Dr. Miller's inquiring what was the nature of her difficulty, Mr. North said that she had been in the deepest distress, saying that the Lord had given her up. "Well, and did she find peace at last? " " Yes, she did, and it was from what I said to her almost at random." "What was that? " " Well her burden was that the Lord had given her up, and would not hear her prayer. So I asked her, ' Are you a believer? Have you placed your trust in Christ? ' ' Yes.' 'And the Lord has given you up? ' ' Yes.' ' Then either you or He must be a liar. Are you telling a lie just now, when you say you have placed your trust in Christ? ' ' No, certainly not.' ' Then the Lord must be a liar; and in that case, if I were you, I would give Him up.' ' Oh, but I can't give Him up, sir.' ' Why not, if He is a liar? ' ' I can't give Him up.' ' Ah!' I said, 'that is because the Lord has not given you up. It's because He is keeping hold of you.' " These words were the means of at once bringing her to peace.

One of Mr. North's characteristics was great shrewdness and quickness of perception, which both kept him from being easily deceived as to the character and condition of those who came to open their mind to him, and enabled him to adapt his counsel to the spiritual state of each soul.

The next case is one which occurred early in Mr. North's ministry, and one to which he often referred.

WHY DID GOD PERMIT SIN?

At the close of one of his services in Edinburgh, a young man asked to speak with him, and was admitted to the side-room, where he was meeting with anxious inquirers. Addressing Mr. North, he said." I have heard your sermon, sir, and I have heard you preach often, now; and I neither care for you nor your preaching, unless you can tell me, why did God permit sin in the world? " " Then I'll tell you," the preacher at once replied; " God permitted sin, because He chose to do so." The man was taken aback by the ready retort, which threw no light on the subject of his question, and yet expressed all the conclusion which the deepest thinkers on that mysterious subject have been able to arrive at, referring it as an unsolved enigma to the Divine good pleasure, which permitted it for reasons altogether wise, but not revealed to us, and to a large extent inscrutable. "Because He chose it," he repeated, as the objector stood speechless, and added, "If you continue to question and cavil at God's dealings, and vainly puffed up by your carnal mind strive to be wise above what is written, I will tell you something more that God will choose to do. He will some day choose to put you into hell. It is vain, sir, for man to strive with his Maker; you cannot resist Him; and neither your opinion of His dealings, nor your blasphemous expression of them, will in the least lessen the pain of your everlasting damnation, which will most certainly be your portion if you go on in your present spirit. There were such questioners as you in Paul's time, and what the Apostle said to them I say to you, 'Nay, but, O man, who art thou that repliest against God?'" The young man interrupted him, and asked, "Is there such a text, sir, as that in the Bible?" "Yes, there is, in the ninth chapter of Romans; and I recommend you to go home and read that chapter, and after you have read it, and learned from His own word that God claims for Himself the right to do whatever He chooses, and does not permit the thing formed to say to Him that formed it, Why hast Thou made me thus?—to remember that, besides permitting sin, there is another thing God has chosen to do— *God chose to send Jesus.*" He then in a few words pointed out to him the way of salvation both from sin and wrath which God had prepared of His own free and sovereign will, and urged him to embrace it.

The following Friday, when sitting in my father's drawing-room, the servant announced that a young man wanted to speak to him. On being shown upstairs, he asked Mr. North if he remembered him, but he could not recall who he was. "Do you not remember the young man who on Sunday night asked you to tell him why God permitted sin?" "Yes, perfectly." "Well, sir, I am that young man; and you said that

God permitted sin because He chose it, and you told me to go home and read the ninth chapter of Romans, and you also told me that God chose to send Jesus to die for such sinners as I was, and I went home and did, sir, what you told me." He said he had gone home, and after reading that chapter, which so many find a stumbling-block, he had pleaded for pardon in the name of Jesus, and for the gift of the Holy Spirit to be his teacher, and was afterwards enabled to believe that he had been heard and forgiven, and now he said, " I am happy, oh, so happy, sir; and though the devil comes some- times to tempt me with my old thoughts, and to ask me what *reason* I have to think God has forgiven me, I have always managed to get him away by telling him that I do not want to judge things any longer by my own reason but by God's word, and that the only reason why I know I am forgiven is that, for Christ's sake, God chooses to pardon me." Mr. North added that the changed expression of the young man's coun- tenance was enough to account for his not knowing him again, as it was radiant with joy and peace.

Mr. James Balfour of Edinburgh narrated this incident, of which Mr. North had given him the particulars, to Principal Cunningham shortly after its occurrence. He listened with deep attention and interest, and said, " That shows me North knows what he is about."

Miss Maitland, a lady long well known in Edinburgh for her successful philanthropic and Christian work, kindly com- municated the particulars of the two following cases :—

ARE YOU WILLING TO GIVE UP THE WORLD?

Mr. North came to luncheon with us in the country. He was living at a friend's house near Scotscraig. He told us that he had had an intimation of a death that morning, and then he gave us the following particulars of this young lady's con- version. She had been one who came for conversation at the house referred to. He said, whenever she entered the room, her appearance impressed him that she was not thoroughly in earnest for salvation, so he just said, " Madam, are you willing to give up the world for Christ?" " Oh, no," she said, " I cannot say that; but what you said last night has troubled me and made me somewhat anxious." "Oh, madam," said he, "it would be mockery for you to go to the Lord Jesus, and say to Him, you want Him to come and dwell in your heart when there is anything else you are preferring to Him. I could not, I dare not, pray with you in these circumstances." She rose and turned haughtily, but sadly, to go away. "Think," he said to her as she was going towards the door, "what these idols, that you are now preferring to Christ, can do for you at your dying hour; and remember, I will be delighted to see you back again when you have decided to take Christ as your Lord and Saviour." She left, and he said he scarcely expected to see her again, for she was young and handsome, and it was something for her to give up the world. Four days afterwards the door opened, and the same lady appeared, but so pale and broken-down-like, that he scarcely knew her. "Oh, Mr. North, I have had an awful struggle, a terrible time since I saw you. I have just come to ask whether you think Christ will take me." "It was easy work then," he said, "so we went to the Lord, and got the matter settled. At the former visit the question was, Would she take Christ? no, she was not willing to do that; but when the question came to be, Was the Lord willing to take her, as a poor hell-deserving sinner? then all the difficulty was removed, for Jesus Christ came to save sinners." About a week after this, Mr. North met her in the street, her face beaming with joy. "I was just coming to tell you," she said, "what joy and peace I have found in believing. I had more pleasure in an hour's communion with my dear Lord last night than ever I had in all the pleasures of the world put together." She joined the weekly class for Bible instruction, and was known to some of our young friends attending it as a consistent Christian, and as an earnest devoted student of the Word. When Mr. North finished the little narrative, he said. "It is her death that I have an intimation of this morning. A friend writes that she was taken suddenly ill, had burst a blood vessel, and died in about ten minutes. Oh," he continued, "was it not well for her that she had chosen Christ and not the world as her portion?"

The next narrative is that of the conversion of a young woman, named Marianne ——.

THE STORY OF MARIANNE ——.

Marianne was wont to be thoughtless and light-hearted, full of youthful frolic and nonsense, enjoying the vanities, follies, and pleasures of the world. But at the same time she maintained a respectable form of religion, and thought herself not worse than her neighbours.

About two years before her conversion, she was much impressed by a remarkable dream. She dreamed that she was seated on a jutting point of rock, near a hill-top. She was in great terror, for the stone on which she sat was rocking, and there was a bottomless abyss below. On the top stood the Lord Jesus, whom she entreated to help her out of her perilous situation; but He only shook His head, as if He said emphatically, "No!" She cried, "Oh, take me up." He again refused. She remembered no more, until she found herself in heaven, among legions of holy angels; and the Lord again appeared, and as He passed gave an approving smile, and said, "You're come." Her soul warmed towards Him as He passed. She thought this dream was a warning from God that she should leave her folly; and it made a temporary impression, which by and by wore away.

About a year afterwards, she was spending a Friday evening thoughtlessly in the theatre, when the above dream rushed into her mind, and terrified her. On the Lord's-day following, a companion asked her to go and hear Mr. North preach. She had intended to go out to walk; but it rained, and she went to church. His text was, "Wilt thou go with this man?" She was struck to the heart by the discourse, and burst into tears when she heard the words, "The blood of Jesus Christ His Son cleanseth us from all sin." As she was going home, she told her friend that she felt herself a lost sinner. He said that it was all excitement, and she should not go back or listen to Mr. North any more. She felt that what had been said was all true, and that she was righteously condemned by the holy law of God, and she defended Mr. North's preaching.

For three days she was in deep distress, and those about her wondered at her unwonted dulness and seriousness, and asked her what was the matter? They were continually trying to divert her attention, and one of the girls took her round the waist, and said, " Marianne, come away, and cheer up, and let us have a laugh as we used to have." " But, oh, I feel I am a lost sinner," said she; " and how can I be happy? " " Never mind," said they : " you should come away, and cheer up, and try to enjoy yourself." She listened to their enticing words, and went with them, although much against her conscience. They sang the cheerful song, and raised the merry laugh, and tried to charm away the melancholy of Marianne's soul, and, sad to say, they succeeded. The Holy Spirit was quenched, and she had no more spiritual anxiety for the next twelve months.

Mr. North returned to Edinburgh, and preached again, in another church, on " Wilt thou go with this man? " Marianne heard him, and her anxiety of soul returned with re-doubled force. Her feelings overcame her, and she cried out in church, and flung her head on the book-board in great agony of mind. She spoke to Mr. North at the second meeting; but was too much agitated to listen to a single word of what was spoken to her, and went home in despair. In the morning she went as usual to her work, but was in such agony of mind that she could scarcely do anything but weep. For seven days there was hardly a word spoken in the work-room, but an awfully solemn impression rested on all about her. Not being able to restrain her feelings one day, she retired into another department to weep and cry for mercy. On her return she cried aloud, " O Lord, will you not hear my cry? " and turning to those around her, she asked, with impassioned eagerness, " Is there none here who can speak to me about Jesus? "

They were all professors; but they made no reply. She thought that she would be obliged to give up her situation, if her prayers remained unanswered; for she was quite unfit to do anything, her soul's anguish was so dreadful, and she feared she would go deranged. She knew salvation was in the Bible, and she must get it there, but although she sought for it, she could not find it.

Her sister, on coming in and seeing her one day weeping and in great distress, asked her if she had had a letter that their brother was dead. "No," she replied; "but I'm dead myself—I'm lost!" When left alone she fell before her Bible, which was open at St. John, third chapter; a blindness came over her, and she cried out in agony, "O blessed Jesus, give me sight to see." At that moment she felt a sensation as if a hand were removing her burden of sin. Then, in a sort of vision, she beheld the Saviour in three positions—extended on the cross, kneeling in prayer, and then in glorious white garments smiling upon her. Her joy was now so great, that she felt as if she could have laughed and wept at the same time, but could do neither. But on her knees she burst out into earnest thanksgiving and praise, and then cried to the Lord for the salvation of her relatives and friends; and her sister coming in, she dragged her down upon her knees, that she might get saved too. Jeannie said, "There's a time for everything, and you are going too far with your religion;" but she knelt, and after prayer left in silence. Jeannie was impressed by it, but was not brought to the Lord at that time.

Marianne had now passed from death into life. She had obtained pardon of sin and the peace of God, and she felt joyful and happy. Her bodily health returned, and she resumed her employment. But on hearing the trifling conversation of those about her respecting ministers and sermons, and feeling that all their talk was soulless and empty, she could not help crying out in the work-room among them. "O fools, what if your souls should be required of you while you are talking about religion, and forgetting the name of Jesus? I have found Him, and He is my Saviour." Two girls were so much impressed by what she said, that they left the room in tears. And as she continued to talk to her fellow-workers of the precious Redeemer from day to day, one said, "Oh, this is miserable! I'm going to give in my warning on Saturday, for I cannot bear this." Another said, "All our pleasure is gone now, since Marianne has become serious." But twelve of them were somewhat awakened, and some of them gave evidence of being truly converted. Mr. North exhorted her to live and work for Jesus, and she commenced at once, and went on working for the Lord Jesus with all her might, and He greatly blessed her efforts.

Mr. Radcliffe was preaching on the street near Holyrood Palace one night, and at the close invited the people to accompany him into a neighbouring church. Marianne was there giving tracts to the people in the street, and entreating them to go and hear the gospel. A group of careless, hard-visaged men rudely refused; still she stood pleading with them, weeping as she spoke. As the tears rushed from her eyes, she wiped them away with the skirt of her dress, and continued to urge them to come in. A Christian standing near was so overcome by seeing her deep religious feeling, and burning zeal for Christ, and compassion for souls, that he said to his wife, " I cannot stand this any longer. I *must* go and help this dear girl with these hardened men;" and he went up to them, and prevailed on them to enter the church.

What effect this had on these men we know not; but the earnest creature's tears and entreaties had a very powerful influence on this Christian brother, and they were the seeds of the " Carrubber's Close Mission," a mission that has been blessed to very many souls.

Marianne was there almost every night for twelve months; and received grace to lead many souls to Christ. Mr. Jenkinson said quaintly to a lady one day, after the work had gone on for a long time, " She *sews* all day, and *reaps* all night, and she is sure to kill herself; for her zeal for the glory of Jesus and the salvation of souls is consuming her." The lady had it laid upon her heart to employ her as a missionary, in which work she was much blessed; and she is now, we understand, the wife of a minister of the gospel in England.

THE DUTCH AMBASSADOR.

In order to recruit from the effects of over-work in the midst of his arduous labours, Mr. North was ordered by his medical advisers, on one or two successive seasons, to try the waters and baths of Schwalbach. As he was never idle, but was always engaged in actively serving the Lord, except when quite prostrated, he took the opportunity of giving one or more addresses to the numerous English visitors, and foreigners who understood English, who frequented that fashionable watering-place. On one of these occasions, he gave his address on Gen. xxiv. 58, "Wilt thou go with this man?" Among other notabilities who were present was the Dutch ambassador to one of the Continental courts, who seemed to be impressed with what he heard. Next day Mr. North met a party on the public promenade, among whom was the above gentleman, to whom he was introduced, and who seemed glad to make his acquaintance. As they were saying farewell, Mr. North touched him on the shoulder, and looking into his earnest eyes said, "Wilt *thou* go with this man?" to which the ambassador promptly replied in his foreign accent, "*Most positively.*" He proved himself to be a true convert and disciple of Christ, and in gratitude got several of Mr. North's tracts translated into Dutch, that he might circulate them in his own country.

It was, if we mistake not, on the very same occasion and by the same sermon, that some persons of still higher rank were deeply impressed. We are able to give this incident in Mr. North's own words, written at the time to a friend in England:

"SCHWALBACH, NASSAU, *July 17th*, 1862.

"I have great news to tell you about what has been happening here since I came. First of all, I was greatly surprised to find Lord and Lady Kintore here, dear Christian friends of mine, and also a Mr. and Mrs. Mahoney, and Mr. Jenkinson, the Vicar of Battersea. I could not help thinking the Lord had brought us all together for some special purpose. And so I think still. It was arranged that I should give an address in Lord Kintore's room. It was crowded. Many were in tears, and after it was over a Prussian general and aide-de-camp to the emperor, and his sister, came to speak to me; also a Dutchman, chamberlain to the king of Holland. Finding Kintore's rooms too small, we took the large room in the hotel for the next week; this was also filled, and amongst the hearers the three Princesses of ——, whose brother is next heir to the throne of ——. After the service, they asked to be introduced to me, and I had an opportunity of giving them some tracts, which they took. They afterwards sent Lord Kintore to my rooms to ask me for more tracts to get them translated into German, and since then they have sent to ask me to go and see them, five miles off from here, and I have been, and had a most interesting conversation with their old mother, the good Duchess. All this is remarkable, for where may not these foreigners carry the seed? They were in again at the meeting on Tuesday, and are to be, God willing, on Friday. I feel all this is of the Lord. Oh may He keep me out of myself and in Christ, and work by me and in me, that I may bring him great glory and do great good. . . . I do think I am better and stronger, though of course this work is hardly giving the waters a fair chance. Still it is too valuable to be missed, and I cannot but think I was brought here to do it."

Many of the letters which Mr. North received gave curious glimpses of soul-history, and would interest even those for whom the sensational alone has charms. Here is an outline of one case.

THE BACKWOODSMAN'S CONVERSION.

Soon after leaving school, this young man had plunged into dissipation, vice, and crime, and brought down his father's grey hairs with sorrow to the grave, and had been shipped off to the Antipodes at the age of twenty-one, to get him out of the way. From the date of his landing in the colony until God's sovereign grace awoke him, fifteen years after, he never entered a place of worship, except once to attend an election meeting; he had never bent the knee in prayer since he was seventeen, except when in danger, or sick from debauchery. Divine grace awoke him to concern about his soul, when living in a solitary hut shepherding, and seldom seeing any human being. He sought company, and changed his situation to get it, yet was no happier. One day when his mate had left the hut with his sheep, the thought forced itself upon him, " Now you have often promised to serve the Lord, do so now in earnest." He fell on his knees and poured out a prayer to

God for forgiveness. He had no Bible, but there was in the hut a copy of Mr. North's little book, "Earnest Words," which his mate had received from a pious sister in the old country. He earnestly pored over its pages, and found peace in believing in Jesus. His mate began to study the book, and was awakened. The little book was never out of the hands of either the one or the other; they got a New Testament, read and studied it each night together, until they parted, three months later. And a year later, and then again at a later period, he wrote to thank Mr. North as the instrument under God of his deliverance. He then said that at first, mixing among a motley company of the refuse of Newgate and scions of English nobility, he often hesitated about being found on his knees, but that God strengthened him and enabled him to confess his Saviour among twenty or thirty of the most profligate of men. The mate to whom he referred as being a shepherd, and whose hut he shared, was the heir of an old Scottish baronetcy. He appeared also to be brought to the Lord, but is since dead, and the baronetcy is extinct.

OPPOSITION OVERCOME.

The next case belongs to a later period of Mr. North's ministry. The lady who communicates it is the wife of a member of Parliament, and was brought to the Lord through her sister, of whose conversion Mr. North had been the instrument.

"An incident in connection with a drawing-room meeting which he held in my house, was the conversion of a lady who was bitterly opposed to Mr. North and his teaching, the reason being that I, who used to enjoy with her the frivolities of life, no longer could as a Christian do so, and the blame was laid at Mr. North's door, although he was not the means directly of my conversion. My relative would not come to the house while Mr. North was our guest. Well do I remember when addressing cards of invitation for the drawing-room meeting, I said, 'We need not ask J——, she won't come;' but my husband urged me to do so, saying, 'Ask her; if she does not come, that is her affair. You do your duty.' I did so, and prayed for her much, and she came, heard a full, free gospel, was awakened to a sense of sin and danger, and shortly after, through converse with Mr. North, who held up *Jesus,* she was enabled to believe on him. A week later she was stricken with paralysis, but all was peace and comfort, and she gave a clear testimony of her resting in Jesus."

The cases we have here recorded are narrated not to magnify the servant, but the Master, who in His infinite wisdom devises such varied means to bring his banished back again, and who deigned to employ one who was for long a vessel of wrath, fit only for destruction, as a vessel unto honour so meet for the Master's use, alike in saving the perishing and in conveying clearer views of the grace of Christ to those who had already received it.

CHAPTER XIII

Later Evangelistic Work in Large Towns of England

AFTER having devoted the first ten years of his evangelistic labours chiefly to Scotland, which had become to him a second home, doors of usefulness were opened to Brownlow North in many of the cities and large towns of England, and he felt himself providentially led to preach the gospel of the kingdom widely there. He returned to Scotland chiefly to rest and recruit his exhausted energies, or to fulfil special engagements, such as being present at the Annual Religious Conference in Perth in the month of September of each year.

A considerable portion also of his autumn months of repose he devoted to writing and carrying through the press his various publications, which, though far from being pretentious in their aim, were the result of much prayerful study of the Divine Word, exhibiting a thorough mastery in handling his subject, and as the reader may perceive from the evidences adduced in this volume, have been not only widely circulated, but widely blessed. In addressing the public through the press, as well as from the pulpit or platform, Mr. North was following in the steps of more than one of his ancestors, who had published works and treatises of some worth in their day. The third Lord North, who was the discoverer of the medicinal virtues of Tunbridge Wells, published in 1659 "A Forest promiscuous of several Seasons' Productions." The first Baron Guilford, who was made Solicitor-General in 1671, and was Lord Keeper of the Great Seal, wrote several legal treatises; while the fourth Lord North in 1682 published a volume of essays on such subjects as Light in the Way to Paradise, Truth, Goodness, Eternity and Original Sin.

The earlier years of this decade were largely devoted to England, and were far from fruitless, although from the wider extent of the field, and its distance from the scene of his former labours, it was only the most intimate among his Scottish friends who knew how the Master was owning His servant's unwearied efforts to gather in souls.

In the spring of 1868 he visited Swansea in Wales, whence he wrote:—

" I have to tell of such a meeting! The last day has been the great day of the Feast. Yesterday it was blowing a gale of wind and raining hard at the time of the meeting, and I did not think it possible I could have any people to speak to. Yet, though the storm continued, I found the place crammed, and it is an enormous place. It being the last night, I had determined to have a second address for inquirers. I began, and so far as sympathy goes, I felt that as I warmed the people warmed, and I spoke to an audience that was almost breathless through interest the whole time, for two hours and ten minutes. So far as I can judge I have not spoken so for years, but the issue is with the Lord."

In the spring of the following year he paid a visit to Sunderland, and of the work there he writes:—

" SUNDERLAND, *March* 11*th*, 1869.

" I had a most precious night last night (on the cxlv. Psalm), the congregation quite carried with me. Many ministers there. After speaking for more than an hour I said something about time failing, when two or three voices cried out, ' Go on, go on,' and I went on for half an hour more. There was evident impression, and the ministers were delighted. To God be all the glory!"

In place of giving an account of detached services in different years, we shall give a brief, fragmentary sketch of his labours in one year, that of 1870.

In the spring of this year he held services in Birmingham. He writes on the 3rd March :—

"Last night was wonderful. Loads of young men were unable to get in, and they were just the kind I wanted. Hundreds of them were, I should say, thoroughly 'fast' young men : but they behaved very well; first quiet, then attentive, then solemnized. The only disturbance was from one or two fainting from the heat. I preached in my fur coat! At the end a paper was handed up to me, begging for another address, which I announced for Friday, the 25th, amidst loud cheers, which I stopped. I don't, however, expect to get such another meeting. We shall see. I am rather headachy, as you may imagine after last night. I forgot to say I preached for an hour and a half fully. Too long for speaker or hearers.

"Yours affectionately,
"BROWNLOW NORTH."

Of the closing meeting he was able to write :—

"I must send you a line on my last day in Birmingham, my visit to which I cannot but think has been of much moment to many. Two men have just left me who found me out in consequence of last night's meeting. It was a very remarkable one. The enormous place was full; mostly men—many of quite the rougher sort, who all sat, about 3,000 of them, deeply attentive for over an hour's sermon. I do think good has been done here.

"A man from North Wales wants to translate ' The Rich Man and Lazarus ' into Welsh."

A few days later he was in the midst of equally exciting and engrossing work in London, of which he writes to the late Earl of Kintore :—

LONDON, *March 9th*, 1870.

"MY DEAR OLD FRIEND,—I know that you will be very glad to hear that I had a most encouraging meeting last night, in St. James's Hall. After the service, Sir Thomas Beauchamp got General Russell to introduce him, and told me

that Mr. ——, an old shooting friend of mine, and a large
proprietor in N——shire, had been impressed by one of my
books, and would like to see me, so I agreed to go and dine
with him some day to meet him: then came a young man
into the waiting-room to say I had been the means of saving
his soul when last in London. ' Yes,' said Fishbourne, as the
man left the room, ' and *he* has been the means of saving
hundreds of others since.' All this is very pleasing."

According to the arrangement, he met his old sporting friend
at dinner; and after the ladies left for the drawing-room, Mr.
North began a very personal conversation about spiritual and
eternal things, and got the whole of the gentlemen to bow their
knees together in prayer. His friend was just starting for a
long cruise in his yacht, but came to hear him preach before
he sailed, and seemed much interested in the sermon. Thus
it was that he continued to sow beside all waters, not observing the wind, lest he should stay his hand from sowing the
precious seed, nor considering the clouds, lest he should with-
hold his hand from reaping the precious sheaves. There are
many who are ready to work in a time of revival, who stand
all the day, and day after day, idle in a time of spiritual
apathy. These are little-faiths and little-hopes; but men and
women who are strong in faith and hope will look more to
God's promises than to human probabilities, and as with him
whose work we are recording, their gleanings in the years of
drought will outweigh and outvalue the whole vintage of others
in their years of plenty.

In May, 1870, Brownlow North visited Plymouth for the
first time. Of his work here he thus writes:—

" I do hope a wide-spread impression has been made. The
church, the largest here, was crammed to suffocation; but for
all that the minister, a good man, came up to the pulpit after
the prayer, and told me there was a large crowd outside, and
the doors were locked; so I got up, and asked the congregation to squeeze as close as possible, had them opened, and got
in another hundred. A Church dignitary was preaching
within a hundred yards or so of me, and many of those who
were hearing him in the morning were hearing me in the even-

G

ing. I trust the chapter and verse I was able to show them for what I told them may have dissipated his false teaching. He preaches the wisdom of man."

On leaving he received a long and warm letter of earnest thanks from a young woman for the spiritual blessing he had been the means of conveying to her. The letter is anonymous, but it shows us how the heavenly plant of grace will grow under the most adverse conditions. She writes:—

"My parents are ungodly, living utterly careless of their souls; they do not even pray to God, or say prayers at any time. I never heard them utter a word of prayer in my life. I do not know how to express myself. My soul is over-whelmed with love to Christ. I never felt nor thought in my whole life as I do now, and have ever since I heard you preach of Christ. Yes, I know God our heavenly Father did specially send you to me. You have, by your preaching, thrown fresh life across my mind, you have caused my eyes to open, and my ears to hear, and my heart to understand the boundless love of God towards us, His tenderness and compassion. You have, by the Spirit of the Lord, caused me to understand more of the love of Jesus Christ our Lord; you have caused me to put my whole trust in Jesus, and to cast myself utterly and completely on Him. I shall never, never forget you."

Many persons complained of the hardness and even severity of Brownlow North's preaching, and those who only heard him in public addressing sinners, and warning them to flee from the wrath to come, may not unnaturally have supposed that he looked solely at the terrors of the law, and did not himself fully realize or communicate to others the sweetness and infinite fulness of Divine love. Yet those who read the above letter, and several others in this volume, will find that he was likewise largely used by the Divine spirit in conveying a sweet, assuring, and overpowering sense of Christ's love to broken and contrite hearts. This was especially the case in regard to those with whom he had opportunity of conversing in private; and although, perhaps, it was a more predominant

feature of the later years of his ministry, it was not by any
means confined to these.

We are inclined to think that Mr. North did not quite do
himself justice, or perhaps the children of God either, by confining himself so much as he did to the discourses and the subjects with which he had begun his ministry. In new towns
and districts these continued to the end to be largely blessed,
and probably this made him averse to deliver many new
discourses. It was certainly no indolence that led him to pur-
sue this course, and no inability to work out fresh addresses;
for the three hours of prayer and hard study of the Word of
God by which he began each day are as much time and toil as
most ministers devote to the preparation of two wholly new
sermons each week; and the richness and variety of his original
annotations in his Bible, on almost all the books of Scripture,
attest the freshness of his mental powers, and the successful
results of his constant study. But those who merely heard his
evangelistic addresses, or even perused his published works,
could form but a very imperfect idea of the fulness, the richness, the variety, the tenderness of his meditations on the Word
of God which he gave out in family worship, and which he
committed in a succinct and often epigrammatic form to writing on the interleaved pages and margins of his Bibles.

It was an interesting trait in Mr. North's Christian character,
that while as a natural orator he had a passion, and almost a
weakness, for addressing very large audiences, whom he could
keep spell-bound, hanging upon his lips, he never refused to
go to address a small gathering when he felt that this was a
leading of providence and a call from his Master; and in speaking in the Lord's name to such an assembly as a hospital for
the incurable, or a ship's crew, or a police force, he from time
to time received not a few precious souls for his reward. To
one who once remarked to him, "You must feel it a great
responsibility to address so many thousands," he replied, "I
feel it a great responsibility to address half-a-dozen people."

Mr. North now returned to his home in Elgin, and on Tuesday, the 9th of August, 1870, a public meeting of the inhabitants of Bishopmill (the suburb of Elgin, where his residence

was situated) was convened, to receive from him the gift of a Mission Hall, which he had erected for their benefit, on a piece of ground close to the gate of his own residence. This beautiful residence of the Knoll, on the banks of the Lossie, had originally been purchased by him with a sum of upwards of £2,000, which was presented to him in the end of 1860, as a testimonial by a number of his friends, after he had been for several years preaching without any pecuniary remuneration, in order to provide a home, where he might rest for part of the year, and where Mrs. North might remain while he itinerated through different parts of the country. Since commencing his public career as an evangelist his time had been so thoroughly occupied, and his strength so utterly exhausted by his labours in the large centres of population, whose claims upon him he rightly felt to be of the first importance, that when he returned home he was obliged to take entire rest. He felt, however, that his neighbours in Bishopmill had claims upon him, some of them being too aged and infirm to go to the regular services of the sanctuary in the adjoining town of Elgin, and others having lapsed into indifference and non-church-attendance; and he knew that these could only be reclaimed by having the gospel brought to their own doors. Accordingly, not possessing the means himself, he resolved to make an effort among his personal friends to raise a sum of money sufficient to build a hall, that would be available at all times for missionary, evangelistic, and Sabbath-school purposes, etc.

Thus, both in the starting of a town-missionary and the building of a Mission Hall, was Mr. North the means of conferring signal spiritual advantages upon the town where he for many years resided.

In the autumn of 1870, when it was known that Mr. North had somewhat unexpectedly, both to himself and others, formed the resolution of changing his place of stated residence to London, the inhabitants of Bishopmill and its neighbourhood drew up and presented to him an Address, urging him to remain in their midst. This gratifying memorial has signatures appended to it to the number of 502, and was conveyed to him on the 12th of January, 1871.

During these years of hard and incessant work he often suffered a great deal from ill-health; and it shows the intense energy and earnestness of the man, that though now upwards of sixty years of age, he still undertook and carried through such an amount of exhausting labour. A letter to Lord Kintore a year or two before he left Elgin shows that he felt the increasing infirmities of age telling upon his frame.

"THE KNOLL, ELGIN, *Oct.* 31*st*.

"MY VERY DEAR KINTORE,—It is always a pleasant post that brings me a line from either of you.

"Though better, I have had several of the sciatic attacks I had, and was obliged to send an excuse on Saturday to Inverness, where I was to have preached on Sunday. Today is our fast day here; and though I am better, I am not able to leave the house, yet hope to get down to the Lord's table on Sunday. I suspect it is the Lord's will, if my years are lengthened, that they be years of suffering. Glory be to God! May they be years of improvement to my own soul's good, and of patient enduring to the glory of Christ. I have grown far too earthly-minded of late. Be sure that God's best blessing to man is *not* freedom from earthly care and trouble. With all this, however, I feel the Knoll is very pretty, and I am longing for you to see it again.

"We have got a minister who is filling our church. I have a carriage from the inn, and go regularly to the weekly prayer-meeting.

"God bless you. God bless my lady. God bless your children!

"Your always affectionate friend,
"B. N."

The last five years of his life were very much a repetition of the year of which we have been able to give pretty full notices. In the spring of 1873 he visited the fashionable watering-place of Bournemouth, and his addresses there seem to have been owned by the great Master.

He wrote from his own house in London on his return,—

"Such a whirl at Bournemouth, yet I believe it was a very blessed time. The dear old baron with whom I was staying certainly seemed to get good. The last morning at prayers he wept like a child, and said afterwards, 'Oh, you naughty man, you have made me cry: I had left that to my wife.' And then, on a large tray of beautiful flowers being brought into the room, he said, 'Ah, they are very beautiful; but it is North that has strewed my path with flowers.' To God be all the glory! His was only one case of many. I came here on Saturday, to preach for Saphir last Sunday. The church was very full, and the people attentive. I preach for him again, God willing, next Sunday, and on the Sunday following at Cambridge."

These services in the Rev. Adolph Saphir's church were not fruitless, for among his correspondence we find a long letter of gratitude from one in her youth, who was then brought within the safe and blessed enclosure of the fold of grace. She says,—

"Indeed I am wonderfully happy and blessed in my new and precious possession, and trying to make everybody I meet be the same. Oh, the joy you will have in heaven when many, many point to you as the means of their conversion! How I pray that I may never be cast away! I am learning a great deal of my precious Bible now. Six weeks ago was to me the beginning of days, when you preached in Mr. Saphir's in the evening. It was then I determined to give up, God helping me, my whole heart to Jesus Christ."

CHAPTER XIV

Last Year of Earthly Labour

THE greater part of the last two years of Mr. North's life was devoted to evangelistic work in the great city of Glasgow. This city contains such a vast and rapidly increasing population as to more than overtask the utmost efforts of all the churches to meet its spiritual necessities. Many of the non-church-going multitudes in that teeming hive of industry and commerce belong not to the sunken and pauperized, but to the prosperous and intelligent artisan class, and it is clear that the desideratum is powerful preachers of the gospel as much as places of worship. For after all, it is the preachers, and not the churches or the ritual, that must attract, and arouse, and convert the people.

The Rev. W. Ross Taylor, an intimate and valued friend of Mr. North, in giving a narrative of his work at this time as it fell under his own observation, wrote,—

"We may certainly regard it as a mark of God's kindness to our honoured friend that, in 1874-75, he was permitted to reap another harvest of rich blessing before being called to his rest.

"Friends did not know at the time that it was the sunset hour with him; they hoped that further years of usefulness were still in store; but afterwards, when the end came, they could not but observe with gratitude, even while the pain of bereavement was at their hearts, that his course had closed as it commenced, amid the warmth and glow of earnest and successful work.

"Mr. North was at this time far from physically strong. He was constantly suffering more or less from liability to chills, and from a feeling of exhaustion; but his spirit was as intense as ever, and he threw himself into the work of the revival with all the enthusiasm of his powerful nature. The feeling of weakness which weighed upon him at other times vanished as soon as he found himself face to face with a congregation of eager listeners; and no stranger witnessing the energy with which he preached for fully an hour, could imagine how carefully he required to husband his strength before going into the pulpit, or how ' done ' he felt after the service was over. The conviction was indeed forcing itself upon his mind, that he would require to curtail the number of his weekly services, but he was most reluctant to accept the thought, and battled against it to the last.

" In the earlier months of 1874, while Mr. Moody and Mr. Sankey were holding their wonderful meetings in the various districts of Glasgow, Mr. North was at work in the large and populous suburbs which girdle that city,—Govan, Partick, and Hillhead. Reports of the remarkable results which followed the meetings in Govan were given at the time at the daily noon meetings, and tended greatly to encourage the hearts of God's children to abound in prayer for a large blessing. Of the work in the west-end suburb of Hillhead it is my privilege to speak from full personal knowledge, as the meetings were all held in Kelvinside Free Church, and extended over the entire month of March. On the first Sabbath of that month, Mr. Moody occupied the pulpit in the forenoon, and in view of the services in which the veteran evangelist was about to engage, strove to arouse the Christians among us to earnest co-operation, by preaching his powerful sermon on the text, ' To every man his work.' Mr. North followed in the evening, and preached to an overflowing congregation on ' The rich man and Lazarus;' a sermon with which he frequently commenced a series of services, as being eminently fitted to awaken spiritual anxiety, where previously indifference had reigned. And not a few in his audience that night felt their hearts tremble as they listened to his solemn and fervid words, and of these a number remained in their seats at the close of the service, to ask the old question of stricken hearts, ' Men and brethren, what shall we do?'

" During the weeks which followed, greatly encouraged and strengthened by the beginning which had been made, Mr. North occupied the pulpit on three evenings of each week, and preached to large congregations with rare freshness and power. There were words for all classes of hearers, for the thoughtless and thoughtful, for the presumptuous and the doubting, for the inquiring and the enlightened, for the babes and those of mature experience; and speaker and hearers alike were sensible that the living energy of the Spirit was with the word. At one time the realities of the unseen world were portrayed with overpowering vividness; at another the loving calls of Christ were urged with persuasive tenderness; at another the absolute sufficiency of God's word, as the ground of faith was so clearly unfolded as to dispel many long lingering doubts and misconceptions; while on other evenings, choosing Psalms for his theme, the preacher analysed with admirable insight, the varied states of feeling experienced by the people of God. Many of the evangelistic or arousing addresses I had heard him deliver in other places, and I was prepared for those features of vivid representation, direct appeal, and intense urgency which always characterized them; but the addresses on the psalms were new to me, and I was greatly struck by the richness of his exposition. He appeared himself also to have special pleasure in dwelling on these themes, although he never seemed to lose the very groundless impression that his one talent was to awaken the unconcerned. Hence it was under something like a mental protest that he allowed himself to indulge in the treatment of those topics which were becoming the most congenial to his ripening spirit, and hence too he selected those psalms only out of which he could unfold, sometimes ingeniously enough his favourite doctrine of ' righteousness through faith.'

" At the close of each Sabbath evening service, a large number, about four or five hundred, remained to continue in prayer for a blessing; and at the close of these second meetings, inquirers remained in increasing numbers to get further guidance from those who waited to converse with them."

During the same winter Mr. North held services in the Barony Church, and concerning these the Rev. James Wells wrote :—

" In the winter of 1874, Mr. North conducted a series of meetings in the Barony Free Church. His addresses then

seemed to me the best I had ever heard from him, and justified the statement Dr. Duncan used to make, that he had a
fine theological mind. Along with all the freshness and glowing intensity that marked his first public appeals, his utterances had a peculiar richness and mellowness. Some of his
expositions of Scripture were very striking. I remember that
he had a great desire to reach the hard-headed men: and, so
far as I could judge, his success was chiefly among that class.
I had satisfactory evidence that several of them were then
brought to personal decision."

During this period of labour in Glasgow, as Mr. Taylor has
noticed, Mr. North came into contact with Mr. D. L. Moody
of Chicago. Mr. Moody was at this time the centre of attrac-
tion, so that Mr. North, whose name had been wont to ring
through any city in which he had come to labour, was not
even known by many Christian people in Glasgow to have
been steadily preaching for about a year in their city. His
work was quieter than formerly, but his labours appear to have
been not less fruitful. But what we desire to call attention
to, is the entire absence of anything approaching to jealousy
in this honoured man of God, when he found himself, for perhaps the first time in his experience, not forgotten at all by
the Master, but to a certain extent, overlooked by the crowd.
Mr. Moody had everything in his favour. He had the excitement of novelty, of Mr. Sankey's beautiful voice, of instrumental music, and of sacred songs, both the words and melo-
dies of which had a great attractiveness, and all the charm of
freshness. He had a marvellous faculty for organization,
which Mr. North lacked, and the Lord was making him the
instrument of a very widespread revival movement. As a
theologian and preacher, however, Mr. Moody would be the
first to acknowledge that Mr. North was greatly in advance of
him. We know how common it is for men in the position in
which Mr. North unexpectedly found himself to judge somewhat harshly of those who have the flood-tide in their favour.
But his heart was filled with joy at seeing such true and successful reapers busy wielding the sickle; and in private notes
to his most intimate friends he expressed his happiness at

witnessing the Lord's work thus carried on by others who were drawing the popular eye from his own labours; and he who had been accustomed to stand first proved his meetness for that honour by being most willing when called upon to take the lowest room. The Lord was thus preparing for His own presence His servant, to whom he was about to address the invitation, "Come up higher."

A letter written to his old friend the late Earl of Kintore, from Liverpool, where he had come for a short time during Mr. Moody's visit there, shows his own sense of the precarious state of his bodily health, and also his opinion of Moody and Sankey.

"SANDFIELD PARK, WEST DERBY,

"LIVERPOOL, *March 4th*.

"MY DEAREST KINTORE,—I was very glad to get your two kind letters, as was Mrs. H——. I am getting older and uglier and deafer every year, not attractions with which to make new friends, so I am more jealous of the old ones, and I should be sorry to lose many of them if I could help it, and none more so than yourself, dear Kintore, for we have travelled together as friends over many a long year of good report and evil report. My ending, I suspect, is not very far off, for I am full of gout and rheumatism, added to which Sir William Gull, whom I consulted, says I have a weak heart and enlarged liver. Notwithstanding all this, however, I had accepted an invitation to speak in the enormous hall here, built for Moody and Sankey, on next Sunday, but fortunately for Liverpool and myself, they are not ready for them in London, and we have got them here for another Sunday. Their success is a miracle, perfectly superhuman! Every service crammed, and after every service the inquiry room also. Of course the devil rages, as he always does when God works: and He *is* working, I most firmly believe, *mightily*. I cannot tell you how sorry I am to hear of dear —— being such an invalid.

"The whole household are gone in to hear Moody and Sankey, or I am sure would send you every kind message. I am sipping barley-water in single blessedness. I am so glad to hear —— got such a blessing from M. and S. May the

Lord increase it more and more! for she has had much trial lately.

"Always and ever yours most affectionately,

"BROWNLOW NORTH."

We shall next record an instance of blessing in which the beginning and the close of this good workman's sowing the seed of life were linked together in a wise and watchful providence.

After one of his services in the Free Church of Sighthill, Glasgow, a young man came into the vestry, and thanked Mr. North, with the tear in his eye, for having been the instrument of his conversion in another church in the city some months previously. He then related to Mr. North the substance of the following statement, which we are enabled to give in his own words.

He says:—

"On the Sabbath in question I called to see a young friend at the south side of Glasgow. Conversation getting stale, I proposed a walk to pass the time. We passed Mr. Riddel's church: my friend told me that Mr. North was preaching, so I said, 'Let's go in.' I may remark that my friend had very serious views on religion. Mr. North preached from the words, 'Jesus Christ, unto the Jews a stumbling-block, and unto the Greeks foolishness.' I came away from the church no better than I entered it, save that I had got one idea from the sermon. And reasoning with myself, I came to the conclusion that up to the present time I had been a 'fool,' and that Jesus Christ was to me but 'foolishness.' My friend offered to accompany me part of the way home, and as we were crossing the Clyde I felt as if all the powers of hell had put their heads together to tempt me: so strong were my feelings, that I stopped on the bridge, and said to myself, 'This matter must be settled, either the one way or the other, before I cross this river.' I heard the jeers already in my ears from my mocking companions, and the scoffs of the world, but by the grace of God I was enabled to view the two sides of the question, and I decided for God. And no sooner had I done so, than joy which words cannot express filled my heart. My companion noticed the change, and I explained to him the cause. I felt so light, that I did not feel my feet touch the ground. By the grace of God I can say that Jesus Christ is still to me ' the wisdom and the power of God.' "

When he had related this to Mr. North, he told him he was the son of a minister in Morayshire, who had asked Mr. North to preach to his people at the very beginning of his career, but had himself been removed by death before the dawn of the Sabbath fixed on, three weeks later. That service had been a solemn one, the crowds being such that they had to adjourn to the open air. Mr. North had spoken to the people with great feeling, on the death of their revered pastor, whose recent removal caused many to weep tears of heartfelt sorrow. Sixteen years had elapsed since then, and the Lord had guided His servant's son, now training as an engineer in Glasgow, to hear the gospel, and be brought to the saving knowledge of Christ by the lips of this very evangelist whose course was now nearly finished.

Mr. North was much overcome at the recital. and as a friend who was present was about to assist him on with his top-coat, he took it from him, and handing it to the young convert, said, " Let *my child* help me on with it."

It was not Mr. North's habit to remain in church or vestry after preaching to converse with anxious inquirers at an after-meeting. He preferred to see them the following day; his reason being that he was so heated and exhausted by the exertion of preaching, that he was liable to be chilled, unless he returned home at once.

In the year 1872-3, when assisting Mr. Riddel in Glasgow, being specially asked, he stayed to converse with some inquirers one evening, the consequence being that he caught a chill, and was prostrated the next day with a painful illness which confined him to bed for many weeks. Yet so eager was he to preach that, in spite of all dissuasion, when the hour of each advertised service arrived, he rose from bed, wrapped up and drove to the church, preached amid much bodily pain and weakness, retiring to bed again the moment he returned home. This course he continued three times every week until the month of services he had arranged for in that church was concluded, because he had evidence that the Lord was at that time blessing his message.

The physician who saw him on his death-bed said that his heart was in such a state that he might at any time have dropped down in the pulpit, and from Sir William Gull's opinion he was fully aware that that organ was seriously affected. Yet so anxious was he to fulfil his ministry, that he preached often when physically unable for the effort.

As an evidence of the widespread fruits of his ministry, a friend has told us that when he was staying in her house in Edinburgh on one occasion for six weeks, not a single day passed in which the bell did not ring, bearing a message of thanks to him, either by word of mouth or by letter, for his having been the means of bringing the speaker or writer to the knowledge of the Saviour. Even in localities in which Mr. North never preached, not a few instances of conversion under his ministrations have been traced. It was so in the village of Moffat, in Dumfriesshire, where, a few months before Mr. North's decease, the writer of this volume came, within a short interval, upon two persons who spoke of him as their spiritual father. The first was a gentleman who was passing through, lecturing upon Sabbath-school work, in which he had extensive experience, and who mentioned that he had been converted and brought to the Lord under Mr. North in Edinburgh, in Free St. Luke's, in 1858. The second was a young domestic servant encountered in pastoral visitation, whose bright smile and ready answer to some question about the state of her soul, told that her heart had been given to Jesus. When asked if it was long since she had known the Lord as her Saviour, she said it was only a few months since she had been brought to Christ under Mr. North, in Kelvinside Church, Glasgow, in the beginning of 1875.

One of the last letters we have found in his repositories, apart from those of personal friends, was addressed to him by an English gentleman in the autumn of this year, 1875, thanking him for his prayers with his wife after a carriage accident at Tarbet, and for an exposition he had given of John v. at that place, and also for instruction and help they both had derived from reading one of his books which he had kindly presented to them. Thus his useful and busy life drew to its close, filled with work for the Saviour who had bought him with a price, and who, when He came suddenly, found His servant at his post, distributing to friends and strangers, in public and in private, a portion of spiritual meat in due season.

CHAPTER XV

Last Days and Death

THE reader must by this time have been able to form a pretty correct estimate of Mr. North's character, at least on its spiritual side. In order, however, to present him, before the memoir closes, with a full portrait of the man, it may be well to preserve in these pages some delineations of his traits and characteristics, as they have been sketched by those who from their intimacy with him, and also by reason of their wide knowledge of men and manners, are well qualified to form and express their judgment on this point.

"Among the most striking features of his character were intensity of purpose and force of will. Earnest and strenuous in whatever cause, he was never more earnest than in that cause for which he eventually lived, and in devotion to which he died. That nature which is never eradicated, however subordinated to a higher impulse and a nobler will, still clung to him, and now asserted itself with all its native force and determination in the service of his new master. His powerful will and native force of character were shown in every action; he could do nothing by halves; and whatever he did he did well. It was the combination of the two natures, the thoroughly human with the true Christian, that presented him to my mind as so remarkable a person; and hence the difficulty of attempting to crystallize, or to gather into a focus so many-sided a character. For undoubtedly it comprised seeming contradictions, and yet such as are sure to be found wherever a powerful influence has been manifested. His was a character that drew to it the love of many. He never lost a friendship worth the possession, nor a confidence once inspired.

His life was indeed a true life, for it was true to self and to nature."[1]

"It was impossible to know Mr. North without being bound to him with a cordial attachment. He was thoroughly a man, and in many qualities both of head and heart he was a great man. He was genuine, transparent, outspoken, sincere in his affections, and thoroughly free from all that was artificial in his religion. His talents were of a high order; and with his athletic frame and vast energy he was fitted to take a foremost position in any line of life he might have chosen. In everything he was extremely practical; and in religion he saw clearly what was great and solid, with even too little taste for the sentimental. He spoke to his hearers as in the transaction of a great business; and this practical dealing commended itself to the multitudes. From the time when eternal truths had broken in upon himself, as his own practical concern, he was borne forward with an inexpressible earnestness to communicate them to every living man whom his words could reach; and in his own special sphere no recent preacher has equalled him in vividness and power. But those who heard the masterly clearness of his theology, the decision of his statements, and the boldness of his address in the pulpit, could scarcely conceive how childlike he was in private, and how ready he was to listen to any teaching.

"The hand of the Lord was with him, and when he was reminded to make the most of Divine help while he had it, he thought it impossible that he could ever lose his vivid apprehension of things spiritual and eternal, or relax in zeal for his Redeemer and for the salvation of men. But when towards the close of his life, he saw the Lord's hand with the American Evangelist, and his own work at the time but little in comparison, he said to me, 'This would not have been if I had persevered as I began.' In many respects, as well as in this, the defects and the faults which others saw in him were not unknown to himself, and he had an extreme frankness in owning them. Even to the most devoted ministers and members of the Church of Christ, these words of our Lord, 'Nevertheless thou

[1] Admiral Baillie Hamilton.

hast left thy first love,' seldom fail to be spoken at some period of their course, and Mr. North learned that he formed no exception; but as with many others so with him, there was a gracious recovery.

"In so far as has fallen under my own observation, the fruit of his preaching has been more abiding than that of any other evangelist. In not a few instances known to myself, these conversions have stood the trial of twenty years, with much more than the average of Christian life and fruit. This is due in part to the great foundation the preacher laid in the Divine judgment, sovereignty, and law, as well as in mercy and love; but also, and in immediate connection with these great truths, it is perhaps even more to be ascribed to his unceasing reference to the word of the living God. The permanence of the conversions under the preaching of Mr. North has often recalled to my memory the words of an English minister in my church some time after the beginning of his work : ' I have seen many sung into conversion, but few of them stood; I have seen others prayed into conversion, and more of them stood, but many fell away; but I have seen those stand who were converted by the Word of God.'

" It was what he believed for himself that he spoke to others, and he spoke it only because he believed it. He once said to me that he would like to go through the streets bearing a large board on his breast with such a text as this printed on it, ' The wages of sin is death, but the gift of God is eternal life through Jesus Christ our Lord.' If he had been sure that it would do good he was willing even to become such a fool for Christ's sake. Eternity was to him as great a certainty as time, and if equally certain, infinitely more important."[1]

Regarding the secular side of his character, Mr. Balfour wrote : —

" Among those whom he knew intimately, and who were congenial with him, he was capital company, full of liveliness and spirit, quick at repartee, entered into a passing joke, even if the fun should be against himself, and told a story

[1] Dr. Moody-Stuart.

admirably. In his earlier years he had been fond of private theatricals, and was, I believe, no mean performer. Children he used often to amuse by his imitations of foreigners or well-known characters, and he always made himself a favourite of young people by his warm sympathy with them."

Mr. North himself once laughingly quoted a friend's description of him as being not so far from the truth, that he was a big man, a big woman, and a big child rolled into one. If the illustrious moralist's definition of a great man be correct, that he is not a man who has fewer weak points than the ordinary run of men, but a man who is stronger in his strong points, we might advance for him some claim to the epithet. At all events, Brownlow North assuredly was a man who did a great work, a work whose greatness and extent only the Great Day will fully unfold. He was a man who preached the great truths of revelation with great powers and great results.

In the twenty years of labour allotted to him in the great harvest field he did as much as most active men do in fifty years, and perhaps there is no one of his contemporaries to whom spiritual and vital religion in Scotland owes more than to Brownlow North, if so much. He gave it an aggressive force and character which it was not exercising when he came forth as its herald, and under his leadership evangelical religion, instead of standing on the defensive, assaulted the strongholds of worldliness in all classes of society, from the highest to the lowest, with the most undaunted prowess and success. The hour now came when his Master summoned him home from his labour to his reward.

In the autumn of 1875 he went to pay a long-promised visit to his friend Lord Polwarth in Berwickshire. They had first met at Haddo House at the close of 1862, just previous to the marriage of Walter Scott (later Lord Polwarth) to his cousin, the eldest daughter of the Earl of Aberdeen; a memorable occasion. They had occasionally met since, and Lord Polwarth wrote, "When I saw him previous to Mr. Moody's visit to Glasgow, I thought him a good deal shaken in constitution, and no wonder, as I afterwards learned how he had often laboured on in positive bodily suffering. Those who knew him well, who were with him in prayer, can testify to the fervent simple faith which he exercised in the living God, on whose Spirit he relied for all true result in his work. His prayers were very unadorned, very plain, very direct and very humble. He never forgot what he was in himself, and his characteristic expression when speaking in prayer of himself was 'this poor sinner.' He evidently was to the last deeply conscious of the marvellous grace which had called him out of darkness into light, and made him a chosen vessel for God's service. His prayerfulness was truly one secret of his power, no less than the constant study of the Word of God, which he thoroughly knew. His own call by the grace of God was a frequent subject of conversation, and was ever a vivid reality to him. The tears would start to his eyes as he spoke of God's goodness to himself, and he was ever under a sense of gratitude to the One who had loved him and washed him from his sins.

"When he visited us in the autumn of 1875, we were at Humbie, where he spent a week with us, greatly enjoying himself in the woods, and taking a lively interest in the agricultural improvements going on. He was in particularly good spirits, and seemed to feel stronger. How little did we then think the end was so near! At a little Bible-reading in our house he met a gentleman who told him that he had been the means of spiritual blessing to a dear one many years before, who had lived and died a consistent Christian. Mr. North felt this very much as encouragement concerning work of years gone by. Possibly they are dwelling on all that now. He was very sympathetic in nature, and there was nothing which did not awaken his sympathetic interest. He was able to accompany us to Mertoun, where he stayed for another week, as bright and happy as before. Indeed, we look back to those days as a time of peculiar joy and gladness in friendly intercourse with one who rejoiced in the Lord, and as His child in all that was lovely and of good report. There was nothing of gloom about him. He loved to see others happy. He went on Sunday to preach in the parish church of Kelso, which was largely filled. I fancied he had not his usual vigour, but he preached earnestly on a favourite passage. After the service an old man requested to see him, and informed me that Mr. North had been the means of his conversion eighteen years previously at Newcastle. This was another token of God's blessing on past work which gladdened his heart. I shall not forget the times of quiet spiritual intercourse which we were privileged to have together at that season. He left my house on October 20th, and that day fortnight he left the earthly house of the bodily tabernacle, to depart and be with the Lord."

" He was to begin his winter's campaign [Mr. Balfour wrote] that year by holding meetings at Alexandria in Dumbartonshire; and during the time he was to be there, James Campbell, Esq., of Tullichewan Castle, invited him to be his guest at his lovely residence on the banks of Loch Lomond, well known for two generations for the hospitality of its owners. When passing through Edinburgh, on his way there, he spent a night with us. We sat up pretty late in his bedroom, talking together of a great many things. I remember among others that we spoke of the uncertainty of the time of our dying, and he said, ' We don't know how soon we may die, but no tongue can tell how important to us through eternity is the manner in which we spend the time, whatever it may be, till we die. Our eternity will be proportioned to our lives on earth, so that everything we do till we die will be multiplied by eternity.' "

" He left us next morning for the West. As he was driving in a cab to the station, with a friend of many years' standing, he referred in his usual emphatic way to the Word of God. Miss— said, ' Mr. North, you always send one back to the Bible,' when he replied, ' That's just it; there's nothing for any of us but the Bible.' "

The Vale of Leven Young Men's Christian Association had asked him to conduct services which they arranged for in the town of Alexandria, Dumbartonshire, and on the 21st October he became the guest of Mr. Campbell of Tullichewan. On his arrival he was a complete stranger to the family, but his agreeable society and Christian conversation soon made him a general favourite. On the Lord's-day evening, the 24th, he preached in the Public Hall of Alexandria to a crowded and attentive congregation. About 1,200 persons were present, some of whom were able to remember the deep impression made by his earnest preaching in Alexandria sixteen years before, which had left behind it abiding and saving effects. His text on this his last Sabbath in the pulpit was Rev. xxi. 5-8, "Behold, I make all things new," etc. He preached for nearly an hour in his usual pointed and searching style, but seemed to feel the effort, and asked the Free Church minister, the Rev. W. Sutherland, to announce and read the Psalms to be sung, which were the 100th Psalm, and the 67th paraphrase in two portions, which begins—

> " Lo, what a glorious sight appears
>   To our admiring eyes!
> The former seas have passed away,
>   The former earth and skies."

He preached in the Free Church on the Wednesday and Friday following.

The last address which he delivered was on this Friday evening before he was struck down with illness, and between 600 and 700 persons were present. He took for his subject the 86th Psalm, on which he commented throughout, making frequent and touching references to his own spiritual experiences. He regarded preaching the everlasting message of God to man as the highest honour, as well as the greatest responsibility, that can be conferred on any child of God; in it he took the greatest delight, and the Lord permitted him to exercise his gift and grace to the very close of his life with unimpaired vigour, and to die in harness. Indeed, at the time of his death, his list of engagements was completed up to the summer of 1877. But as he showed his list to his friends at Ramornie he said, " I have booked myself for meetings with you in October, 1876, that is to say, if I am alive, for we must always feel that our days are in God's hand."

We extract the following account of this his first and last visit to Tullichewan from a letter from his kind hostess, Mrs. Campbell, dated 24th November, 1877.

"Mr. North came a stranger to us personally, in October 1875, and (although we did not altogether sympathise with his views on religious matters) he impressed us all as being a thoroughly earnest Christian. He never lost an opportunity of speaking for Christ, and indeed sought opportunities of speaking to people about their souls and eternity and Jesus Christ. He had a great impression of the horrors of sin, and of God's wrath, rather than of His everlasting Fatherhood and mercy, and spoke much of the awful punishment of sin."

"We had a dinner party one night, to meet Mr. North. After the ladies left, he introduced the subject of religion, and spoke very impressively. We had some young people with us another night, when he did the same thing. He spoke of marriage, I remember, and of the evil and sin of believers marrying unbelievers, and impressed some of the young people very much. Although Mrs. Campbell has not been able to furnish us with recollections of his exact remarks on this the last of those occasions when he spoke in a drawing-room on behalf of that Lord whom he had so zealously adored, loved, and served, we are able to give correct notes of his remarks on this very subject on another similar occasion, and introduce them here, as this may be regarded as in a sense his parting testimony. His advice was, " Never marry a man who you are not fully persuaded is a thorough, true Christian, and not only so, but one who has as high a standard of Christianity as yourself, and one whom you can respect, look up to, and lean upon. The wife is the weaker vessel, and the husband should be one to lead her and draw her on. She should not have to do this to him. Remember these words, ' Be not unequally yoked together with unbelievers; for what fellowship hath righteousness with unrighteousness? and what communion hath light with darkness? and what concord hath Christ with Belial? ' Observe how Christ identifies Himself with His people, and also the children of this world with the wicked one. It was the sin that destroyed the old world when the sons of God intermarried with the daughters of men (Gen. vi. 4). Then ' the wickedness of man was great in the earth, and every imagination of the thoughts of his heart was only evil continually, and it repented the Lord that He had made man on the earth.' It was also the sin that Nehemiah so strongly reprobated in the Israelites, after their return from captivity, when they had intermarried with the Ammonites, the people of Ashdod and of Moab. Nehemiah says, ' I contended with them, and cursed them, and made them swear by God, saying, Ye shall not give your daughters unto their sons, not take their daughters unto your sons, or for yourselves.' And keep away from worldly acquaintances; that is the way these attachments are made, and then it is such a trial to break them off. The trial will come to you some day. No progress in religion can be made without a cross of some kind; sickness will come, death will come; but *then*—to stand before your Saviour, face to face, and look up to Him, and say (here he stopped from emotion at the thought of *seeing Him*)—You are *married* to Him, you are the bride of Christ. ' I have espoused you to one husband, that I may present you as a chaste virgin of Christ.' ' Be married to another, even to Him who is raised from the dead, that ye should bring forth fruit unto God.' Is it not wonderful? beautiful? "

Mrs. Campbell continues: " On Sunday night he had preached a very arousing discourse upon the awfulness of sin and of God's wrath, addressed to the unconverted. His two discourses on Wednesday and Friday were addressed more to the Lord's people. He was quiet, and spoke much of the blessedness of the Christian life. He said that week-night services were generally gatherings of Christians, and he changed his style of preaching accordingly. He spent much of his time in his own room, and when he preached in the evening he did not appear till five o'clock, and when he returned from preaching went direct to his room. Preaching was a very great exertion to him. The doctor said from the state of his health he might have died at any time in the pulpit.

" On the Saturday he was taken ill, our son-in-law, Major Gildea, was in the next room to him, and heard him fall,— went in and found him on the floor, and got him to bed. The doctor hoped he would get better, and he was kept as quiet as possible. Mrs. North was sent for, and was with him immediately, and never left, night or day, till the solemn close." His illness came on on Saturday, the 30th October, and lasted ten days, terminating in his release from his labours and his suffering on Tuesday, the 9th November, 1875. As both heart and liver were seriously affected, the physician took from the first a gloomy view of the case; but for a week he rallied occasionally, and in the bosoms of his anxious friends hopes alternated with fears. One of those who attended him afterwards told a stranger, who spoke to him on the concerns of his soul, that it was while watching by Brownlow North's dying bed that he was first impressed with the fact that there was reality in religion. During his illness, he had interviews with his attached friends, the Rev. Walter Ross Taylor and Mr. James Balfour. The latter, to whom he had addressed a letter the very evening he was taken ill, has furnished us with the following relation of his last intercourse with his old friend :—

"He was ill for only about ten days, and occasionally during that time he rallied so much that hopes were entertained that he might recover. But these hopes were extinguished on the eighth day, and I was telegraphed for on Sunday, to go and see him. I went by the first train on Monday morning, and arrived immediately after breakfast. On getting to the house I saw the doctor, who told me how hopelessly ill he was. I was then taken to his room, but he seemed, when I then saw him, to be very near death; and although I took his hand, I can hardly say that I thought he was conscious of my doing so. I remained at Tullichewan all day, and was well rewarded for staying. About four o'clock I returned to his room with Mr. Campbell, when I found him much revived and perfectly conscious. He first said a few tender words to Mr. Campbell, and I then drew near him, and took his hand, saying, 'Do you know me, North?' He looked up, and with a smile pronounced my Christian name. It was touching as he continued to hold my hand, to look on him lying there, like a weaned child, able to speak only in whispers, and slowly, and with an effort. He again looked at me, and said very softly, 'Jesus came to me and said, 'I will never leave thee nor forsake thee,' and up to this time He never has. But,' he added, ' I have been a beast.' I said, ' I have often thought that the verse on which I should like to die is, " The blood of Jesus Christ His Son cleanseth us from all sin." ' ' That,' he replied, ' is the verse on which I am now dying. One wants no more.' I said, ' This dying is what you and I have often spoken of.' ' Often,' he answered. ' Have you peace? ' ' *Perfect peace,*' he said, with such meaning. I proposed to pray, to which he gladly assented. After a short prayer he wiped his moistened eyes, and I had to leave him. That was the last expression of his faith and hope. But a day before that he had said, ' I used to have a great terror of death, but that is quite gone from me; I have no fear of it now; I am resting on Christ.' He also at that time said to one standing by, ' You are young, in good health, and with the prospect of rising in the army; I am dying : but if the Bible is true, and I know it is, I would not change places with you for the whole world.' As I looked at him, he seemed like a great ship of war slowly entering the harbour, the sails all furled, the guns unshotted, the excitement and the perils of the voyage over, and the desired haven reached. The next day the gates were swung open, and he spent that first five minutes in heaven, of which he often used to speak, when he was wont to imagine that Christ would come to him, when He saw his amazement, and say, ' Said I not unto thee, if thou wouldest believe, thou shouldest see? ' "

During his illness, while consciousness remained to him, his thoughts often turned to his friends. In his last will and testament, dated 2nd November, he says, " There are a few other dear friends to whom I should have liked to leave something if I had had anything. I leave them however, my love, which heartily is and has long been, theirs and their children's. May the blessing of the Lord be on them all ! Let a copy of this sentence be sent to those named."

It was arranged that he should be buried in the Dean Cemetery, in Edinburgh, and that the funeral should proceed from the house of his friend Mr. Brown-Douglas. It is touching to notice that this distinguished servant of the Lord, whose delight for twenty years it had been to go from place to place preaching the gospel of Jesus Christ, was struck down in the very midst of his loved work, died in the house of strangers, who received him and bestowed on him every attention that friendship could suggest for the sake of their common Master, and was carried to his grave from the house of an attached friend, to which twenty years before he had also come as a stranger on his great mission of preaching the gospel. The funeral was a private one; but many of his sorrowing friends met with heavy hearts to pay the last offering of respect and love to the dust of one from whose eloquent lips they had often listened to the soul-stirring message which his Master gave him to deliver.

A portion of Scripture from the 15th chapter of 1 Corinthians was read. The sorrowful company joined in singing the sixty-sixth paraphrase:—

> " How bright these glorious spirits shine!
>   Whence all their white array?
> How came they to the blissful seats
>   Of everlasting day?
>
> " Lo, these are they from sufferings great
>   Who came to realms of light,
> And in the blood of Christ have washed
>   Those robes, which shine so bright."

The effect was tender and solemnizing. It seemed to take us within the veil, and unite us with the worshippers there, of whom we felt assured he was now one, whose robes were washed and made white in the blood of the Lamb. Touching and suitable prayers were offered by Dr. Moody-Stuart and Mr. Ross Taylor, in brotherly fellowship with the former of whom Brownlow North began in Edinburgh that public minis-try which, after an interval of twenty years, he closed in Glasgow in intimate association with the latter. The congrega-tions of both of these ministers will long bear evidence to the power and success of the faithful preaching of the everlasting gospel by those lips which were now sealed with the silence of death. The thoughts of all present rose to the great general assembly and church of the firstborn above, and to the ever-increasing company of the spirits of just men made perfect.

His body was silently laid in the tomb, beside the remains of his daughter-in-law, and doubtless many who were not present then have visited the spot since, and thanked God for the work of faith and labour of love of His departed servant. A grey granite obelisk was erected by his friends in the Dean Cemetery, to mark the place of interment, and bears this inscription:—

"BROWNLOW NORTH,

ONLY SON OF THE REV. CHARLES AUGUSTUS NORTH,
Prebendary of Winchester.

Born January 6th, 1810: Died November 9th, 1875.

At the age of forty-four years he was turned from an ungodly life to serve the Lord; thereafter he preached the Gospel with singular power and was greatly honoured in winning souls to Jesus.

IN TESTIMONY OF THE LOVE AND RESPECT OF
MANY FRIENDS."

The words that will rise unbidden into many hearts as they close this record of his labours, or visit the resting-place of his dust, are, " Well done, good and faithful servant; thou hast entered into the joy of thy Lord! "

On perusing a short sketch of his labours in the *British Messenger,* written by Mr. Ross Taylor, the Archbishop of Canterbury (Dr. Tait), wrote to a friend, on 15th November, 1875, words that well express the feelings of very many. " We have been reading the account of Brownlow North which some one sent to us. He will leave a great blank among those for whom he laboured. No one could know him without seeing that his heart and life were devoted to his Master's service, and that he burned to preach to others what he had found so precious to his own soul."

Taking a retrospect of the great work accomplished by Brownlow North, and reflecting that two-thirds of his life were worse than wasted, some may be disposed to find fault with the Divine procedure, and argue that it would have been more suitable had this work been performed by one who had feared the Lord from his youth. To such objectors we retort with the inspired Apostle, "Nay, but, O man, who are thou that repliest against God?" or with Beza, who, when a detractor threw in his teeth his early sins, replied, "Hic homo mihi invidet gratiam Christi" ("This man envies me Christ's grace"); or with Augustine, who answered a like objector thus, "The more desperate was my disease, the greater honour redounded to the Physician who cured me." Indeed, we cannot better close this imperfect record of the life-labours of Brownlow North, than by again quoting from lines written on St. Augustine, to whose experience of Satan's sway, and of the power of Divine grace, that of Brownlow North bore a striking resemblance:—

> " I lov'd Thee late, too late I lov'd Thee, Lord;
>   Yet not so late, but Thou dost still afford
>   Good proof that Thou hast borne, with winning art,
>   One sinner more upon Thy loving heart:
>   And may I prove when all this life is past,
>   Though late I lov'd, I lov'd Thee to the last."

The epitaph of one of the Lord's most distinguished servants in a still more ancient church may not unfitly be uttered from many a sorrowing yet thankful heart over the tomb of Brownlow North:—

" AFTER HE HAD SERVED HIS OWN GENERATION BY
        THE WILL OF GOD, HE FELL ASLEEP."

The Sovereignty of God
A. W. Pink

At a time when there is renewed discussion on this controversial subject, this popular reprint of A. W. Pink's well-known work provides a clear and forthright statement of Divine Sovereignty in Creation, Providence and Redemption. But the author does more than expound the Scriptural doctrine. At every point he applies this truth to present-day conditions and shows its relevance to much contemporary teaching:

"From every pulpit in the land it needs to be thundered forth that God still lives, that God still observes, that God still reigns. Faith is now in the crucible, it is being tested by fire, and there is no fixed and sufficient resting-place for the heart and mind but in the Throne of God. What is needed now, as never before, is a full, positive, constructive setting forth of the Godhood of God."

A revised and shortened version.   Paperback. pp. 160   2/6

* Redemption—Accomplished and Applied
John Murray

"This volume deals with themes which lie at the very heart of the Christian faith. Every chapter is worth reading and re-reading. It should have a place on the shelves of every student and minister of the Word. . . . It is one of the very finest of recent works on theology."—*W. J. Grier.*

Paperback. pp. 192   3/-

* Not for sale in U.S.A. or Canada.

The Work of the Holy Spirit
Octavius Winslow

This is a popular work on the subject and readers will find themselves helped by the author's vigorous style. In his Introduction, Winslow makes clear the primary purpose of the book:

"To impress the mind more deeply with the glory of His person and with the necessity and value of His work, and to awaken a more ardent desire and more earnest and constant prayer for a greater manifestation of His influence, and a more undoubted evidence of His glory and power in the church and in the believer, are the object of the writer in the following treatise."

Paperback. pp. 224   3/-

Five Christian Leaders
J. C. Ryle

"The first want of our day," says the author, "is a return to the old, simple, and sharply-cut doctrines of our fathers; and the second want is a generation of like-minded and like-gifted men to preach them. Give me in any county of England and Wales a man like Grimshaw or Rowlands, and there is nothing in the present day which would make me afraid."

Biographies of William Grimshaw, Daniel Rowlands, John Berridge, William Romaine and Henry Venn, leaders in the Great Awakening of the eighteenth century.

Paperback. pp. 192   2/6

Five English Reformers
J. C. Ryle

Never did Ryle write with greater urgency than in this work and nowhere has he stated more clearly the spiritual peril which England has incurred by her departure from the Reformation:

"The danger is very great, far greater than most people suppose. A conspiracy has been long at work for *unprotestantizing* the Church of England, and all the energies of Rome are concentrated on this little island. . . . The ship is among the breakers—breakers ahead and breakers astern—breakers on the right hand and breakers on the left. Something needs to be done, if we are to escape shipwreck."

A stirring account of what John Hooper, Rowland Taylor, Hugh Latimer, John Bradford and Nicholas Ridley did and taught, and of what they suffered at the hands of the Church of Rome.

Paperback. pp. 160   2/6

The Life of Robert Murray M'Cheyne
Andrew Bonar

"Read M'Cheyne's Memoir," urged C. H. Spurgeon, "read the whole of it; I cannot do you a better service than by recommending you to read it . . . it is the story of the life of a man who walked with God."

"This is that rare type of biography in which the subject is allowed to speak for himself in his own way, and M'Cheyne's oft-quoted prayer: 'Lord, make me as holy as a pardoned sinner can be made', casts its hallowed breath over every page."—*R. A. Finlayson, The Life of Faith.*

Paperback. pp. 192   2/6

A Lifting Up for the Downcast   William Bridge

These thirteen sermons on Psalm 42, v. 11, preached at Stepney, London, in the year 1648 are the work of a true physician of souls. In dealing with believers suffering from spiritual depression, Bridge manifests great insight into the causes of the saints' discouragements such as great sins, weak grace, failure in duties, want of assurance, temptation, desertion and affliction.

A correct diagnosis is more than half the cure but Bridge does not leave his readers there. He gives directions for applying the remedy. For example in dealing with "great sins" he says, "If you would be truly humbled and not be discouraged; not be discouraged and yet be humbled; then beat and drive up all your sin to your unbelief, and lay the stress and weight of all your sorrow upon that sin."

The general causes of spiritual depression are the same in every age. Downcast Christians of the twentieth century can find help here as surely as did past generations.

Paperback. pp. 288   5/-

Heaven on Earth   Thomas Brooks

(A Treatise on Christian Assurance)

"All saints shall enjoy a heaven when they leave this earth; some saints enjoy a heaven while they are here on earth. That saints might enjoy two heavens is the project of this book."—*Joseph Caryl.*

Brooks, Rector of St. Margaret's, Fish-Street Hill, was one of the greatest of the later Puritans and no writer of the seventeenth century, with the exception of Baxter and Bunyan, has been so widely read. "As a writer," says Spurgeon, "he scatters stars with both his hands; he hath dust of gold; in his storehouse are all manner of precious stones."

Paperback. pp. 320   5/-